50!

THE LIFE, LOVES & PSYCHE OF A MALE MID-LIFE CRISIS:

Volume 1 - The Journey

50!

THE LIFE, LOVES & PSYCHE OF A MALE MID-LIFE CRISIS:

Volume 1 - The Journey

CORY Y. STANDBY

**BECAUSE
BAD
DECISIONS
MAKE
GOOD
STORIES**

Library of Congress Control Number:		2015903118
ISBN:	Hardcover	978-1-4990-9587-6
	Softcover	978-1-4990-9588-3
	eBook	978-1-4990-9589-0

Print information available on the last page.

Rev. date: 03/02/2015

To order additional copies of this book, contact:
Xlibris
800-056-3182
www.Xlibrispublishing.co.uk
Orders@Xlibrispublishing.co.uk
704726

CONTENTS

Prologue ix

'You weren't created to stand on the sidelines and just get by. You
were created to get in the game, make every moment count and
leave your mark in this world' (Billy Cox)

Introduction xiii

'Sometimes what you're looking for comes when you're not looking
at all' (Anonymous)

Part I   Childhood & Teenage Angst 1

'When I let go of what I am, I become what I might be'
(Lao Tzu)

Part II   Deaths & Births; Marriage & Divorce 35

'If you can find a path without any obstacles, it probably doesn't
lead anywhere' (Anonymous)

Part III   Drinking & Dating; Secretaries & Strippers 103

'Never get so busy making a living that you forget to make a life'
(Anonymous)

Part IV Growing Older: The Penultimate Chapter? 254

'Enlightenment means taking full responsibility for your life'
(William Blake)

Epilogue 265

'In the end we only regret the chances we didn't take, the
relationships we were afraid to have, and the decisions we waited
too long to make' (Anonymous)

To my family & loved ones

'There is only one way to avoid criticism:
do nothing, say nothing, and be nothing' (Aristotle)

PROLOGUE

'Life isn't about waiting for the storm to pass; it's about learning to dance in the rain' (Vivian Greene)

The concept of writing this book has been swirling around the author's head for years. The transition from random thoughts to some kind of outline structure and then actually committing to paper and recounting the tale itself makes an elephant's gestation period seem like the blink of an eye by comparison. Although it is at the very least a semi-autobiographical tale, all real names have been changed in order to protect the innocent and especially the extremely guilty too. As the saying goes, 'the truth will out'. Fortunately, the truth is (from a legal perspective) a defence. There is some poetic licence in the telling of the tales, but the facts are accurate and the incidents recounted are all real events which occurred. No doubt many will speculate as to who, what, when, where, and probably even why – but that's all part of the fun, isn't it?

This is the story of life. It is about love and relationships; about the importance of family; about how real life and human emotions invariably mess each of these up. It looks at death, divorce and dating; losing loved ones; family feuds and other intertwined issues; grief and stress and how we seek to cope (or spectacularly fail to do so) with all that fate and fortune throws at us on our journey through life. It is a series of personal anecdotes intertwined with the author's view of the world, both then as it happened and especially now he is older and hopefully much wiser. It is written with the benefit of hindsight. If he'd had such clarity and understanding at the time, much of it would never have happened. But he didn't. As we all know:

'To be old and wise, you must first be young and stupid'
(Anonymous)

The aim has been to strike a balance between the main themes and recurring messages of the book, alongside some kind of chronological overview of his life events, particularly his relationships with women. The purpose being to seek to explain why he did what he did; why he made the decisions he made and if possible, to understand and explain it all more clearly now, looking back with a more rounded view of the world. It is not intended to be hugely introspective or overly personal, but more a series of examples to show how, to paraphrase the saying, rarely does each element of your life go well at the same time. Many people endure far worse in life; he knows that he has been lucky. He is grateful for all that he has had and done and hopes that these tales may even offer some help, solace, or guidance to others as they cope with some of the pain we all go through. The author is very sorry about the people he has hurt along the way, but this book is not intended as any form of excuse or attempt at personal apology (this is not the right forum for that); rather, it is an exploration of why things happened the way they did. Some things happened by choice, some by chance, fate, and circumstance. In no way should it be read with the author as a victim, and if at any stage it comes across like that, he apologises. He accepts full responsibility for all his actions, good and bad. He is truly sorry for all the bad and accepts that:

'Circumstances do not make a man, they reveal him'
(Wayne W. Dyer)

All of the quotations which appear throughout this book have been carefully chosen by him as reflecting his views on life, perhaps best epitomised by the following:

> 'Reality is we are born and then we die, whatever happens in between is up to you. Cherish every day, don't waste a second of it' (Rashida Rowe), and

> 'In the long run, we shape our lives and we shape ourselves. The process never ends until we die. And the choices we make are ultimately our own responsibility' (Eleanor Roosevelt).

He has grabbed his life by the scruff of the neck and shaken it, at times far too vigorously. He reacted as he felt was appropriate at the time; he clearly got it wrong often. With the benefit of hindsight and the wisdom life's experiences have brought him, he would have done so many things differently. But life isn't like that. We live and learn from our mistakes and should aim to make the best of what we have, who we are, and what we want from life. There are constant extraneous factors, of course, and things happen to us that we wouldn't chose and can't control. But that is all part of the rich tapestry of life, isn't it? We each are given one life to live and we choose how to live it; how to respond to things that happen to us outside our own control; and how to make the best out of whatever life throws at us. Cory is the main protagonist in his own life, never a bystander, no mere witness; he chose how to act and react throughout, undoubtedly far too strongly at times. It was always his choice how he dealt with life's travails, especially when fate brought him some bad times. Even when lost in grief and losing our way in the world, it is up to each of us individually always to take responsibility for what we do, whether we are thinking rationally or not.

It is written in the third person, not because the author has the same egocentric pretentions of grandeur seen in many public figures, but rather because it is easier to recount tales more dispassionately like this. Let's see if it works.

INTRODUCTION

'Everyone makes mistakes in life, but that doesn't mean they have to pay for them the rest of their life. Sometimes good people make bad choices; it doesn't mean they are bad. It means they are human' (Anonymous)

As Cory sat at his desk staring out of his window observing the beautiful autumnal landscape of the southern English countryside, he smiled wryly to himself. Here he was entering his fiftieth year; he felt more empowered, free, and generally just more content with life than ever before. That is to say, inner contentment was finally his, after years of striving for the perfect life, but is that just an illusion? What he had come to realise as he approached his half century in this world was that the old saying was so true – *'The less you give a shit, the happier you will be'* (Anonymous).

This book is an exploration of his path through life, the ups and downs and where it had now brought him. He had first thought of writing a book many years ago, having been told by his lovely, mad, eccentric English teacher decades earlier that he had an eloquent writing style that should be explored further. He doubted that she had meant this much later, but real life kind of got in the way in the intervening thirty-plus years. Mind you, she was also full of praise for his stylish handwriting back then too, but that (like so much else) has been destroyed by real life grinding it down over the decades ever since. It has descended from beautiful calligraphy then to an illegible scrawl now. That really is a true metaphor for life!

Actually, his earlier thoughts on the book had been a variation on the theme, which crystallised after England's then latest major football tournament failure at Euro 2000. The football fans amongst you will remember the last minute penalty we gave away to snatch failure from the jaws of our qualification success, but life as a frustrated England sports fan is a whole other story and perhaps too close in subject matter to Nick Hornby's superb benchmark of that genre *Fever Pitch*. For numerous reasons, it didn't happen and that leads us to where Cory sits now – a decade and a half on. What a journey it's been since then! And that really is the point of this book, because in the summer of 2000, rather than settling down to write his book, Cory instead left his marriage to the woman he'd been with for thirteen years, had met at university, and with whom he had four wonderful kids.

This book isn't however a study in what specifically went wrong in that relationship, though who knows whether future volumes may explore such themes further, should this tome find critical or even mass approval. It is more an examination of whether Cory has spent the subsequent years desperately trying to make up for all he lost, and it is entirely possible that could be the conclusion and the salutary tale for every middle-aged man. At this stage, as he sits here contemplating life – having spent years *getting his shit together*' – it is intended as an exploration of that incredible phenomenon: his male mid-life crisis. It is obviously written by Cory, from his perspective and through his eyes; no doubt others will have different views and interpretations, but the facts are correct whatever spin either side may wish to put on them. As the saying goes:

> 'When writing the story of your life, don't let anyone else hold the pen' (Harley Davidson)

In order to look at this amazing journey, we shall explore its highs and lows; the purpose being to see whether, as he enjoys single life with the opportunity to reflect properly for the first time in decades, any sense can be made of it all. It is hoped that with the benefit of hindsight, even if not necessarily with any greater wisdom, some kind of order can finally be brought to the chaos he has lived through. He has divided the tale of his life (to date) into four broad parts; but certain issues and themes will recur throughout and he makes no apology for that; indeed, he relies on Churchill's guidance:

> *'If you have an important point to make, don't try to be subtle or clever. Use a pile driver. Hit the point once. Then come back and hit it again. Then hit it a third time – a tremendous whack'*
> (Winston Churchill)

Before we get to the main part of the story, we look briefly at those crucial formative years; so let's start at the beginning.

PART I

Childhood & Teenage Angst

'Everyone had gone through something in their life that has changed them in a way that means they could never go back to the person they once were' (Anonymous)

Childhood Bliss – Running Free

Cory recalled a visit to a stress counsellor, an anger management specialist (psychotherapist/psychiatrist/trick cyclist or something similar) at the height of his divorce, when the learned professional had insisted his then issues all stemmed back to Cory's early childhood. Utter bollocks! As you'll see here, Cory and his brothers had a loving, safe, normal upbringing by great parents, with no issues outside the ordinary growing pains of boys. There were two distinct parts, their respective births and early years in the north, then the move south and real formative years down here (though with regular visits back to the remaining family in the north to maintain their roots up there).

Cory is the eldest of three boys, all born in major northern industrial cities. Their dad was a teacher, who moved around with the family in tow, from Leeds to Newcastle, on to Liverpool and then down to the Home Counties. Although this peripatetic life was interesting, growing up at different stages in different places, acquiring different dialects and accents depending on the stage the boys were at in each place, it was disruptive and meant childhood friendships came and went as the family followed a slightly nomadic existence. However, there is no criticism at all of his parents for that (despite during his teenage angst repeatedly claiming such travesties as part of a litany of issues he set out forcefully in the late 1970s/early 1980s!). It was all clearly for the betterment of the family, as Dad moved each time for a promotion, a better job, more pay, a school-house etc. This was essential back then in the bleak late 1960s and 1970s, when teachers still earned very little; and mums roles were firmly to stay at home and look after the household, kids, and family – no dual income nonsense back then. Their dad worked hard and was a highly respected professional, of whom the boys were all very proud, as well as a loving devoted parent along with their mum, who brought them up on little money but in the kindest most loving way anyone could ever have wished for. It taught the boys the value of family stability, love, and affection and being happy with what you had – a far cry from today's materialistic world.

They made their own fun, unlike this current generation's indolence. They had one black-and-white TV in the house, showing programmes from some time each morning until midnight if lucky – the test card filled the screen the rest of the time. BBC 1 and ITV were the stalwarts, with BBC 2 as the back-up; nothing more. When Cory now tells his own kids that that was all they had for most of his childhood, they are aghast. He recalls Channel 4 being a major development when launched in the 1980s; there was no Sky or Virgin, Freeview, DVDs, digital, or even VCRs (until the 1980s); no all-night TV, multi-channel options, no pause and play, no recording programmes, no wall-to-wall sport – just *Match of the Day* and *The Big Match* for footy, and *The World of Sport* and *Grandstand* generally for everything else. He fondly remembered the mad rush to get to a radio (no portables, laptops, iPhones/Pads, PCs or similar were even contemplated back then) to hear the classified football results on a Saturday evening after going to real football games. What a very different world it was then! In so many ways, it was far less complicated and better than that in which we now live with the increased wealth, prosperity, and numerous technological advances, certainly not necessarily what *Tomorrow's World* had in mind when it told us of how the world and our lives would change; and is it really what the visionary technology gurus of our age (Gates, Jobs et al) envisaged for our brave new world? As the Dalai Lama accurately says in *The Paradox of our Age*:

> 'We have bigger houses but smaller families;
> More conveniences, but less time;
> We have more degrees, but less sense;
> More knowledge, but less judgement;
> More experts, but more problems;
> More medicines, but less healthiness;
> We've been all the way to the moon and back,
> but have trouble crossing the street to meet the new neighbour.
> We build more computers to hold more information to
> produce more copies than ever but have less communication.
> We have become long on quantity,
> but short on quality.
> These are times of fast foods but slow digestion;
> Tall man but short character;
> Steep profits but shallow relationships.
> It's a time when there is much in the window,
> but nothing in the room.'

The early years of their family started in the early 1960s, when their parents romantically met on a Yorkshire railway station in their early twenties. Dad was a university student embarking on his teaching career in Leeds; Mum was brought up in an archetypal small

Yorkshire working man's village (where the Working Man's club was the focal point, more of that later) and was starting her secretarial working life. They were a beautiful young couple, clean cut and attractive and married in the mid-1960s. At the time of writing this book, they have just celebrated their golden wedding anniversary. This is not something Cory will ever experience, and he is in awe of their lifetime together. Fifty years of marriage – wow! It is perhaps not something many will experience in current and future generations, which is a shame, but is symptomatic of much this book will seek to explore in subsequent chapters. Cory's birth followed a year later, on a bleak winter's night, snowstorms and high winds whirling around the old granite and stone of Leeds Maternity Hospital (perhaps the gods' rumblings on the anniversary of JFK's assassination – we could read all sorts of omens into such signs!). The three of them lived happily for the first few years of Cory's life within sight of Elland Road and still close enough to both families for regular contact and support – as people still did in those days, but not as much anymore (despite what the TV soaps would have you believe).

Cory was loved by his parents and by his maternal grandparents (the jovial local plumber and local wool-mill worker) whose bungalow and land in the village became his constant northern base and 'other' home as they moved around in subsequent years (and continued until fairly recently when his lovely down to earth grandma's longevity finally expired in her early nineties). And his matriarchal paternal grandmother, whose husband (Cory's granddad who he never knew) died after World War II, as a result of shrapnel injuries apparently, leaving her to bring up six children as a single mother in true Irish Catholic style. She was a pillar of the local Catholic community in Leeds and known as Lady Rosemary, or the Duchess, for her middle-class bearing! Many of his parents' siblings and cousins were still based in and around Leeds too. The extended family on both sides was something Cory grew up very appreciative of and enjoyed for many happy years at family parties and gatherings. The family expanded as his cousins were born to his uncles and aunts. These happy memories led to his own desire to have a big family in later years. As a child, Cory was blissfully unaware of the inevitable family tensions behind the scenes, which were never discussed openly (that was just the way it was back then). Certainly any hint of discord was hidden from the dozen-plus cousins as they played happily together throughout their childhood years. Church hall venues on his dad's family's side (the Duchess's influence with the priest securing use of the Catholic church near her home seemingly endlessly!) and the Working Man's club were regular venues for Christmas parties and the like in his mum's family's small village just outside Leeds. Joyful times all round.

As Cory has recently discussed with his own kids as they grow up, life as a child is great, blissfully ignorant, happy and carefree with no responsibility. And yet, being human, one of life's ironies is always to want more. As children, we always want to be older and reach the next stage, to be a teenager, and then to be an adult once we reach that point. Yet you get to adulthood and look back fondly on how simple life was as a child. Obviously this is based on personal experience, coming from a secure, loving family – no doubt it's not the same for those who have had abusive or deprived childhoods, which must be awful. It is clear how much the quality of your childhood affects us all as we develop into adults. Cory recalled one his mum's work colleagues in Oxford, a very jolly, apparently happy young lady who was terribly posh and well-spoken, who had a well-paid professional job in the health sector and came from a very wealthy family. And yet she apparently poured her heart out to his mum, saying she would have swapped all the money and privilege for some love and affection from her parents, to be a normal child living at home with them as she grew up rather than packed off to the poshest boarding and finishing schools. Cory recognised the type, very prevalent in the City of London ('the City'). Outwardly brash, confident types, with loud braying voices, clothes and behaviour

crying out, 'Look at me. Aren't I great?' But it's all a front: people
with real confidence don't need or demand recognition from others.
A couple of sayings sum this up perfectly:

> 'Confidence is not, they will like me. Confidence is, I'll be fine if
> they don't' (Anonymous), and

> 'Work hard in silence. Let success be your noise' (Frank Ocean)

People with inner security and confidence just get on with their
own lives and generally don't seek attention and adulation from
others. They aren't usually bothered about others' opinions or what
most people may think of them. Often those who do are invariably
making up for deficiencies in their own personalities, mainly caused
by a lack of affection and true love when we all need it most, as we
grow up. Cory would not have swapped all the wealth in the world
for the loving security his parents had given him and his brothers
– and yet even that wasn't necessarily enough, as we will see later,
sadly. The three brothers enjoyed their childhoods, now living on the
North Sea coast, just outside Newcastle. Their mum walked them
to and from school when they were small and took them on to the
beach in the afternoons, where the wind was always blowing and
the North Sea was always cold, even in summer. They learned to sail
little boats in the shallows and in the harbour area too. Cory had the
terrifying experience when a solid wooden rowing boat caught a wave
as they tried to sail out from the beach, being flipped over and he
was trapped underneath in the dark water washing in until the adults
lifted the boat off. He was too young to understand fully how scary
the situation was at the time, but certainly has never lost his respect
for the awesome power of the sea ever since. Undoubtedly, it was this
open-air life and being 'at one with nature' that made him love the
space and beauty of nature as he grew. He feels trapped and confined
in the concrete jungles of our major cities and loves the commute
back out to greenery and space. He loves the beauty of the rolling

countryside, the raw force of the sea against coastal rock formations, and particularly the tranquillity of exclusive beach resorts, with their azure waters and golden sands. He hates modern offices and hotels, with their hermetically sealed windows; he hates internal rooms with no natural outside light, the nonsense of internal atria, and not being able to see the real world outside. He feels trapped, confined, caged, and claustrophobic, desperate to break out. He craves natural sunlight, its warmth on his face, the smell of fresh air – no doubt why he loves tropical island resorts so much. The joy he feels every time he hires jet skis on holiday and glides (or bounces!) across the Caribbean or Mediterranean is intense. He needs to feel free, as this was his childhood. It explains a lot about his personality, as you will see.

The boys played with their neighbours' kids, exploring the fields and empty spaces behind their houses, long before it was all built on with never-ending new housing estates and developments in later years. This was the early-to mid-1970s and life was simple. Cory's best friend had a sister, who not only was one of their playmates, but became Cory's first girlfriend at the tender age of five or six! They had secret snogs in the coal sheds attached to their houses (as houses still had in the industrial north in those days, before Thatcher destroyed it all in subsequent decades). They used the trampoline at the gym in the school where their dad taught; he took them swimming at weekends and life was good. Cory only really had two bad memories from that period: the first being his beloved (and then still mighty) Leeds United losing to huge underdogs Sunderland in the 1973 FA Cup Final – not ideal when living in the north-east. Fortunately, in their area Sunderland fans were outnumbered by Newcastle fans, but the teasing was still painful! Secondly, the boys' bedroom was at the front of the house, which meant that apart from the main road and a timber yard behind it, it was not far from the beach and the crashing waves of the North Sea. Whether it was the howling winds, shapes and shadows swaying at night or just his fervent imagination, Cory recalled many nights believing the house was haunted or that witches were flying in to get him. He would run full pelt along the long corridor to the sanctuary of his parents' bedroom at the back of the house. As a then sensitive soul, he was prone to a number of these incidents, seeking the security of being in his parents' loving embrace. He recalls this nervousness led to something of a sensitive bowel too, which was bad enough at home, but particularly awkward when he started at the Catholic primary school. On too many occasions, he didn't make the outside toilet block across the playground under the shadow of the church in time; all very messy and embarrassing, but his parents never shouted at him for it, just reassured him all was fine and would be okay. He soon outgrew the problem, as children often do (as long as there are no further psychological reasons involved).

There were the inevitable childhood injuries. Cory still bears the scar above his left temple, where he cut his head falling off a huge, industrial-sized cricket roller (the type pulled by a tractor, not pushed by a person) as he and his friends played on it. As he was climbing up it, he slipped and fell, hitting his head on the solid metal roller on the way down. As the blood poured down his face, he felt dazed and was concerned to hear his friends screaming, 'He's cracked his head open!' As always, his parents looked after him as stitches and butterfly strips were applied at the local hospital. They became regular visitors, as his brothers also injured themselves often. It was the nature of things back then; they were allowed to be adventurous, making their own fun without any of today's distractions. On one occasion, a smaller garden roller at his grandparents', in Cory's hands slipped and the spring-handled solid metal stanchion hit his brother on the head. Their dad had to drive from home in Liverpool to Leeds to take them to the hospital. Another time, a brother fell off a slippery wooden ladder on to sharp stones beneath at one of the docks, badly cutting the back of his head. There were no health and safety issues back then, nor when they shimmied across the huge industrial pipes in the dock, with no safety elements at all in place. Life was freer and simpler. They had huge freedom, going out on their own and with friends to play outside all day long. Parents would not necessarily know where they were as they wandered off, but in those days, that's what kids did. They disappeared for hours. They had none of the gadgets today's youth do, and it was regarded as natural and healthy for kids to go off and explore. The fear that abounds in today's society wasn't a feature of life then; they literally ran free.

Although this nostalgia is lovely, the point of it is simply to show that life was good. Cory and his brothers were happy, loved, secure, free and enjoyed the basic freedoms life offered with relish. A happy home and loving immediate and extended family was enough. Holidays with grandparents, parties with cousins, family gatherings on both sides were all great fun. But then of course, childhood innocence gives way to teenage years, and life changes. Confused hormones replace innocent happiness; doubts and questions interfere with simple childhood truths; those loving parents who cherished, loved, and supported you for over a decade become irritating old codgers, ruining your life. In short, the beauty and sweetness of childhood innocence gradually gets lost in the mists of time, as the growing pains of moving from that period of blissfully naive ignorance to adulthood lead to every parent's worst memories of their once-sweet kids – the teenage years!

Teenage Angst

After their childhood tour of the north, at about ten years of age, Cory and his family moved to the south. His dad had secured a promotion to assistant principal of a residential school for delinquent types – a reform school, as it was known in the old days. Quite what the current politically correct term is Cory is unsure, perhaps a residential facility for emotionally and behaviourally maladjusted boys? His dad had a stint at a similar school in the north, as well as teaching in a grammar school and lecturing at college level. Although it was all far more intense, given the nature of the kids in his care and the fact you lived on site, one of the perks was housing for the family, so it suited them well. Mum later explained that they had struggled financially on just a teacher's salary with three hungry boys to raise, particularly when having to buy a house to fit five of them. Given their dad's seniority, they were given one of the new senior staff houses built on the edge of the school grounds (an old farm, so there was plenty of land which has subsequently all been sold off privately after the school closed a few years ago). They were happy as they grew up in a decent home; their dad worked hard, long hours, evenings and weekends, but at least he only had a five-minute walk to work. As the boys became teenagers, their mum also resumed her working life, initially away from the school, but after tiring of the commuting, at the school itself. It was a good community to grow up in; the other senior staff became friends of the family. If they had kids of a similar age to Cory and his brothers, they all became friends too. One of Cory's closest friends was a year or two older, but they got on very well. They played football and tennis, used the school's gym, swimming pool, and other facilities, especially in the holidays, when the resident boys weren't around. It was all very idyllic. This friend had a sister Cory's age, Abbey, who was a tomboy, joining in with their games in the early years, who went to the same school as Cory and was the closest thing he ever had to a sister (for a few years, at least). Their paths diverged in mid-teenage years, as Cory pursued his studies, and Abbey, who by then had grown into one of the most beautiful girls in the school, was less academic and busy with her constant array of male suitors. However, their childhood bond and friendship was always there, even when they were parts of the different groups at school and therefore didn't hang out together socially any more. Although Cory missed his friend, he understood he had to work hard for his exams and couldn't party as much as the types Abbey was hanging around with, one of whom was another of his best friends as a child, Gez, who went on to become a professional footballer, marry Abbey, and then ruin it all by so predictably having an affair with a hairdresser.

One day, Cory got the bus back from school to his home with his brothers, at the end of which they had to walk over a field to their house. As they left the bus, he noticed a beautiful girl out of the corner of his eye, and to his delight, she got off the bus too. He realised it was Abbey, who by then he hadn't seen for some time, even though they only lived ten minutes apart; their lives had gone in different directions. She was as beautiful as ever. He was confused. This was his friend, his childhood tomboy mate. His good friend's little sister. His own quasi-sister. And yet as Cory looked at her, he realised his feelings were far more than that. Teenage hormones were at play and all the more intense, given their previous (albeit innocent) history as childhood friends. They talked excitedly with each other, catching up on what each had been doing for the past year or so since they'd had any proper contact. Back then, in the early 1980s, there were no mobile phones, Internet, etc., so contact was face to face or landline phone calls occasionally. Cory was besotted, but didn't know how Abbey felt. Fortunately, she started babysitting for his neighbours' younger kids around that time, so they bumped into each other much more regularly. Cory had a few relationships at school, and he knew Abbey was still, not surprisingly, very popular with many boys and in constant demand. But he felt a connection and wondered if she did too. He wasn't sure if she just saw them as reunited friends. Being a slightly awkward teenager, still learning the mysterious ways of women and how best to approach them, he took it slowly. Eventually, after far too long dallying, talking, and being unsure if he would ruin their friendship if he finally made a move, one evening he did. He thought, 'What the hell!' He would never know if he didn't try, after months of not trying for fear of having read the signals wrong – every teenage boy's eternal dilemma!

He made his move and kissed Abbey, and the passion between them exploded. She said she had been waiting for him to make a

move for months (as girls do) and felt she had been giving signals
which he had ignored. He explained he was nervous, as they were
such good friends; he hadn't wanted to ruin it. And because they had
spent years growing up together, he wasn't sure if she was just being
friendly. They had a summer of fun, but sadly were never able to build
what could have been an amazing relationship, as his parents moved
at that stage to another school, his dad having secured a headship.
Cory in turn completed his exams, worked, and went travelling, then
off to university back in the north. Although he kept in touch with
Abbey, she settled down with Gez. They had occasional contact over
the years, but after her divorce, she eventually remarried, as did Cory,
and their lives again went in different directions. Even now, Cory
believes she is the one that got away (well, her and possibly Chloe, the
current on/off love of his life, but she features in much later chapters).
If only they could have got their acts together at the same time, they
could have converted their summer fling into the solid relationship
it should have been. But that's life, sadly. You don't always meet
the right person at the right time. It did however teach him a very
valuable lesson, namely that if you find a girl attractive, whether a
long-term friend like Abbey or someone new, you tell them and avoid
all the awkward uncertainty. As their circumstances prevented them
building their relationship by the time they finally got together, he
resolved then he would never again in life let that happen to him.
So all the girls subsequently who have accused Cory of being too
direct, that's why! Although the bond and connection with Abbey was
amazing, based on childhood friends eventually growing into teenage
lovers and possibly therefore being his first real love, she wasn't his
first real, serious relationship. That was Penny.

As a young teenager, Cory had been the quiet type. He preferred
to watch and listen and only speak publicly when he had something
to add. Initially, his teachers had worried he was shy, or reserved,
but eventually realised he was just a bit more selective in his social
interactions than some of his peers. Interestingly, Cory worked out

that although he was good-looking, the girls at school responded better to his more garrulous mates. At this very early age, he realised what he came to know as a truth in later life, that women respond much more to guys with a personality than just the strong silent type; another valuable lesson learned and another reason he has been the way he is with women in adult life. Cory had dated a few girls in the early years at school, but like many adolescent boys, preferred the company of his mates, football, other sports, and just being lads to all that soppy relationship stuff. That was all fine in the early teenage years, when having a girlfriend wasn't a serious issue. Those he did have were okay, but never particularly serious. Strangely, looking back now, Cory can see that all his relationships with women have been one of the two types – either the intensity, strong bond, and connection (is that love?) that he had with Abbey and Penny or the short-term, okay-but-not-serious, and ultimately not-going-anywhere episodes (whether all the women knew they were in the latter, he was less certain of). Certainly those Cory has loved have talked of the incredible connection and emotional intensity; those he hasn't have talked of emotional distance, coldness and almost lack of interest. Cory is an all or nothing man; no shades of grey.

Cory was happy as a teenager until the stress of his O levels, revision, and the build-up to them coincided with his inexorable teenage hormonal rage. Looking back, he realises what a complete pain in the arse he was. Having now been through it with his own teenage kids, he sees how utterly bewildering it is for all concerned. As Harry Enfield so accurately portrays through his teenage character 'Kevin', everyone is at a loss to understand how the sweet, lovely child of the previous thirteen or so years suddenly changes into a bundle of conflicting emotions, raging hormones and incredible mood swings. The first real manifestation of this in Cory was his gradual refusal to attend Catholic church any more. When they lived in the north, he had always attended Catholic schools, so it was all part of the school day, general life and wider community. There was no question of not going to weekend Mass, First Communion, becoming an altar boy (although luckily, one of his parents' moves had scuppered this for Cory, or who knows what additional tales of Catholic priests he would have had to relate now!). Generally being part of the church community was a big, inescapable part of your life. In the south, however, the small Catholic church they went to seemed like an outpost in the heathen southlands. There was a much less religious feel to life generally down here, and the schools were largely non-denominational, certainly in the area they lived in. So that weakening of the Catholic Church's inherent vice-like hold over their lives coincided with his hormonal teenage maelstrom of changing views and challenges to any authority – particularly his parents and the Church. As he played football on Sundays, that became his real religion and focus. Sunday Mass got in the way. Having been a good boy and attended classes to take his Confirmation and Mass regularly for years, he now suddenly felt empowered as a stroppy teenager to announce that he didn't agree with Catholicism and no longer wished to attend church. This debate raged at home for some time, but ultimately his parents gave in. Church became less regular and eventually no longer part of his life at all. Cory's primary motivation was, firstly, to avoid the hassle of Mass on Sundays, when sleep and football mattered much more; secondly, to assert himself and make changes from his childhood's subservient ways. Attending church was simply now boring and irrelevant to his new life in the secular south. His considered views on religion (if he really had any) were largely ancillary at this stage, but as he skilfully pointed out, how could he have apparently known as an eleven-year-old that he wished to confirm himself to God if he now didn't know as a thirteen-year-old that he did not?! Early signs of that fine legal mind at play? Or just a bit of a stroppy teenage twat being awkward? Probably a bit of both, but mainly the latter. As things were to play out a few years later though, Cory ultimately felt vindicated, as we shall explore shortly.

The crux of the teenage problem is that despite their apparent strident, dogmatic views on everything, the teenagers themselves are more confused than anyone. Cory knew this himself at the time, but of course could never admit it to his parents. He stomped around raging against their life, where they lived, how noisy and disruptive his brothers were and the house was, and anything else he could think of. Apparently, his parents dreaded the evening meal time, as he would often launch into his diatribes at the end of the meal. Cory has related all this to his own kids, now that hopefully they are largely through their own teenage issues, anger and resentments. They agree that it's just some weird shit we all go through as we grow! Apart from the obvious physical manifestations, the oddest part of that side of the teenage years was to see (both when Cory was a boy and watching his own kids grow) not only their own changes, but also those of their friends. It's bad enough to watch your own kids' transformations, but to see their sweet, cute little friends also morph into dodgy teenagers is so sad. It truly is the loss of the innocence of youth. On the football pitch especially, the effects can be soul destroying – the small skilful pre-pubescent star player can turn into a lumbering uncoordinated oaf, cruelly ending his parents' lifelong dreams of him becoming a professional footballer. Cory did all he could to channel his teenage rage, being generally as active as possible. He played every sport he could, all year round, and cycled to his Saturday job in the kitchen of a local hotel and his summer holiday job labouring for a local builder. But the reality is that all of this is never enough; his own kids now don't even do a fraction of that, as they vegetate in front of the TV and game consoles. They appear listless and lifeless unless plugged in to some form of online device; they even use iPads for every lesson at school now, for God's sake! But there is no shortcut to getting through the teenage years. You just have to go through the full gamut of teenage pain, angst, confusion, uncertainty, anger and frustration, whilst hoping that what you say and do during the hormonal tsunami that hits you doesn't leave any irreparable damage. Cory hopes and believes that was the case for him, as it has been for his own kids subsequently. It is not always the case sadly, however, as we will touch on later.

Cory enjoyed his school years. There was the sporting side, where he captained very successful school football and rugby teams throughout and was an accomplished athlete, holding various school records for sprint events. The group of boys in these teams was generally the same, many of whom were also members of the same local Sunday league football team, which was managed by Gez's dad and coached by Cory's. The only bad memory Cory has of these times was breaking his nose as an eleven-year-old, when an opposition player headed him in the face rather than connecting with the ball. The shock and realisation that blood was pouring from his nose, the hospital visits, and operation to re-set it (pointless as it turned out, as you will read later) were all unpleasant experiences. But they were nothing compared to the post-operative discomfort of waking to find packing wedged up his nose to the back of his throat. Disgusting, uncomfortable, and not something he would ever put himself through again, as is evident from his nose now. He'd had a tonsillectomy as a five-year-old but didn't recall this level of discomfort. Looking back now, he would put it on a par for unpleasantness with the laser eye surgery and post-operative pain following a minor umbilical hernia repair he subsequently had. When he broke his nose again in later years, he refused to go through this again, as the memory was so bad. How the hell women go through childbirth, time after time, he will never be able to comprehend!

The football team was good and they were a great group for many years; playing sports together, socialising around the local town, knowing each others' families well, and generally enjoying growing up in a small Oxfordshire market town. As everyone finds, though, as you grow from eleven-year-olds through to sixteen-year-olds, not only does life change, but your friends do too. The sporty guys who aren't as academic, who were your best mates in the early years, become less so as you stay in at weekends and evenings to do homework and revise for exams. They don't; they go out more and more, socialising, womanising and enjoying life. Although Cory was torn and sad to lose his friends, he knew he was making the right choice. It was a small price to pay generally to be regarded as a swot. As mentioned, Gez became a professional footballer (which had been Cory's dream) but at a time before the big money brought by Sky and the Premier League had arrived in English football. His promising career was curtailed by a series of injuries and he ended up in the lower leagues and running a sports shop. Far worse though, he blew his marriage to Abbey – the biggest crime any man could ever commit, in Cory's view! The rest of that group ended up running shoe-heeling bars and other similar jobs in their local town, marrying girls they'd known at school, drinking in the same pubs they had as teenagers, and never leaving the local town or progressing with their lives in the wider world. In comparison, the group (of swots) that Cory gravitated towards for the final years of his school days, who he stayed on in the sixth form with, all moved on, attaining successful careers all over the world. It was an interesting socio-economic experiment for Cory to witness and indeed to be part of, albeit inadvertently. Although it was sad at the time to have his erstwhile friends turn against him, as he was no longer one of them as he put his studies first. This turned out to be another important one of life's lessons for Cory – you do what's best for you, whatever those around you say, even if you have to go against the crowd; you never let anyone's comments, barbs, or unpleasantness deter you from achieving your own goals and ambitions; and just because someone has apparently been your close friend for years, it doesn't mean they always will be. Life moves on, and we have to move with it, looking forward, never dwelling on what was in the past. Sadly, Cory has brought this attitude into relationships in his adult life, when they have run their course (in his opinion at least, although not always mutually agreed by the ladies in question, it seems).

The transition to a new group of friends was okay, as they were all decent kids and of course they had a mutual aim in studying hard to get good grades and progress – not something necessarily always shared by Cory's kids' generation those days, it seems! A number of them were sporty too, so they had played in the same teams as Cory over the years. He didn't necessarily have the previous years' closeness to them and the bonds that they had developed with each other, but that didn't really bother him. Given the transitory nature of his childhood, due to his dad's peripatetic teaching career, he was used to making friends for a few years, then moving on and losing them. Cory vowed that when he had kids, he would bring then up in one place. Although he fully understood his parents' reasons for moving around and the necessity of it to improve their quality of life, as his dad won promotions, he did not want that for his own kids. He accepted that his brothers' and his own quality of life had been far greater than his parents had been able to afford, due to the nice house provided by the schools, but determined that he would do all he could to give his own kids more. Whether he achieved that, perhaps only time will tell. Or rather, did he end up by giving them security and stability to begin with, that was then lost in the divorce from their mum and subsequent acrimonious years and then trying to compensate by spoiling them? All to be investigated much later.

So this new group of more academic types became Cory's new friends. These were the nerds and swots of earlier years, who Cory's old group of cooler kids hadn't liked. But as the saying goes, 'the meek shall inherit the earth' – just look at Gates, Jobs, Zuckerberg, et al. They were a good group and they all got on well as they progressed into sixth form together. The new headmaster's son was part of the group, and as he was from Leeds they had that mutual connection too. They shared the piss-taking of their Northern accents (Cory having avowedly never lost his Northern pronunciation of those tell-tale words such as glass, grass, after, ask etc.) and a mutual love of Leeds United, which led to trips on the bus from Oxon to London to watch them play. This was in the early 1980s, when English football was still a rough game, with rougher-still crowds. They stood on terraces in those days; no respectable fan ever had a seat (well before Hillsborough and the Taylor report changes). A typical vivid memory was standing on the dirt terracing at Stamford Bridge, as Chelsea stewards taunted Leeds fans, who responded by ripping up clumps of the mud and decaying concrete terracing to launch at the offending stewards. These were teenage boys from a nice middle-class Oxfordshire market town, studying ultimately to become lawyers, doctors, and scientists, caught in the war of hatred between those rival football tribes. Cory and his friends were penned in by the police for hours after games, escorted miles from train stations to grounds and back (whether they wanted to go there or not!) and generally treated like cattle. Any efforts to communicate with the police, let alone reason with them rationally, were flatly rejected. All very scary indeed. On the safety of the bus out of London back to their middle-class world, they would pontificate about the perils of Thatcher's police state and other suitably political topics, such as the validity of the Falklands War, her destruction of our Northern industrial homelands, entire mining communities, steel and wool mills and generally the demise of industrial Britain. Although they were technically, chronologically (sadly and reluctantly) Thatcher's children and their parents' generation appeared to support her as their lives became more affluent, the boys were free of such financial worries and generally hated her for all she represented. That view never changed as Cory grew older. He once saw her through the window of a Mayfair private club decades later as she was in her final years and felt the same rage at her destruction of much of Britain and the polarisation of the haves and have-nots (continued apace, in true Tory style, by her party ever since). After her death, Cory stridently refused to be anywhere near her funeral procession, although he was working in the St Paul's area of the City, as many of his colleagues poured out to watch.

As well as Leeds games in London and across the south, their little gang also ventured to Wembley (the old, original version with the twin towers) to watch England play. The highlight undoubtedly was the nine goals scored against Luxembourg on a cold December night in 1982, when Luther Blissett scored a hat-trick, supported by half of the rest of the team getting a goal each too. Cory and company had also discovered the pubs in their small market town that would serve them under-age, en masse. Ironically, the best one (the Row Barge) tucked down some back street was closest to the small police station in the town – the received wisdom was that as long as the police knew the teens were all there, then they weren't causing trouble elsewhere. Ultimately, the landlord was prosecuted and the pub closed, as such early 1980s' lenience and pragmatism was swept away by rules, regulations, and jobsworths, the effect being to drive the disenfranchised youth into the public parks to drink, smoke, experiment with substances, and the like. It was more fine planning by bureaucrats with no real understanding or knowledge of the local community and certainly no provision of any suitable facilities for bored, restless teenagers. Remember, they had no online and social media diversions in those days. So they drank themselves silly with ridiculous concoctions like 'Depth Charges', 'Snakebites' and other suitably horrible mixed drinks designed to get these teens drunk as quickly as possible. There wasn't really the culture of 'pre-loading', as Cory witnessed now with his own teenage kids. The pub was king back then or the party at someone's house if their parents were away, which certainly hasn't changed between generations. Cory and the gang had so many of these. The view seemed to be that as they were all bright, well-educated, serious, hard-working kids, who studied and didn't mess around, they could be trusted. Oh dear, how wrong! Whilst all of that was true, they were teenagers after all, who did study hard and take the important bits seriously, which meant when they came to party, they did it in style! It started, inevitably, with bottles of cider bought cheaply from dodgy corner shops (supermarkets wouldn't serve them under age), supplemented by whatever could be raided from the host parents' drinks cabinet. Cory cannot now even smell whiskey or port without feeling sick, let alone drink them as a result of those days. There was the usual smoking, as it was cool, and weed around too, but no other drugs in those days. Cory, as a non-smoker, was somewhat hampered and after a few feeble efforts to inhale, finally gave up after a party at his own house one Christmas when his parents were away visiting relatives in the North. He had naturally promised to have no parties and, using the same logic his own kids do now too, and had justified inviting a few mates round in breach of this promise, but as 'a gathering' rather than a party. Such semantics rarely impress parents, but it's good to see every generation instinctively try it. Teenagers are just teenagers after all, whichever era they are born in. As Cory prepared his parents' house for the impending arrival of his friends, he obviously drank a few cans of strong lager, some suitably horrible cider, and thought he should probably practice his smoking, so lit up a fag and inhaled deeply. The violent eruption from his mouth all over the kitchen floor of all he had drunk, as he coughed, spluttered, and gagged was enough to put him off smoking for life - well that and having to change his clothes and clear up the mess all over the kitchen floor. The lingering aroma didn't help his pulling efforts that night either!

Those parties were very popular as this group of teenagers got to know each other better and as they started exploring each other sexually too; lots of kissing, petting and sometimes more. Although they were all young and inexperienced, some swapping around happened too; but as they were all friends, it was regarded as normal behaviour – though usually not when people were a couple (although that did occur occasionally and cause much angst, see below). Cory, to his shame, recalled on one occasion pretending to have passed out as one girl (who he had been told was keen on him but the feeling was unfortunately unrequited) started kissing him! Not his proudest moment, but sadly not his worst either (but more of that later). It is fair to say that many of the more intimate moments happened privately or on subsequent one-to-one meetings; and although the group all knew it was going on, as long as no one was a couple and straying, it was fine. As part of his invaluable life lessons, Cory had two experiences over this period, where his then girlfriends became intimate with another of his male friends (in both cases, there was previous history, which was perhaps part of the explanation). That said, to be clear, Cory did also go with girls he knew were liked by or involved with other boys he knew; everyone was at it, and the lines were rather blurred. Or rather, more accurately, as has worked out and we will return to a few times in this book, the male species is made up largely of predatory beasts; and where sexual activity with females is concerned, there is very little (if any) loyalty to other males. Look at all the affairs that occur between married neighbours, couples' best friends, work colleagues and so on. Sadly, the cliché that too many men think primarily with their balls rather than brains is scarily true.

Benji and Penny had been an item in their early years at school. Cory didn't really know Penny then; she was part of the geek and nerd grouping when he had been part of the cool crew. Benji was in the same form group as Cory, so although they knew each other, they weren't close friends at that stage, as he was more in tune with the other group. Cory couldn't recall if he knew Benji and Penny had been together – probably not, as they weren't really relevant to his life at that stage. Weird how things change, isn't it? She evidently moved away from the school for a year or so, as her dad was relocated somewhere (he was some eminent scientist). Cory didn't know whether Benji and Penny had reunited on her return, as it was irrelevant to him. But that all changed once they all entered the sixth form. The story of Cory and Penny will be recounted shortly, but for present purposes, it is enough to record that they became friends and developed into much more. Benji was by now one of Cory's very good friends too. Cory spent little time thinking about Benji and Penny's previous childhood romance, as he and Penny were happy together and Benji was a good mutual friend to them both.

Cory was about to learn another of life's cruel, but vital, lessons he would never forget. Beware of men who claim to be 'just good friends' with attractive women. As Billy Crystal's character pronounced so wisely in *When Harry Met Sally*, men and women can never just be friends, as the sex thing always gets in the way. Oh, so true! Not necessarily from the woman's point of view, but almost invariably from the man's; particularly if she is attractive, he will want sex with her. Looking back now with the benefit of many years' experience, his view has not changed; in fact, it has hardened and been reinforced at every turn. Cory regards it now as a universal truth, with many personal examples to back this up. Every time one of Cory's girlfriend's would tell him X was just a good male friend, he knew the truth and was always proved right. The problem is that invariably, that's really what the girl in question honestly thinks. Her belief is that X is lovely and sweet and just a very good friend, as that's how she sees him. She wants nothing more than that from him, and she naively believes he knows and accepts that. A classic example of men and women being so different in their thoughts and emotions – men truly are from Mars and women from Venus. The reality is that each of these 'best friend' men are obsessed and in love with that girl. They adore and worship her and crave her so much. Either they have been rejected and pretend they are okay just being friends, or they have never had the courage to try progressing, so live in eternal hope and frustration at their unrequited love. They spend hours with and talking to these girls in the hope that she will realise his love, have a revelation about what a fool she's been not recognising it, and they will fall in love and live happily ever after. X will have rescued her from all those bad men she prefers to him and he will be her saviour. Cory relates further evidence of this weird phenomenon in later chapters to prove his point. The one exception to this is the gay man who is every girl's best friend. Every girl wants one, if she doesn't already have one. She gets all she often really wants from a man, the kind, sympathetic ear, the best friend, in short, the nicer version of normal men, without any of the testosterone-fuelled sexual desires for her that ruin all other friendships and many relationships too!

As Cory and Penny's relationship developed, they decided to go to see *Dire Straits* (who were cool and happening back then!) in concert at the Hammersmith Apollo. Benji, as their good friend, came along too. It was a great concert, a good night out, and everyone was happy and in a party mood. This however was all soured and ruined by the following turn of events. As Cory returned to his seat from a brief toilet break, he was staggered to see Benji leaning in towards Penny and the two of them snogging each other's faces off. Cory approached and asked what the fuck was going on. Penny went bright red and said she was sorry; it was a temporary aberration. She had got caught up in the mood of the concert. Although the details of the rest of the evening are hazy, Cory did not speak again to Benji from that moment for many months. He managed to resolve issues with Penny by her apologising profusely and promising to have nothing more to do with Benji. She came out with the classic line that she had been taken by surprise when he leant in for the kiss, as she thought they were just good friends. Benji had however admitted that he still had feelings for her, and she had temporarily been swayed to not resist, slightly drunk in the good mood of the evening by her ex declaring his ongoing feelings for her. Cory said it was her choice; if she still wanted Benji, she should go for it, but Cory would no longer be part of her life. She decided to stay and cut Benji out until the anger subsided. Therein lies another of life's eternal truths – you can never lose real friends. Yes, you can argue, hate each other, feel let down, and betrayed by them, and vow never to speak to them again. But if they are real friends, no matter how long the impasse, how big the schism in your friendship, one day, you will both think, 'Fuck it – our friendship matters more than whatever we fell out over.' If this never happens, then the sad reality is they were never truly a real friend. Naturally, those were not Cory's thoughts at the time, and he avowedly ignored and avoided Benji for a long time. It was awkward in a small town, and for a while in the sixth-form environment, though helped by the summer holidays intervening. Eventually, after a long period of reflection, they were reconciled. Benji was his friend. Benji and Penny had been together years ago, long before Cory was with her. She was a very attractive, vivacious young lady, who many boys lusted after. Cory decided that as long as there was never any repetition, it was an understandable one-off that could be forgiven. So he did. Given what was about to transpire, he was very glad he had done so.

Adrian and Nina was a very different scenario. That said, it was also scarily similar in too many ways to the Benji-and-Penny incident. Adrian was the headmaster's son mentioned above. He and Cory were friends, they went to football matches together, and they spent time together outside school. They got on well. Nina was also in the sixth form with them. Apparently, there was some sexual history between them, but then that applied to many of the randy teenagers in the sixth form! Cory had paid little attention to Nina previously, as he had been happy with Penny. After Penny though, Nina had made it obvious quite quickly that she was interested in Cory, and in true teenage boy style (which sadly many men never outgrow), he thought, 'What the hell! Why not?' She had seduced Cory at one of the regular house parties, and he had gone along with it. He knew very little about her, but teenage male testosterone levels don't need to know very much. They got together, and much later, Cory found out that she had a habit of seducing boys at parties. She had with Adrian and a number of others before and since. Cory took the view that he was enjoying their time together, the sex was great, and it served its purpose there and then. He went along with the relationship for the period of months it lasted. He knew it wasn't love. The intensity and connection he had enjoyed with Penny was not there, partly because they were very different girls, but mainly because Penny had been a very good friend before anything romantic developed. As Cory came to realise (especially now looking back over the decades), his best relationships have always evolved from some form of friendship first. His least meaningful or concrete encounters have been those where he met someone he didn't know and immediately fell into a relationship with them (with a few hybrid types too thrown in for good measure). Perhaps this is all overly analytical, though that is inevitable at times in a book such as this. Frankly, if he'd known then what he does now, with the benefit of decades of experience, wisdom, hindsight, and failed relationships and generally just 'getting his shit together', he probably would never have done a lot of it. But that's life, isn't it? We live and learn (or not, in many cases), don't we?

Nina was from a friendly working-class family. Her dad ran a local business in which her elder brother worked. He still lived at home with Nina and their parents, along with his much older girlfriend (who had kids nearly his age from her marriage) and their new baby. Her mum ran the house and was always friendly and welcoming, providing hot meals at lunchtime for all the family, organising the regular family nights out in the local pubs, and holidays. Her granddad lived two doors down from them and joined in all the above activities. This was all a new world to Cory though, and he took a while to adjust to these 'salt of the earth' types. He was told he was too polite and formal by Nina's mum over the first few weeks and gradually learned to just join in. It was an interesting change to his own middle-class upbringing. What shocked him though, apart from Nina's apparently insatiable desire for male attention and sexual favours offered in return, was the wider shenanigans that probably explained Nina's attitudes and behaviour. He became immersed in their family, as that's the way these traditional families are, open and welcoming and you become one of them. His slightly sheltered, blinkered upbringing by his caring, loving parents, but who weren't very worldly, was eye-openingly changed. The scales didn't just fall from his eyes; they were ripped off and destroyed forever. Although it was all quite shocking at the time to a still somewhat naive eighteen-year-old, it was all invaluable life experience. Like everything else in this book, vital life lessons were learned that have made him into the middle-aged man he is today, for good or bad, for better or worse.

It transpired that Nina was evidently known as something of an easy lay around town. People asked Cory why he was with her, especially when compared to Penny. All he could say was that given the way that had ended, he was just having fun. He came to realise he was just on the rebound and seeking solace and comfort, given the emotional trauma he had been through. Although it was never at the time as callous as it now sounds, he had used Nina to get over Penny. But as she had initiated things, he didn't feel guilty. It probably explained his attitude to her reputation and much of what he learned about her. She was known to have had a whole string of one-night stands, often with older guys, but then many attractive girls do as they grow up, and many men exploit this. What shocked Cory though was to learn that she had even shagged some of her dad's mates. Even worse, one of them was also having an affair with her mum at the same time! These were mind-boggling scenarios for Cory to comprehend. Her brother's older girlfriend also turned out to have been the wife of another family friend, until she started her affair with their son. Against this background, Cory thought, well she's okay when they were together, and if he found out she'd done anything behind his back, with any of her other older men, he would work out how he felt and deal with it at that time. No need to worry unnecessarily now and to stop his regular sex life just yet. What he didn't expect however was the scenario with Adrian, his friend. Cory divided his time between nights at Nina's and time at home studying for his imminent A levels. One Sunday morning, as he was leaving after another night of passion, she started asking him to spend the day with her. He said no, he had revision to do, as did she. Although she was bright, she was less academic than Cory and got upset with him. He was resolute though; he had to go and study. She said she might catch up with some of their friends, which he thought nothing of. She jokingly (or so he thought) said also that if he wasn't going to have sex with her again, she would get one of their other male friends to do so. Cory laughed and said, 'Yeah, fine.' He of course did not mean it. As it transpired, she evidently did! She chose to revisit her previous assignations with their mutual friend Adrian; not just as a one-off apparently, but as a bit of a fling. Although Cory was still relatively naive, he gradually realised over the following weeks that she was acting differently. One night when he wasn't due to see her, he suddenly decided to check where she was, not something he had ever contemplated before. His view was (and remains) that if you don't trust someone you are involved with, you probably shouldn't be with them. She was not at her friend's, where she had claimed to be, but at Adrian's (her car parked outside being conclusive proof). Cory confronted them, all sorts of arguments ensued, and it was all highly charged and very emotional. Adrian's dad, their school headmaster, subsequently learned of it all and, as a devout Christian, disapproved of his son's actions, whilst pointing out to Cory he should get out of this rebound relationship. Adrian and Cory went through the inevitable period of silence and eventually tried to repair the damage, but never could. Months later, an argument between them over something completely unrelated led to this issue arising and as the old tensions re-surfaced, Cory knocked Adrian off his feet with one punch. Nothing more was ever said about it, but their friendship was over. As for Cory and Nina, after their exams they went to Ibiza on holiday to see if they could fix things. Another valuable life lesson learned there: a holiday with your partner is a great way of finding out how compatible you really are, stuck together without a break for a week or more! He has used it very successfully many times since. It became clear that they couldn't fix the damage. Cory decided that although sex had been good and fun as a release from A level study tedium, now that was all over and he was going away to university (after a gap year), he no longer needed her in his life. It was at that stage that he and Abbey finally consummated their long-term friendship into something more physical and tangible, but the timing just wasn't right to make it into a longer term relationship. Sadly. But all of these incredibly important life experiences, good and bad, have undoubtedly influenced him over the decades since. The fact that he can recall them now, over thirty years later, so clearly shows how engrained they are in him. Sadly though, they pale into insignificance alongside the next major event and perhaps one of two main things in his life that have made Cory into the man he became.

Cory had achieved good O level grades in his exams (pre-GCSEs, coursework assessments, and all the modern changes) and decent A levels. He had no idea what to do, had toyed with joining the forces, but the Falklands War had just happened, so the spectre of real fighting and death (ironically, as it was soon to turn out) was too real and so went to university instead. Many did, as it was always a good option in those days, as you decided what to do with your life, before tuition fees, extortionate student rents, and the prospect of a better job on graduation – all unlike now. He got an excellent degree and then launched his professional career in the City. But it could all have been so different, as he could have been stopped in his prime because of what he did just before his eighteenth birthday.

Finding Love

Cory and Penny got together about halfway through their first year in the sixth form. They became friendly as they were doing some of the same subjects, and through the study and social time they spent with each other in the common room. She was a popular girl, well-liked by all. She was attractive, intelligent, sporty, musically talented and from a lovely, posher middle-class family. She was particularly popular with the boys. Cory noticed that the older boys in the upper sixth spent a lot of time around her. But he and Penny got on very well, and the bond between them appeared to be growing daily. Do please remember, though, that at this stage, he was still a shy seventeen-year-old and less confident around girls – very hard for women these days who know Cory to appreciate, no doubt! Cory valued their friendship, increasing closeness and connection, but given that she was being pursued by the older boys, thought it would just have to stay at that, at least until the older guys left at the end of the year. He subsequently learned from Penny that she was having similar thoughts. Indeed, her contemporaneous diary talked of liking Cory but being unsure if he liked her romantically, as although they were so close, he never made a move. Although she wanted him to, she wouldn't make the first move (as good girls didn't) so if he wasn't going to, she may as well start seeing one of the older guys. She recorded that maybe she would have Cory as her closest male friend, whilst being romantically involved with one of the other guys. The traumas of teenage emotions, love and lust!

Fortunately, the situation soon resolved itself. One day, Penny invited Cory over to her house to study, to discuss some of the work they were doing, and to hang out. He was delighted. It confirmed what he had hoped but been unsure of, that she liked him romantically too. Any such invitation always has a sub-text, as he knew even then. He arrived at her house, they had pleasant chats, discussed work, and then the moment came. He resolved it was now or never; they were alone, they liked each other and got on so well, so what the hell?! He was nervous, as he really cared about Penny but had to know how she felt. So he leant in for a kiss. Their lips met, and wow! All doubts evaporated. It turned out they had both been feeling the same for some time; nervous excitement and wondering if the other felt the same. They did. It was so sweet, so lovely, such a beautiful culmination to months of an increasingly strong connection growing between them. They laughed at how stupid they had both been to almost lose out on this, given their relative inexperience and naivety. After this and the subsequent events with Abbey, Cory was a changed man. Never again, he vowed, would he ever be left wondering if a girl liked him. But for then, he and Penny enjoyed their burgeoning romance, building on their already close friendship. All their sixth form colleagues asked why they had waited so long, as it was so obvious to everyone else how close and attracted to each other they had been for months. The only surprise was that it had taken them so long to finally get together. Seemingly, the only person who wasn't happy for them was their mutual friend, Benji. They spent even more time together, got to know each other's families, and their great connection grew quickly into teenage love. It was the first serious, deep, grown-up real relationship for both of them. Life was great. They enjoyed the spring and summer together in the sixth form and out. Over the summer holidays, they went to Wales camping with another friend and grew ever closer. They went up North for her to meet his extended family. The culture shock for her, particularly in the small working man's village was marked. These blunt-speaking Yorkshire people, with their strong views, opinions, and directness were a far cry from her genteel, socially correct, posh Oxfordshire village tennis and dinner party circle. She struggled to understand their accents, casual profanities as part of every other sentence and local phrases. She was thrown by their politically incorrect views of the world, their inherent racism (although to them, it wasn't), as they used names and labels, long since banned in polite society, that had been prevalent on 1970s' TV shows such as *Love Thy Neighbour* and those of a similar ilk. Her visit with Cory and his family to the working man's club was educational. She had asked for a gin and tonic with ice, please, as a posh southern girl would. The barman bluntly replied in his broad Yorkshire accent that they didn't do cocktails and 'if tha wants ice, tha'll 'ave to get up on't bloody roof in winter, lass'! She survived the experience; they were together, happy and in love.

They returned to sixth form to start their final A level year full of the joys of life, looking forward to making their university applications, and started discussing their possible future life together.

They intended to study different subjects at Uni, and that meant they weren't necessarily applying to the same places, but they had started to talk about whether they should or whether they should at least be close by. They knew deep down that they might meet new people and go their separate ways at Uni, so there was even talk of a temporary break once they got there to get that out of their systems without destroying what they had. It was all very sweet young love. Looking back now, Cory sees it for the tragic romance that it was. At that stage, they were very good for each other and very happy. Cory had even not done some of his assigned essays over that summer holiday, as he was enjoying his time with Penny so much. That was a first for him, as he had always been so diligent previously about doing school/college work. He was beginning to realise though that sometimes, you just go with the flow, enjoy what's happening, and don't stress. As things turned out, he was so glad he had taken that decision. It caused a few fraught discussions with the head of sixth form at the time, who noticed the change and encouraged Cory to keep a balance. As Cory has gone through life since, he realised how important that advice was. We rarely achieve a proper balance between our home, work and social lives, and we are all the poorer for it. They got their studies back on track but carried on seeing each other regularly outside sixth form too. As Cory's home was slightly outside the local town and Penny's village was on the other side of it, relying on lifts from parents and long bike rides had become tiresome, so Cory had bought himself a moped with the money he earned from his Saturday and summer jobs – no spoilt teenagers then, unlike Cory's own kids now! His parents worried about him out on it (ironically, as it turned out), but it gave him a new freedom he fully exploited. It also meant his image at sixth form suddenly changed into something of a biker boy, albeit a very mild, middle-class, small Oxfordshire market-town version. This was all rather ironic, as he was at the same time elected head boy of the entire school, probably as recognition of his good behaviour in the main school for five years and lower sixth the previous year. Such are the teenage years though, just as he achieved recognition, he was finding love and his perspective on life was changing. Penny was elected as one of his deputies, reinforcing her popularity too. They were the golden couple, bright, young, attractive, sporty, intelligent people, recognised by the school as Head Boy and Head Girl, a great couple together, deeply in love (well, as much as you can be at seventeen), with glorious futures and their whole lives ahead of them. Or so they thought.

As mentioned, there was a great social scene amongst the sixth form group; gatherings in local pubs were more regular now, as although all still under age, many pubs would serve them without question. The regular haunts in town were now becoming boring after too long drinking in them. It was decided that they would start to explore the more rural pubs in the beautiful Oxfordshire countryside in which they lived, as a number of them were passing their driving tests and had access to parents' cars on certain occasions. One Friday evening at the end of September, it was agreed that a crowd of them would meet at one particularly isolated pub in the middle of nowhere, down endlessly long, winding narrow country roads cut out between the trees and fields. So they all piled into a few cars and descended en masse on to the hostelry, where they had a great night. At closing time, they clambered back into their cars and headed off back to town to drop off the various passengers at their homes. Everyone was in great spirits; they were a crowd of decent, bright, well-educated young things from nice homes, all about to apply to the universities of their choices, enjoying their final year of sixth form together. How quickly that happy mood was violently shattered. The cars drove away from the pub in convoy down the dark, narrow country lanes. At one of the junctions, they split and went in different directions. The car Cory and Penny were in with three other friends proceeded further along a long, winding, single-track country lane. Cory recalled that they had to pull over at least once to let an oncoming car pass, but other than that, they were in splendid isolation. The car gathered speed on the long straights, then slowed as the bends in the distance came into view under the full headlight beam. That was the general pattern as they approached the outskirts of civilisation again; just around the corner and down the last stretch of country lane lay the main road, fully illuminated, unlike these dark, treacherous country lanes. But they never quite made it; they suddenly swerved at the final corner, the driver losing control on a sharp bend, and as he tried to steer back the other way, over-compensated (as young, inexperienced drivers do) and ended up in the ditch. The left-hand side of the car had hit one of the huge trees bordering the ditch and left the car crumpled on that side. The impact was loud and the full force was felt in the car. Bang. Crash. Darkness. Eerie silence.

PART II

Deaths & Births; Marriage & Divorce

*'Don't confuse your path with your destination. Just because
it's stormy now, it doesn't mean you aren't headed for sunshine'*
(Anonymous)

Death

It was the hardest phone call Cory ever had to make in his life,
from the local A&E, after the police and ambulance had eventually
arrived and sorted out the aftermath of the crash. No one had mobile
phones back then. They were on a deserted country lane approaching
midnight on that fateful Friday late September night, and passing
traffic was minimal. The nearest houses were still a mile away ahead
of them, and there were only endless rolling fields behind them.
There were various injuries, blackouts, and other consequences of the
crash. Cory had hit his nose and apparently broken it again and had
also seemingly blacked out with the impact. As he came round, it was
just deafening silence. He managed to clamber out of the car and
then looked back to assess the damage. The left-hand side of the car
was wrapped around the huge tree. It was crumpled and crushed on
that side. He ran around to the side Penny was on. She wasn't moving.

He thought she must have passed out too. He shook her, increasingly frantic. She looked so peaceful. The other passengers were extricating themselves from the car, one with a leg injury, another with arm/shoulder damage. The only one not moving was Penny. Eventually, a car arrived behind them. Cory had no concept of time at that point. He had no idea how long they had been there, how long ago the accident had occurred, how long until this car arrived. The driver stopped and surveyed the damage. Cory and the others implored him to drive to the nearest phone box (as we had to in the early 1980s) to call 999. He said he would do so and then asked what had happened. The teenagers explained they had been in the pub on a night out and had lost control on the way back home on the bend. The driver suddenly started screaming abuse at the group about the dangers of drinking and driving and asking what had they done. Cory and the others said they knew all of that and understood his comments and anger, but they needed an ambulance urgently for Penny. They weren't interested in debating these points with him; the police would deal with the aspects he was screaming at them about. He angrily drove off but apparently did call 999, as some time later, the police and ambulance arrived. The road was closed off; breathalysers and preliminary statements were taken by the police. The ambulance crew attended the injured. Cory begged them to wake Penny up; he had become increasingly upset that she still hadn't regained consciousness. He was screaming at her to wake up, that he loved her, 'Come on, Pen, come back!' She never did. Penny was declared dead at the scene. The late-night call he made from the hospital to his parents to tell them that will haunt him forever, as will the vision of Penny's parents answering that late-night knock at the door every teenager's parents dread, only to see the sombre-looking police officers there to tell you they have some very bad news. Even typing this now, over thirty years later, Cory is in floods of tears. It shattered his world. His beautiful, vibrant girlfriend, with her whole life ahead of her, had been violently ripped from him. All of her vivacity, her sweet personality, had been snuffed out in one fatal moment. As if all of that wasn't bad enough, who could Cory vent his anger on? The driver of the car naturally, as he had killed Penny. The problem was – Cory was the driver. He had killed the love of his life.

Penny had been sitting in the front passenger seat. She was wearing a seat belt, as the law making this compulsory had recently come into force, and yet that killed her. The impact on her side of the car was so intense that as she flew forward, her seat belt locked so sharply that the diagonal part across her chest had ruptured her aorta. She died instantly. She had been dead the whole time Cory had tried to revive her and had begged and pleaded with the ambulance crew to bring her back. The worst had crossed his mind the longer she hadn't revived, but he kept thinking, 'No, she can't be dead. Bad things like this can't happen to us. We have so much going for us, so much to look forward to. She has to come back.' This was the harshest lesson of all ever for Cory. Not only had he tragically lost the love of his life, he had killed her. A beautiful young seventeen-year-old girl with a glittering life and career ahead of her had been killed by the boy she had made the mistake of loving. This fucked Cory up for a long time, maybe permanently, forever. He still feels the guilt now and has never really got over what he did.

It was obviously an accident, caused by his inexperience, and Cory had only drunk two weak shandies along with soft drinks in the pub all evening (being a sensible and worried new driver); yet he still had managed to fuck up in the most extreme way. He kept telling the police he had killed Penny; he didn't care what happened to him now; he didn't deserve to carry on. He didn't want to be without her. He was breathalysed and wasn't drunk or over the limit. He had further tests at the police station after the hospital; all were negative. The subsequent accident investigation cleared him of speeding or driving at excessive speeds (apparently the tyre marks from braking are evidence of this). He was simply guilty of being an inexperienced young new driver who had fatally misjudged a corner on the dark country lane. The crash and actual impact had been caused not by his initial feeling that he had lost control around the bend, but by him over-compensating as he steered back the other way (the way people do when they skid on ice and snow and are advised to steer into the initial spin, never against it, as this merely makes matters worse). None of this was any consolation to Cory. He wanted to be punished. He didn't want to be excused. The way he felt then, lost and lonely, desolate and despondent, completely crushed, he wanted to go to jail for killing his girlfriend. Those around him tried to support and console him, but he was a lost soul. He was only happy in isolation and especially asleep, where he could reconnect with Penny in his dreams. He had no interest in anything else. He despised all those who told him it was God's will and only the good die young. If he hadn't already largely turned his back on religion, that was the final straw. It was all bullshit. It wasn't fate or pre-ordained; it was his fault for losing control of the car, hitting a tree, and literally destroying Penny's life.

He had also desperately let his parents down, obviously by killing another person, but on a more mundane and practical level, by writing off their new car, which they had reluctantly allowed him to drive as long as he promised to be safe and sensible. They weren't wealthy and only had that one car, and indeed that was the only new car they had ever bought only a short while before. His shame and guilt was all-consuming and he lived in a state of shock for weeks, if not months after. He can't now recall how long he was away from sixth form or when he went back. It was all a blur, all irrelevant, all pointless and meaningless. He went to stay with relatives who owned a hotel on the Devon coast and spent his days staring out to sea thinking about Penny, his nights dreaming about her and trying to connect with her again. The crushing realisation every day when he woke that it was all now just dreams, that he had lost her forever, was devastating. But the worst part was facing Penny's parents. He imagined if he were in their position, he would hate the person who had killed their daughter and would press for prosecution and punishment. He fully expected that. He accepted that if it happened, he may well face a custodial sentence, and then his life would take a new direction from all that he had planned. But he felt he deserved it. Penny, after all, no longer had a life. He had killed her. It nearly destroyed him. But he survived; not least because Penny's parents were amazingly gracious. They had lost their only daughter, killed in an (all too common) teenage car crash, and yet they apparently had no anger or bitterness towards Cory. Even as a basic human reaction, there must have been some, but he spent a lot of time with them in the months after Penny's death and never saw any at all, ever. What truly incredible people they were. They said the following: it was just a tragic accident; there was no evidence whatsoever of Cory doing anything wrong other than being an inexperienced driver, and they had allowed her to go out in the car with him. He was as devastated as them and had clearly loved her; they were so pleased she had found love even so briefly in her tragically short life; and there would be no purpose in ruining a second young life by pressing charges against Cory. His eternal gratitude and debt to them for their magnanimous approach to the worst time of their lives cannot be expressed in words. His life could (and possibly should) have been very different from the moment Penny died, but gradually, Cory got back on track and carried on. He will never be able to thank her parents enough for allowing him that opportunity. As the world-weary London loss adjustor who assessed his parents' damaged car said, any death by driving, whether accidental, careless, or reckless in his experience always led to some form of prosecution, as a matter of public policy. He said he was surprised that her parents' compassion led the local police not to pursue any charges at all against Cory. Even if he would probably have got off ultimately, as it was clearly a tragic accident, it was apparently unusual for the police not to take it to court to verify that. Cory has never forgotten that and the immense gratitude that he was allowed to carry on with his life, when she was not. Nor has he ever lost the guilt that he caused Penny's death (nor should he). He never will. Perhaps that's why he has put off writing this book for so many years, as it meant confronting many old demons, this being the greatest of them. The long-term effect this (along with another young death seven years later) had on Cory cannot be underestimated. It explains a lot of what he has done since and his attitude to life.

Back then, it led to his rebound relationship with Nina, and his A level grades being okay, but not as good as they would have been; but that was a small price to pay in the greater scheme of things. In his later career, Cory would always wince when colleagues dismissed candidates' 'extenuating circumstances' claims as reasons for worse grades than expected, as he knew first hand that sometimes it really is true. As with so many things in life, with perceived wisdom and attitudes, only those who have been through the worst of times can truly appreciate it when others suffer too. If you haven't experienced true pain, you can never understand why people sometimes act as they do and don't always conform. It is the difference between empathy and sympathy. As people often say, we learn far more from our mistakes and any pain we go through in life than from all the good times. Cory was unsure whether to defer going to university for a year, as he and Penny had planned to take a gap year together and work and travel their way around the globe. In the event, the decision was made for him by the dean of the law school he was to join. He said that due to his third A level grade not being quite as strong as their offer, but understanding fully the reasons why, they couldn't accept him that year, but would be delighted to the following year. The dean also suggested that a year out may be advisable anyway to help Cory clear his head and try to sort himself out fully before starting his law degree, as clearly he had been through a very traumatic year. It was excellent advice and one of the best decisions ever made for Cory. He loved his year out, and by the time he went back 'home' to Leeds University to start his LLB course, he was refreshed, reinvigorated, and in many ways, a changed young man. He worked in various local pubs and bars; a posh local hotel (where his big claim to fame was serving Michael Caine and his beautiful wife drinks and having a discussion about how to make Pimm's properly!); as well as his usual builders' labouring work, although by now, as a driver, he was allowed to drive the builder's van around at times, which was infinitely preferable to pushing a barrow full of rubble up a narrow plank on to the back of lorries (as he had for previous years). He enjoyed all of the jobs, mixing and matching between them for a few months each to raise the money to go travelling. But the mind-numbingly boring nature of the work, the dead-end nature of the jobs, and the lack of ambition of many of the older people he worked with (who did these jobs full time for life) made him all the more determined to achieve a good degree and successful career. This was in marked contrast both to the undecided, uncertain young seventeen-year-old who had no idea what to do (before Penny's death) and to the bitter, disillusioned, guilt-ridden, don't-give-a-fuck eighteen-year-old afterwards, who could so easily have flunked his A levels and messed it all up. As ever, his own parents were constantly there for him. Their love and support got him through the painful months after the crash. Even though he had been a stroppy teenager, they always loved him unconditionally and that is something he has learned and brought to his own kids. That frankly is the greatest gift any parent can give their child, and Cory was indeed blessed to have such loving parents. He hopes his own kids will say the same. As well as helping him to cope with Penny's death and his burning guilt over causing it, they also encouraged Cory to get back to his studies, with his A level exams only six months away. He no longer had the same drive and desire to achieve the best grades possible; it all seemed so pointless and insignificant now. He slowly worked himself back into his studies, but now alongside his increasingly external distractions of partying, nights with Nina and general teenage debauchery. Perhaps that's why even at times of stress now, decades later, Cory still has a recurring nightmare about having imminent exams for which he is wholly unprepared, particularly in subjects he hates and has never understood (maths and sciences). The human mind is a strange and dangerous thing! Maybe he should seek advice at some point on whether it has any deeper meaning than its recurrence when he has deadlines and is stressed! Back then, he recognised that he should at least try to get good grades, as he had applied to various unis to read law simply as he had no idea what else to do. When he got his A level results, his third and weakest subject (French), which had suffered most during his time out after the crash, had cost him his preferred Uni place. Before the accident, he had however interviewed for a place at Cambridge; his sixth form being keen to push the brighter students in that direction, as it obviously helped their image and statistics. Cory has never seen himself as an Oxbridge type, nor frankly does he regard himself as a City type, despite most of his career so far being there. To complete the trilogy of things Cory certainly is not - a public school boy. The irony of ending up working in a profession in the City full of many fulfilling each of those criteria is not lost on Cory!

After the investable post-traumatic hiatus following the accident, he discussed with his tutors how to gradually get his work back on track to at least try to rescue his A levels. It was recognised that he was unlikely to get the required grades to get into Cambridge (he hadn't applied to Oxford simply because it was too close to home; but loyalties now firmly lie with the dark blues in all matters). Cambridge Uni therefore said that he would be welcome to take the entrance exam after his A levels, as he had apparently shown promise at the interviews and they would encourage him to try again. This posed a quandary for all concerned. His sixth form could not offer such tuition; they had no experience of it, and as a state school some things were beyond them. It was suggested one of the local public schools could do so. Cory was initially not keen, not least as it would involve his parents having to pay for him to attend for a term, but several of his tutors encouraged and persuaded him to do it. His parents struggled to raise these unexpected fees, but did so. Bless them. So for a term at the start of his year out, Cory attended the public school part-time, only going in a couple of times each week, which was enough for him. He had evidently impressed the admissions tutor at the interview through some written work. This chap was his tutor too, and although from such different worlds, he and Cory got on well. Without him, Cory would have hated every minute of it. They prepared him on how to approach the Oxbridge entrance exam and, more importantly, had chums in the respective colleges they put a word in with. Although it was an interesting experience, intellectually stimulating and worth trying, as his tutors had encouraged, overall Cory hated it. The public school boy culture was as bad as he had imagined. He found the snobbery and social elitism so deeply engrained in these boys that they were oblivious to anything outside their pampered, cossetted, insular world. But his parents had paid for the advancement of his education, so he attended for ten weeks and took the exams; he was invited for interview by a couple of colleges, but his heart really wasn't in it. His fear being that if everyone at Oxbridge was like the public school boys he had met, he would hate that too. But as always he prepared properly, read all the dull scripts he was going to be examined and questioned on, but just felt no excitement at the prospect of potentially being one of the elite. Perhaps that showed. He did not receive any offers and was delighted to be able to go back to Leeds after his year out to normality and real people he would get on with. He has never regretted it. It may explain why he has never been a huge fan of the City and of many of those types in it. It may explain why he has never socialised with any of them and has avowedly brought his own kids up to be as normal, worldly wise and well-rounded individuals as possible.

After earning enough money, Cory then took off to the USA, initially to work on the Camp America scheme (where English students go out to work on American kids summer camps), and then to explore the United States. He loved the experience. He felt slightly like a fish out of water at first, being the only Englishman at his camp in deepest, darkest Kentucky. He was surrounded by extremely loud and outgoing Americans, and those were just the fellow counsellors, as the job attracts extroverts. But he grew to fall in love with it all, the people, the place and the good bits of their culture. He enjoyed it so much he subsequently ran the local BUNAC association at Uni, encouraging others to go (and a good way to meet new girls, he found); he went back each of the next three summers, working again on the camp and travelling even more extensively afterwards from north to south, east to west, along the coasts, and across the vastness of mid-America too (Greyhound and Trailways buses becoming his best friends). Then in his final year, with his then girlfriend, driving coast to coast from Florida to California in a week stopping at all the major places they could en route - that was one hell of a ride. He did all the tourist things (including the Twin Towers, as they were still there then) in every one of the many states he visited or travelled through. He also did some non-tourist stuff, like being shown around Congress on Capitol Hill through the underground tunnels and to see the Senate sitting presided over by the then vice president, George Bush (Senior). Ronald Reagan was president and changing the national minimum drinking age to twenty-one. Cory noticed how vehemently the police enforced this at many student parties he went to. What struck him as odd though was how many of the American teenagers he knew therefore used a whole array of illegal drugs instead. A slightly odd scenario, he thought. To digress too fully into his US ventures and his views on that nation would be however a step too far for the intended purpose of this book. Suffice it to say, he had a great time, made some great friends, many of whom he saw again as they came to London in subsequent years (and which Facebook has now allowed him to reconnect with thirty years later), and got to see a lot of that amazing country properly. As he says regularly to his own kids now they should get out there and see the world while you can, before you settle down and get bogged down by real life, work, relationships, mortgages, kids and the like. Enjoy life as much as you can, while you can. But then that may not surprise you, as you may have spotted that is one of Cory's main themes. And maybe that's the crux of why he has done everything he has. His motto being: 'Life can be short; make the most of it'.

University

University life suited Cory. He was almost twenty, felt he had been through quite a lot which had matured and hardened him to the world; he'd had an invaluable year out where he'd worked and travelled extensively and was ready for a new life. He enjoyed the intellectual stimulation of being back in education after his gap year. But of course, as is the case with most students, he loved the socialising most. He enjoyed meeting new people, the huge drinking and partying culture and the freedom to enjoy life. Nina visited him a few times at Uni, just for sex (as that bit had always been good in their relationship); he and Abbey had agreed that she would come up to see him too, but sadly, such a beauty doesn't wait around for long, and she was enticed away again by Cory's now professional footballer friend, Gez. He lived in the south in the same town as her; Cory was at Uni, 200 miles away. Gez was a young up-and-coming professional footballer in London; Cory was a penniless student in Leeds. Both realised that men always compete for girls, especially the attractive ones, and that's just the way life is (and he has seen nothing at all to change this view in the subsequent thirty years) so they remained friends. Cory had the weird experience of not only watching his childhood friend and teenage football teammate playing for his London club at Elland Road (against his beloved Leeds United), but then join him for a beer in the players' lounge after the match. Amazing, but he would have swapped it for Abbey!

But Abbey was once more taken; Nina was just an occasional booty call, and Penny (God rest her soul) had by now been gone for two years. Cory had dabbled on his travels and during his year off, but no one had ever developed into anything serious as he flitted around. Now here he was back in Leeds for the next three years. He was older and wiser, more confident and had learned not to prevaricate from his cautiousness with Penny and Abbey. He was ready. First came Freshers week. It lived up to all expectations. The worst part, and probably Cory's most embarrassing time ever with a girl, was early in that frantic week of excess. They had chatted at some point in one of the bars and ended up going back to her halls together at the end of a very long night. The fact that it was an all-girls hall didn't deter either of them, and they ended up in her room. Initially, they simply crashed out together. At some later point, the ensuing fun and frolics were all too energetic for the volume of cheap fizzy lager bloating Cory's malnourished student stomach. As he tried to explain to his equally inebriated hostess, mid-coitus, that he felt sick, he threw up all over the back of her bedroom door as he tried to find the door handle. She was naturally unimpressed. After a basic cleaning operation, many mumbled apologies, plus Cory's awkward early morning visit to the female-only toilet and shower block (and lots of withering stares from the other occupants), he rapidly made his excuses and left. He saw her once more that week, but she blanked him. Their paths never crossed again – one of the benefits of being at such a big Uni. Others followed, some more serious than others, but many were just randy students letting off steam together. Everyone was enjoying themselves, and therefore no-strings fun appeared to be the order of the day. Years later, Cory learned from subsequent work colleagues that at least one older girl on the law course, who had bedded him (and many others) a few times, enjoying her older woman status, had gone on to do the same thing at the law firm she trained at. It's very strange when you discover as a thirty-something lawyer in conversation over beers with your new workmates that you have shared sexual conquests! Or rather, more accurately, they had all been her conquests as she worked her way through as many younger men as she could find a decade or so earlier. This laissez-faire attitude did lead to some awkward situations. These included the roommates that Cory ended up sleeping with at the same time (sadly not as a threesum but at separate times). It seemed one apparently tried to steal him from the other, and which horny young man doesn't love such attention? The first girl being a beautiful athletic blonde, with whom Cory had great sex, was very shy, quiet and seemed to be struggling to cope with the drinking culture and was often very drunk or even unconscious. Her roommate was the opposite, a gregarious Welsh girl with an amazing personality, but clearly envious of her roommate's looks and body. What a sordid tale! Nearly as bad as the girlfriend of one of his flatmates, who started to make advances to Cory and ultimately left her man for him, which was awkward enough for Cory to have to change flats. It transpired her mum had suddenly died a year earlier, and this young lady was determined to live life to the full, taking what she wanted, when she wanted it; not dissimilar to Cory's attitude, which drew them together for a few months. Needless to say, she wasn't ever one man's girlfriend for too long, either by choice or him discovering she was dabbling elsewhere. So the pattern continued.

Apart from all the socialising, the course was interesting, and the people on it were generally great. Many ended up as lawyers in the City and are still in touch. There was a wide cross-section of society on the course, from the extremely serious and studious, through the posh types venturing North for the first time, to the average guys and girls who were bright, with enquiring minds, but who loved to party. There were also those at the extremes, the tall, dark, handsome guy who spent his entire time shagging his way through LGI's nurses' accommodation next to the Uni; the hardened Northern drinking boys, whose lives revolved around the Uni bar and pub opening times (this was just before all-day pub opening times was introduced);

and of course, the eternal students. There were two in particular on the course, good-looking foreign guys, whose parents were wealthy, senior government officials back home. They weren't therefore overly concerned as long as they got through the course, as their futures were mapped out for them. Thus, they spent their lives moving from Uni to Uni, course to course, and girl to girl. What a life! And then there was Lisa.

Cory and Lisa met socially in the early days of the course; they were at law faculty drinks, all getting to know each other. They continued to get to know each other as the course went on over their three years in Leeds, and ultimately, they got together in the final year. There had been the usual build-up and flirtation as their friendship had grown and developed; it was both very exciting and a natural culmination when they finally decided to make a go of things. The timing felt right too. Fun had been had over the Uni years, but now as graduation approached, something more solid was perhaps in order. Once again, what was to become his strongest and (to date) longest relationship had grown out of prior friendship. It also supports his firm belief that the timing and circumstances have to be right for it to work too. Look at the Abbey situation and at further evidence later on as well. Cory has no doubt, looking back now at his thirty-plus years' life of assignations and relationships, that there has to be an alignment of it being the right time and situation in both people's lives (along with the mutual attraction and other chemistry required) for it to work properly. Probably one of the major reasons so many relationships fail is the difficulty of ensuring all such factors, on both sides, are all in line at the same time. Of course, people do enter into relationships without all of this being the case (whether consciously or not) and invariably encounter problems when the disparities become apparent – such as one person wanting the relationship to be more serious than the other and the tensions that causes. Cory has encountered this from both sides, as we shall come to explore later.

Coincidentally, Lisa's and Cory's parents didn't live very far apart down south, and consequently, both had already applied to the same law school for the following year. They knew that they could easily carry on seeing each other if they wished to. They spent increasing amounts of time together in their final months at Uni, keeping their relationship secret initially from others on the course, although this caused some problems. One was at their annual law faculty dinner (where inexplicably, Jimmy Saville had been invited along as the guest of honour – he was a strange character and the girls found him very sleazy, but this was when he was in his pomp and none of his heinous crimes had yet come to light). Cory, his mates, Lisa and hers managed to get a table together. One of the other guys on their course was making his feelings for Lisa very obvious that night, as no one knew they were an item. It was awkward but fully understandable. Cory could see why the chap liked Lisa (as obviously he did), and she was looking stunning in her ball gown that night. Anyway, their relationship soon came to light when people outside their immediate circles spotted one leaving the other's house one morning, and the passionate kiss goodbye was a giveaway. They met each other's parents and decided to go to the USA together that summer after graduation. Time in New York, then a holiday in Florida was followed by the drive from Florida to California. That was an amazing experience. Cory had travelled thousands of miles across the United States over his previous summers there, mainly by bus, some by plane, and now was adding the automobile to complete the set. It was a long drive, but a great way to see so much. Cory and Lisa continued to grow ever closer, so when they returned home and started at law school, it was no surprise that they were spending so much time together. They decided to both give up their separate shared accommodation and live together. This was the start of twelve years living together and all the changes they went through. They grew from young students falling in love, starting out on their professional careers, then balancing marriage, kids, career changes, and all the issues people encounter on life's journey. That was until the sad day it all finally ended well over a decade later. And that, dear reader, in many ways, is the point of this book - what happened? Why did all that love, happiness, and excitement get lost along the way? How did this young couple who had started out as friends, who became best friends, husband and wife, loving parents, and so much more, end up for many years as bitter enemies, as their divorce and the inevitable acrimony resurfaced time and again. Thankfully, although the scars are still there, increased civility has been restored in recent years. The common bond of their amazing children requires them to put the kids above their own issues. They had agreed to do this in the early stages of divorce, but all the usual shit got in the way. Cory's biggest regret in life (apart from the fatal crash, obviously) is the damage their kids have suffered. They obviously know he is writing this book and understand that a large part of it is a cathartic experience, an outpouring of his thoughts, a stream of consciousness, with the benefit of his older, worldly wisdom now looking back on those crucial years and why he did what he did. Whether they choose to read it, Cory has no idea - it is obviously painful and personal, perhaps more for them than him. As he recently explained to them at a boozy family birthday lunch, apart from trying to explain to them the way men think (and he thought), if it can help anyone else who is going through the inescapable relationship issues we all encounter at some point, then maybe it is worth the painful bits. That is for others to decide. As stated at the outset, it is not a forensic investigation of every aspect of that marriage, as that would be too personal, painful, and intrusive. It is rather an overview of the issues and why often men react and think as they do. At the time, Cory struggled with his thoughts and decisions, and it tore him apart inside. He has come to realise decades later that (a) this is all part of growing up generally and (b) a lot of men think in the same way, if not worse. Maybe this sorry tale can help people to focus on why.

Love

After initially living in a small bedsit, with shared toilet and bathroom facilities with the other residents of the large town house which the resident landlord had converted, they realised that they needed more space. An upgrade to a 'real' flat was possible (despite the landlady's initial reluctance to rent to students, even to respectable post-graduate lawyers), thanks to Cory having secured a training contract (or articled clerkship, the antiquated term still used back then) with a major City law firm. Not only had they generously contributed to his law school course costs, but given the booming City market, they also kept awarding pay increases. Cory's initial indicative starting salary when he accepted the offer had been just under £10,000 p.a., which had increased to £15,000 by actual start date. Money talks and the landlady was persuaded that she could make an exception in this case. Another important life lesson learned! The flat gave them space to study properly for their law society final exams – an intense regurgitation of a year's worth of course notes, frankly a pretty pointless exercise and subsequently changed years later. Cory felt it was akin to going back to O level years, completely ignoring the five years' progress to essay writing answers for A levels and degree level since. There was no room for any thought or interpretation, literally just showing you knew the facts and being marked accordingly. And of course, there was the dreaded Accounts course, double entry bookkeeping and other equally mind-numbingly dull (and baffling) maths-type issues! He, like many on the course, were creative types, essay writers, forced now to learn this nonsense. It was wholly anathema to him, but he learned it, regurgitated it, passed the exam and promptly forgot it all; all very worthwhile (not!) and completely irrelevant to his prospective career in the City. In fact, so much of the course was aimed at sole-traders and small practitioners that the Law Society was forced to change it radically subsequently at the powerful City firms' behest. As Einstein sagely said: '*Education is not the learning of facts, but the training of the mind to think*'. Those who devise our education policies, at every level from kindergarten upwards, should bear this in mind always.

Cory and Lisa were very happy in the flat building their little nest together. They were still relatively impecunious students, so filled their time with some socialising and plenty of studying. They both worked hard at assimilating the huge amount of information they were expected to learn (all very different, it seems, to their own kids' education these days). The flat fortuitously overlooked a local park area which had football matches every weekend, so Cory could watch these from the lounge window when notionally studying! It also had the requisite number of takeaways, pubs and off licences close by to keep them suitably well-nourished. They did not have a car, which as students they thought was normal, though not amongst many of their peers. This affluent southern town attracted a lot of very posh and wealthy students driving their own cars, given by parents to help them through the year, and even often Mummy or Daddy's huge 4 × 4 or executive saloon (why do our upper-classes call their parents mummy and daddy when the rest of us regard this as a childish habit long since left behind – just listen to our royal family!). It reminded Cory of one of the first questions he had been asked during his brief stint at the public school a few years earlier, when he had pulled up in his parents' standard family car. One chap had asked if that was his mother's car. Clearly, it was the family type car their mummies (or more likely their nannies) drove, not the beasts that daddies handled. The concept of the family only having one car that they all shared and drove when needed simply never occurred to them. This world was alien to him and to Lisa, who came from a similar family background to his own (although her parents were long-since acrimoniously divorced and remarried, but that's a whole different story for another time and place). They successfully got through their relentless end-of-year exams, which seemed designed to test mainly how they coped with the pressure of so many exams in one week, often two different subjects each day. Their working lives were due to start at the end of their final summer as students.

They went on holiday with friends, driving through France to a Spanish seaside resort that summer, taking in the sights as they went. It was a great, relaxing holiday and they decided they would live together when they started their respective training contracts. The issue was that he was going into the City; she to a provincial firm where she would get a wider training, as she had no wish to be a City solicitor. Nor did Cory have any such particular burning desire, but he was now on the treadmill and that was the obvious direction to go in. He had no particular idea whether that was really the career and life for him at that young, inexperienced age, but it was as good an option as anything else. Geographically, they sought to compromise by living out of London, near a fast train line in for him and within commutable driving distance to her work. In theory, it was a great idea and they found a cute little one-bedroom house, which they moved and settled into that summer before they began their legal careers. They were both settling well into their jobs, enjoying finally starting their working lives as (trainee) lawyers after the requisite years of studying and passing exams. They enjoyed their weekends in their little home and all was good initially. After a few weeks of the journey, Cory realised that their blissful ignorance of commuting, working long days, and the joys of the London Underground at rush hour had been a mistake. The novelty quickly wore off as the weather turned colder and delays kicked in. He also had been, as a non-Londoner, completely unaware of the hassle involved in getting a tube across London and having to change lines after his train commute, just to get to the office; this all being during rush hour, which until you experience it you can have no idea of how awful it is. As people often point out, animals being transported to slaughterhouses travel in better conditions! It was a huge shock to Cory. He was new to this working life and all that went with it. The three hours-plus travelling each day on top of a minimum eight-hour working day and often more (as City law firms pay well, but extract their pound of flesh in return) meant he was exhausted. It also meant he and Lisa weren't really seeing each other in the evenings, and it was all very strange. These were the first, very early harsh lessons of working life. No matter how happy you are and however well you think you will cope, real life has a habit of getting in the way of everyone's best laid plans and often helps to fuck things up. They discussed matters at length and ultimately agreed that the long-distance commute wasn't feasible long term. They had been naive to think it was. New plans had to be made. They had to give up their little home. Cory moved to rather unpleasant temporary bedsit accommodation in south London; Lisa went to stay with his parents, who fortunately were close to where she was working. He came home every weekend, but they decided to sort things properly. Lisa applied to transfer her training contract to firms nearer to London and was successful. They were able to reunite and take up the rental of a top floor, one-bedroom flat in the huge town houses around Earls Court. Their flat was tiny but they were happy. The commute for both was fine, work was good, and they socialised with their London friends again. Life seemed to be back on track; they had solved their temporary blip and were young professionals enjoying London. They enjoyed, endured, suffered, and went through every possible emotion through the 1990 World Cup, where England had seemed so dire at the outset but proceeded to almost reach the World Cup Final – the pain of that semi-final defeat on penalties was one we as a nation grew to expect and endure even more in subsequent years. They regularly saw the couple they had holidayed with the previous summer and spent weekends and bank holidays with them. It was on the fateful August bank holiday in 1990 that life dealt another devastating blow to Cory's family.

Death

Cory had two brothers: Alfie was two years younger and Joe was almost six years younger. Cory was approaching his twenty-fifth birthday and was halfway through his training contract in London. Joe had just finished his A levels and was travelling in the United States and Canada before going to Uni. Alfie lived locally, having given up on school and gone into the real world of work, aged sixteen. Cory had seen Joe before he went away. He had seen Alfie that bank holiday weekend when visiting the family home. They had argued and parted on bad terms. Lisa, Cory, and their friends had initially been unsure how to spend the bank holiday Monday and, after a lazy morning, resolved to take a picnic to Kew Gardens. They did so, stayed until the evening, then had a few drinks and came home. This was still in the days before mass mobile phone ownership, so as they entered the flat Cory pressed the answerphone machine button to retrieve the message indicated by the flashing light. His dad's voice was sombre as he asked Cory to call back when he could. Cory and Lisa looked at each other concerned and Cory immediately called his parents' house. His dad answered the phone. Although at the time Cory struggled to take in what his dad said, subsequently, he realised the irony and symmetry of his dad making this call to him. Seven years earlier, Cory had called his dad late at night from the hospital and had to say that Penny was dead. This time, his dad simply said to Cory: Alfie is dead.

Alfie had been a troubled soul since his teenage years. Even as a toddler, he was always involved in some scrape or another. He was what one of Cory's aunts described as 'a real boy' (nothing like classic stereotyping, is there?). Cory recalled having to defend him at times as they grew up, as he had a tendency to provoke others and be naughty. But he was Cory's younger brother and they were close, so he defended, protected, argued and fought for him. As teenagers, Cory and Alfie clashed a lot, regularly, and it was quite frightening. There were full-on fights, smashed doors, and simmering tension between them for a few years. It was all just a manifestation of their mutual teenage angst coinciding with usual sibling rivalries. Cory was quieter, more studious and sensible throughout their childhood and teenage years (not so much a 'real boy' apparently – maybe he has spent his later adult years misbehaving trying to make up for it?). Unfortunately, many people committed the cardinal sin of comparing Alfie to Cory. The fact that this included teachers, especially the headmaster, and other professionals was inexcusable. It simply reinforced Alfie's resentment of Cory and the system which only judged him by (unfavourable) comparison to his elder brother. Alfie was intelligent but from the age of about fourteen, had rebelled increasingly. At the time, the family counselling, the issues with Alfie and their ongoing arguments all just irritated Cory. He was a selfish teenager and couldn't be bothered with all the hassle caused by his brother. As they had grown up, they had been very close and great friends, always playing together throughout their childhood, up north and down south, yet they were now distant, and the antipathy between them was palpable. Cory made his views known to the professionals who got involved. He sadly shared the sentiments of all the pompous types who should have helped Alfie but instead wrote him off as not being like his brothers. This, of course, merely reinforced Alfie's anger and the classic middle child syndrome he clearly suffered from – and who wouldn't, when your teachers tell you that both your elder and younger brothers are better than you and you should be more like them? Cory's only excuse for sharing these views was that he was a typical self-centred, stressed teenager trying to study for his O levels and resenting all the distractions Alfie caused. There can be no excuse though for that attitude from teachers, social workers, and family counsellors; no wonder Alfie rebelled more and more at every turn. Looking back, Cory would have done the same. The problem was that no one could understand Alfie and why he acted as he did. He was from a good home, a nice middle-class family, loving parents, growing up in a safe affluent area, and he was (as were all three boys) a good sportsman. But it wasn't enough for him. His rebellious streak seemed to be fuelled by authority patronising him; instead of trying to empathise with him, the school just told him to be more like his brothers. How crass and stupid! He deliberately went the other way. Their poor parents didn't know what to do for the best. As their dad was very senior within the schooling system for emotional and educationally disturbed kids, it was assumed he must know how to deal with Alfie. But we are all much better at our jobs when we are objective, as once subjectivity and emotional connections come into play, it is harder to always see the wood for the trees. Our own feelings and involvement descends like a fog and clouds the clarity of vision we would bring to that very situation at work. As they were always told at law school, a lawyer makes his own worst client; similarly, look at how many others are unable to bring their professional skills to bear in their own lives. Otherwise, no marriage guidance counsellor would ever have marital issues; psychiatrists would have no mental problems and so on. Life doesn't work like that, sadly. Indeed, whatever wisdom and insight Cory may now be able to offer on relationships, love, and human emotions clearly wasn't always evident in his own actions over the years. Real life got in the way. His own temperament and feelings meant that he was rarely as dispassionate as he should have been. But you can't be. When it's your own life, you are by definition too involved. You can't step back and look objectively at everything. You can't strip out all human feelings and emotions and forensically analyse yourself, your partner, and family and come up with objective solutions to whatever the issues (or solutions) are. Some people try to or pretend they can. But it's impossible. Alfie was like that too. Even if he knew what he was doing was wrong, it seemed he couldn't help himself. He was too caught up in it all. He wanted to show the school that he couldn't just be ignored; to take from society what he felt he was entitled to, and to live his life his way, refusing to conform. With access to eminent child psychologists through work, Alfie's parents did all they could to understand him, to find out why he kept doing all he did, through all his apparent cries for help/regular 'fuck yous' to school and society. The most plausible explanation they ever received after years of trying to work him out, shortly after his death, was that he simply had some form of genetic imbalance, some form of hard wiring not quite right. It was the classic nature-versus-nurture scenario. All three boys had been brought up the same; the other two conformed and were well respected; Alfie didn't and wasn't. This meant he seemingly craved excitement, adventure, danger, and rebellion. This certainly explained both his constant issues as a child and subsequent rebellious, resentful teenage years.

Alfie had stolen from his family regularly, from his parents and then from his brothers. It was as if he was taking back what he felt he was owed by them, for the better lives and privileges he felt they enjoyed. Cory and Joe both went to university; Alfie dropped out of school at sixteen, thereby choosing not to. Yet he appeared to think he was entitled to take money to compensate for that. That was the reason Cory and Alfie had argued the last time they saw each other, as Alfie had stolen cheques from Joe while he was abroad. This followed a familiar pattern to what Alfie had done to Cory a few years earlier when he was a student; taking what he felt he was owed. Alfie also had a drink (and possibly drug) problem too. He was a bit of a geezer, a boy about town. He worked in pubs and bars in and around Oxford but seemed to move a lot. He lived with a girlfriend on and off, but came home often when they fell out and at least one occasion when he had been beaten up. He had been sent to a youth offenders institute for a few months at the age of seventeen for stealing from an employer. Although that appeared to shake him initially to sort himself out, it wasn't enough long term. By the time of his death, he was living at home again and had been to see the local doctor about his drinking issues. The doctor had prescribed Heminevrin to help his alcohol withdrawal symptoms. The family hoped that he was sorting himself out as he matured. The problem was that as well as all the other known side effects, still drinking whilst taking Heminevrin was dangerous. It proved to be fatal for Alfie.

Alfie's dad found him dead in his bed in his room at their parents' house that fateful bank holiday Monday. Cory had argued with him the day before, telling him he was fucked up to steal from their younger brother, as he had from Cory and their parents previously. There was talk of possibly getting the police involved, as he evidently never learned. In retrospect, Cory should have realised that a lot of the fight had gone from Alfie. Whereas previously he would have fought and argued back initially, then moved on to apologise and promise it would never happen again and use his inherent cheeky charm to smooth it over, there was none of that this time. He just looked at Cory, lost, scared, nothing to say for himself. Maybe it was partly the effect of the Heminevrin on him, maybe it was his way of showing he'd lost his fight, his desire to keep ducking and diving his way through life. Whichever it was, that was the last time Cory saw his brother alive, as Alfie died in his sleep that night. Apparently, he choked on his own vomit, as his usual gag reflexes and reactions had been dulled by a mixture of the Heminevrin and alcohol. There was an initial working theory that he may have deliberately taken an overdose of the pills, as many were missing, and washed them down with alcohol. He had stolen a case of wine Cory had delivered to the house a week earlier; he had said it never turned up, but then Cory had found the packaging and some of the empty bottles in the woods at the end of their parents' garden. The post-mortem was delayed due to a backlog after the bank holiday weekend, so this apparent suicide theory sat with the family for longer than it should have. It was dispelled when the post-mortem results came back to reveal that he hadn't taken the missing pills and only had minimal alcohol in his system. It was simply a tragic accident evidently. They were told it was akin to (an adult) cot death, the only explanation being that the sedative effects of the pills may have meant he simply didn't react when he started being sick by coughing and spluttering, as is normal human instinct. There was no explanation as to where all the pills had gone. They will never know.

Joe was eventually tracked down by leaving messages at youth hostels to call home urgently on the route it was believed he was taking across North America/Canada. The emotional outpouring between the family as he walked into the Arrivals hall at Gatwick was incredibly intense. Cory still feels it at times, even these days when he walks through that area of the airport, as such profound feelings never leave you. They fade with time and life moves on, but you can never forget. There was a big family funeral. Alfie was cremated in his beloved Newcastle United football shirt and the grief was tangible. Joe and Cory immediately became closer and a bond formed between them that hadn't been as strong before due to their age difference; Cory and Alfie grew up together with Joe as the later baby/little kid in the background. But now, they were united in their grief for the loss of their brother, and it reinforced Cory's firm belief that family is everything. No matter what else happens in life, no matter what arguments and disputes arise, no matter where our paths may take us, family bonds should never be lost. He had thought this as a kid, enjoying the extended families on both sides of his parents' families, but this had faded a bit as they had all grown up. This was particularly so when some of the family secrets had eventually come out, after years of silence and turning a blind eye (as society often did back in those days) ended with an almighty crash as people turned on each other over past indiscretions and behaviours. More of that later. Whatever Alfie's issues, crimes, and own selfishness, he clearly did not deserve to die. Indeed, he was compared to one of their uncles who had been dodgy when younger (and arguably never really changed) but had grown into an older, cheeky charmer. Alfie had been denied that opportunity. Cory resolved that he wanted a big family of his own and for them to be strong and solid with each other. He and Joe, although sharing many family character traits, are also different in many ways, but are as strongly bonded as ever decades later.

Cory wondered if Alfie's death was some form of retribution for the fatal crash that ripped Penny from her family seven years earlier. He struggled to cope with another tragic young death and really questioned the point of everything. Was it worth bothering with qualifications, with working so hard, with trying to have a normal life? He took time off work and his law firm employers were hugely sympathetic. His affection for that firm even decades after he left is firmly rooted in this; in contrast to another City firm five years later, who were quite the opposite. He had regular meetings with Cruse bereavement counsellors, who helped him hugely through the worst of times. He drank heavily to blot out the pain (not that it ever does). A few months later at a work party, Cory was told by someone he vaguely knew (but not well and who didn't know about Alfie's death) that he looked as if he was trying to drink himself into oblivion. He was. And he has at subsequent times of his life, when upset, stressed, and disappointed, not because it offers any solution, he knows that. Indeed, things often seem worse on the downer afterwards, but because for that moment, all of the shit goes away, no matter how briefly (although drinking heavily often creates its own shit too!). Cory regards it as a safety valve in his life. It is his way of releasing tension, of escaping life's pressures even if just for a while. This is not an excuse, just an explanation. He knows those around him hate it when he goes to these extremes. He knows that, yet drinks anyway. He can go for long periods without alcohol, but finds that when he starts drinking, once he reaches a point of no return, he will often go on all night; not every time, but too often over the years, especially when out socially. He is a binge alcoholic. Many people are, particularly in the City. It has occurred often to Cory that of course many people drink for many reasons, but in his experience, driven, intelligent men particularly find it hard to switch off, and this is their default mode. Certainly, the multimillion-pound trade in City bars, clubs, and various other nefarious venues supports this contention.

Cory was again left reflecting on a young death of someone he loved. That was now two in the past seven years. Although Alfie had many issues, he patently did not deserve to die. The timing that he did so (apparently by a freak of nature), the day after they had argued, added to Cory's grief. And to his guilt. He wondered if he was somehow jinxed, if he was destined always to lose those he loved, or even worse, to cause or contribute to their deaths. These thoughts were intense and much of the grieving was both for Alfie as well as the old wounds of Penny's death being reopened. It was a horrendous time, not just for Cory, but for Lisa too. They were physically living together in their tiny flat, but Cory was no longer there mentally and emotionally. Lisa stood by him, but Cory was a lost soul. He no longer knew what he wanted from life, whether it was all worth it. Fortunately, his law firm was so supportive, and luckily, he was in a specialist department at that stage, where there weren't the same relentless hours as in some of the bigger, macho groups. The firm as a whole were kind and sympathetic, and the lawyers he worked directly with were particularly so. They knew his mind was elsewhere but, after a few weeks, welcomed him back (so that he had something to do during the day) without any expectation that his mind was on work at all. Cory was very lucky to have this support both at work and at home. Yet still he questioned the meaning and purpose of life and if it was all worth it. This led him continuing to drink a lot; he started going out socialising with work mates and regrettably strayed and slept with a few other people. He felt torn and guilty as he occasionally cheated on Lisa but also thought, 'Fuck it! Why not?' He too could be dead tomorrow. Random drunken gratification seemed more important than a serious relationship. His life, relationship, and career all felt as if it was in the balance, and he was unsure whether to stay on his original course or to just leave altogether.

The best analogy he could think of was that he was on a tightrope walking across to his original destination and aims in life, still believing that was where he should go. But the rope was wobbling;

he was losing his footing, slipping, and losing the motivation to carry on at times. Yet he couldn't allow himself to fall completely. He knew that he needed to get through the shit and then decide rationally, once his head was sorted, what he wanted from life. He knew he needed to decide properly, both for his own sake and Lisa's, but not during those dark times when nothing mattered. Sadly, he knew from Penny's death and the aftermath that although the pain, guilt, and grief never goes away, it does fade with time. Time isn't a healer, as people claim, but it does generally allow people eventually to re-focus on their lives, to get back on track and to fill the void left by death and tragedy. That is the usual way grief plays out, but there are always instances where people never recover, such as parents of murdered children, who never get over that tragic loss; where partners can no longer cope when their loved one dies and soon follow. Cory can understand why. He was able to articulate this to his Cruse bereavement counsellor and will be eternally grateful that he was blessed to have one who understood. The counsellor didn't talk in clichés, such as time healing; the good dying young, it being God's will, and all the other bullshit Cory had heard after Penny's death. Cory was a rational, intelligent young man who knew there were no answers, but also knew he had to vent his rage and anger at the unfairness of Alfie and Penny both dying young; his guilt at his role in both, but ultimately no one could sort things out for him. We all deal with grief (and stress) in our own ways, and you have to go through the pain and hopefully come out of the other side. There is no shortcut, no way of circumventing it. You can't ignore it, pretend it's not there, or hope it will just go away. You have to confront it. We each find the best way to do that and invariably terrify those around us in the way we do it. People are often out of control, go off the rails, and lose their way during the process. Some work through it and come back. Some don't. The counsellor agreed and let him rant. Over the weeks, they gradually came to discuss that he either had to let the grief overwhelm him, give in to it, drop out for a while to find himself (or lose himself further); or he had to fight back yet again, as he had during his A levels. He wavered, he strayed, he almost gave up on his job, his relationship, and the life he had been so happy in until Alfie's death. But ultimately, Cory knew that it would all be a waste to not fight back yet again. He had survived and come back from Penny's death to get this far, so why let it all slip away now? But it was a close call and he fully understood how people can be crushed by tragedies in their lives and lose the will to fight on.

It was an awful few months for Cory, for his parents, and for Lisa. She stood by him and he knew he had to talk to her properly. Eventually he did. She was distraught that he had cheated. He tried to explain none of it had meant anything; it was all part of his not giving a shit. Although it was a very close call, she eventually forgave him, and they resolved to stay together and make it work, which they did for many years. Naturally, when they eventually split up and divorced over a decade later, Lisa said that she wished she had walked away at that stage. Cory fully understood why. Cory's parents were obviously also very badly affected by Alfie's death. They had always been loving, affectionate parents, never rich, never spoiling their three sons, but doing all they could to give the boys as comfortable a life as they could, teaching them a proper moral code, bringing them up to be respectable young men. The emotional security was key. Yet Alfie had rebelled against this. Cory could see in retrospect that Alfie's rebellious teenage view of the world appeared to mirror his own after Alfie's death: just not caring, hating everyone and everything, and rebelling by doing stupid, hurtful things to those around you. Their mum particularly had battled with Alfie over his drinking, his behaviour generally, and his attitude as she brought them up. She hated drinking to excess anyway (something in her past about her dad, their lovely, cuddly granddad, turning quite nasty when drunk on whiskey evidently) and always objected when any of her sons were drunk, as she still does even though we are middle-aged men now! But she was a practical, down-to-earth Northerner who dealt with whatever life threw at her. Her comment would often be that you just have to deal with life and get on with it. She had raised three young boys on little money, performing fully the traditional mum and housewife role for many years, as that was her duty (even now, you can tell she doesn't fully approve of any woman who doesn't fulfil that role). These days, after fifty years of marriage, she cares full-time for their dad, who has been deteriorating over recent years as he suffers from one of life's cruel degenerative diseases. It is sad both to see him like that and to see how she is now simply his carer, rather than anything else any more. But again, she sees it as her duty; very commendable and not necessarily the way Cory's or the younger generations think. These old-fashioned, traditional ideals and qualities are at her core, as that's just the way she was brought up and always thinks and acts. She dealt with Alfie's issues pragmatically and, although clearly devastated to lose one of her sons, now brought her same stoical approach to life to bear as always. Her advice to Cory was to carry on with his legal career, his life, and to not let Alfie's death destroy all he had to live for. Cory eventually saw that she was right and sorted himself out (for a few years, at least). Cory's dad, however, struggled to cope with Alfie's death.

Their dad was a great guy. He started life as a PE teacher and progressed to become a headmaster. He was always an active parent and, although working long hours in intense jobs dealing with educationally and emotionally challenged kids (and that was just at work, never mind home!), every weekend took the boys to swimming when younger, then to their respective football matches for years as they grew up. He was also their mum's ultimate threat to them when fighting, arguing, etc.: 'Just you wait until your dad gets home' being the dreaded words she used while bearing the brunt of their childhood and teenage fights, their cheekiness and general issues (well that was as they grew older, and her threats with Scholl sandals and the large, illustrated Bible no longer worked!). Depending on the gravity of the offence and how stressed he was from work, this could either lead to him immediately running up the stairs to confront the offending boy(s) or a more measured discussion later in the evening. He was a loving dad and everyone said what a great guy he was, including their friends, other kids he coached or refereed at football, and even the kids he taught. In fact, completely randomly, some guy contacted Cory through Facebook very recently to say Cory's dad had been head of the school this guy had attended twenty-five years ago; that Cory's dad had saved him, had sorted him out, and given his life purpose, which had led to his subsequent successful adult life. Amazing to know their dad had that effect on so many others as well as his own boys! But that was the crux of the issue where Alfie was concerned; why had Alfie been like he was? Their dad struggled to understand it and wanted answers. There were the child psychologist views that he was just born like that, inherently a rebel who rejected authority and couldn't help hurting those around him. There was initially the thought that his troubles had led Alfie to take an overdose of pills (quickly disproved). But then the uncertainty remained as to what effect the Heminevrin had on him and how much it contributed to his death. Their dad almost became obsessed with searching for answers. This was consistent with his personality, intense, enquiring, questioning and wanting to understand matters (all traits which Cory shares with his dad). Unfortunately, the stress of being headmaster of a very demanding school; grieving for the dead son he had discovered in his bed at their home; along with the never-ending circles and lack of answers in his quest for the truth took its toll on their dad. He became stressed and effectively suffered a form of breakdown.

Everyone was sympathetic, as he was regarded as a great headmaster, very good at his job, well-liked, and of course people recognised the devastation of his son's unexplained death (particularly as it was in the house they still lived in, a constant reminder). It was very strange for Cory and Joe to see their dad like this. This proud, vibrant, physically active man seeming a shadow of himself as he appeared to become lost in his grief, stress, and frustration at having no real explanation for Alfie's death. Cory recognised that his dad was going through the same kind of grieving process he himself had after both Penny and Alfie's deaths. Although their dad did rally, he was never fully the same again. Alfie's death and the unexplained nature of exactly what happened knocked the stuffing out of him. On top of decades of teaching, the previous twenty-plus years of which had been as a very hard-working and conscientious deputy, then headmaster, with all the stresses that brought anyway, he was just worn down by it all. Whereas he had always been driven, energetic, and enthusiastic, you could now see that some of the life had been crushed out of him by Alfie's death. He took early retirement on health and stress grounds within a few years. It was desperately sad to see. He did however have a number of years of happy retirement, holidaying with their mum and with the family too on occasions, helping to bring up the grandchildren, teaching them to ride bikes in the local park, and taking them to football and watching them play for years. This sadly is no longer the case, as he was diagnosed with Parkinson's disease around a decade ago, shortly after he was operated on to have an aggressive cancerous growth removed from his prostate. His deterioration since is painful to watch, and Joe particularly appears to struggle with seeing his dad as just a shell of his former self. Cory agrees but is slightly more philosophical and thinks that at least he survived the cancer (which may then have triggered the Parkinson's?); they have had some extra years with him, even if he is now very sadly reaching the end. He is trapped in his own little world now, unable to communicate with those around him anymore and physically now looks a very frail, old man. Cory has discussed with his kids that if he ends up like this, a trip to Dignitas may be in order. They have agreed that if he ever reaches that stage and asks to go skiing in Switzerland, they will know what to do. Moreover, this man devoted his life to his career and family and is a role model to Cory and Joe in so many ways. Cory has no doubt that seeing his dad deteriorate like this over the past decade or so (on top of the direct effect of Penny and Alfie's deaths) has further hardened his heart and made him determined to live his life as fully as possible.

Marriage

Lisa and Cory had decided to try to make things work, after full and frank clear-the-air discussions. They were approaching the end of their training contracts and their imminent qualification as solicitors. Cory stayed on at his City firm, being offered a job in his preferred department. Lisa changed firms, and the nature of her work meant that she had to be within a certain travelling time of the office. They therefore decided to move out of London completely and, within a few months, had bought their first house together. As with any couple, your first home often holds special memories, and that was certainly the case for them. Having learned from their mistakes when trying to live outside London two years earlier, this time they ensured that they were in the right location. They certainly appear to have chosen well, as nearly twenty-five years on, they both still live in the same area – albeit on opposite sides of the town now – having brought their kids up here. They bought a three-storey, two-bedroom town house right next to the local park and only five minutes' walk from town. It was perfect: a huge step up from the small flats they had been renting previously. They settled in, had family and friends to stay, dinner parties, family Christmases, and all the usual young couple-building-their-lives-together stuff. They were both doing well at work as qualified young lawyers, so what was the next step? Marriage was mentioned by others, often female family members, and gradually the drip-drip effect must have started to percolate through. Slowly. Subconsciously. Imperceptibly. They were happy as they were, had managed to put Cory's issues after his brother's death behind them, and were once again enjoying life together. Marriage wasn't something that Cory consciously thought about or something he and Lisa had ever really discussed. But one Saturday evening in winter after a very strange day, he suddenly and spontaneously proposed to her without ever having given it any serious conscious thought until that moment.

Lisa's sister lived in a town an hour or so away from them. She and her then boyfriend had holidayed with Lisa and Cory in the United States a summer or two before but hadn't seemed happy. The sister had subsequently ended that long-term relationship and fallen back into one with a rather strange chap she had known previously. She now regarded that as a mistake and wanted to get out of it but, given this chap's oddness, was concerned about his reaction. It was therefore agreed that Cory would hire a van, drive up, and help her move out one Saturday when the (soon-to-be-ex) chap was going to be out. He did so. Lisa's sister wanted to be safe in her new flat, with all her possessions, before she told the chap, not out of spite, but out of concern for her safety. Cory found the whole thing very sad indeed. He helped her to move; she was clearly very worried about the chap coming back unexpectedly before they had finished, so it was quite stressful. They got it done though, and Cory left Lisa's sister safely ensconced in her new flat, with all her possessions in place, also with her baby safely asleep; the couple had a child together some months earlier and that was what had caused her to realise that he wasn't the man for her. She was going to ring him once he was home, to explain her decision, but safely from a distance. Cory could see how stressed and upset she was but clear in her resolve; it was the best thing for her daughter. It was all incredibly sad, and as he drove back home, he was thinking about it all. Once home, Lisa asked how it had all gone; they opened a bottle of wine and started talking about it. Cory related how desperately sad it was. They opened another bottle and then another and carried on talking, now more generally about life, relationships, babies, and so on. They were close, in love, happy, and had overcome their problems when Cory had nearly destroyed it all. When they talked like this, the bond between them seemed unbreakable. They had been talking for hours, and it suddenly occurred to Cory (admittedly after a lot of wine!), out of the blue, with no prior thought, planning, or consideration: he asked Lisa to marry him. She said yes. She said that as it was a leap year, she had been waiting for him to ask, and if he hadn't, she was going to soon anyway. It seemed odd to Cory, as they hadn't really discussed it, but equally, it just felt right to both of them. They sent a few messages out to close friends but, as it was the early hours, resolved to tell family once everyone was awake the next morning. This they did, even with their hangovers and his waking realisation about what he had done! Everyone was delighted, said it was about time, and that they were all looking forward to the wedding. This was carefully planned over the next few months, with all sorts of changes of mind to every detail. Both sets of parents agreed to contribute to the cost (to varying degrees), and ultimately, a beautiful Thames riverside hotel was chosen for a lavish day of celebrations, following a romantic ceremony in a quaint village church near to where some of Lisa's family lived. It was an incredible period of time, the looking forward to and planning of it and, of course, then the day itself. Cory had a weekend back in Leeds over the summer for his stag do, combining going back to the old haunts along the Otley run with a night in the proper city-centre clubs, which they could now better afford as aspiring young professionals and no longer poor students. One of the many highlights for him was that some of the Leeds' players were out on the town that night in at least one of the clubs they visited. It takes a lot to kill that hero worship most football fans have for their idols, whatever age we are. Or rather, it used to. Too many of the current crop often act like overpaid prima donnas who become millionaires instantly and seem to have no loyalties in life to anyone. Those types are alienating their own fans, both at club and international level; but that is an entirely different story. Going back to the wedding, the only part they didn't enjoy (apart from Lisa obviously having to keep her mum in check as she inevitably tried to take over everything, as mother- in-laws do) was the religious marriage preparation classes they were invited to attend by the vicar. They felt obliged to attend, as although her dad and stepmum lived in the parish, Lisa and Cory didn't; the vicar was being helpful in agreeing to marry them in his lovely church. The classes were excruciating though, run by happy-clappy, 'aren't we so in love', middle-aged Christians. They tried to escape at a break, but the vicar followed them and chatted his way through until it was time to return. But it was a small price to pay for what turned out to be an amazing day, or rather few days.

The wedding date was set for a Saturday in late September, to avoid school holidays and to allow Cory's brother, Joe, to return from his planned student summer travels. They finished work a day or two early, planned, packed, and then decamped to Lisa's family's area; Lisa and entourage stayed with her mum at her friend's lovely country home; Cory, his best man, and ushers, were at Lisa's dad's house down the road (the stepmum seeming very pleased to have so many young twenty-something men under her roof!). Family, ushers and bridesmaids all gathered for a meal in the local pub on the Friday evening, so that everyone could relax into the weekend. The church service was lovely, with family and friends turning out in large numbers. It was a delightful country setting made perfect by the local village pub opposite being open on Saturday morning before the service to keep everyone fully libated before the religious service. This meant that the hymns were sung with unusual gusto. The vintage prestige-car journey was a welcome break from everyone for the newlywed couple, and the excellent wedding reception at the hotel was followed by a very late night party. Reference was made in the speeches to Alfie, which brought a tear to everyone's eye, but that apart, it was a magical day. The happy couple had to be up early the following morning to fly out to Puerto Rico to board their Caribbean cruise liner. By the time they arrived, they were exhausted but very happy. Lisa, as a smoker, was still in those days able to sit at the back of the plane and smoke during the flight. Looking back, this was utterly ridiculous, rather like smoking on the upstairs of buses and specified carriages on trains, because smoke doesn't waft around, does it? All of this changed, of course, following the King's Cross fire, which bizarrely occurred on the day Cory and many of his Leeds Uni mates were in London visiting Parliament. They travelled by bus, but some did later use the tube to explore London. Had they come by train instead though, it is very likely they would have been at King's Cross around the time of the fire. Fate. Perhaps the core message in the *Final Destination* films does have a bigger say on all our lives than we would like to admit.

They cruised around a number of Caribbean islands, taking in the awesome scenery and incredibly laid-back attitude to life. Cory instantly fell in love with the area and has been back there countless times since. The only part he didn't enjoy was the helicopter ride over one of the islands. The scenery was spectacular, and if he hadn't been so scared he would no doubt have loved it. He foolishly agreed to it for the experience and to try to conquer his persistent fear of flying. The problem is though that all such fears which many have on commercial planes are massively accentuated in the tiny cabin of a helicopter. The nadir of the experience was when they went through an air pocket and the chopper just fell, only a few feet, but it was enough to leave Cory a quivering wreck. The only other time he had been so scared was when he naively booked an internal flight in the deep South on his first visit to the USA decades earlier. When they walked out on to the tarmac, he was still relaxed as he looked for the plane, only to become terrified as he was told the tiny twelve-seater in front of him was it. Again, every bit of turbulence they hit had the plane bouncing through the skies. Harrowing.

After a week's cruise, fun and entertaining though it was, they were delighted to disembark for the second leg of their luxury honeymoon, a week at La Sport on St Lucia. Pure indulgent luxury. It had been great cruising between the islands and seeing so many of them, having the chance to explore different ones each day; but now being in a luxury seafront honeymoon suite at this amazing resort, rather than in a ship's cabin, was bliss. The facilities were amazing, the various massage and hydrotherapy treatments, water skiing, snorkelling, and so much more, and obviously amazing food, drink and entertainment. They befriended one particular couple there, lovely, down-to-earth Scots, a refreshing change from the loud Americans dominating the cruise ship and 'little Englanders' at the resort. It was idyllic and all was good with the world. It was a real wrench to leave and to have to come back to reality, especially as it was winter in the United Kingdom: dark, miserable, and back to the daily grind after an amazing few weeks. It just shows how happy we could all be if we could live idyllic lives of luxury, without all the stresses and strains of daily life. This probably explains Cory's dislike for (and envy of) the idle rich and the lives they lead – from the Royal Family, through their acolytes and hangers-on, the other 'old money' English upper classes, to the nouveau riche and each of their trust-fund kids. Just imagine the full extent of the fun Cory could have had leading their pampered, self-indulgent lives!

Fortunately, Christmas wasn't too far away and that gave them something else to look forward to. They had a relaxed family Christmas and then drove up to Leeds for New Year's Eve to party with another couple they knew through Cory's work, who had become good friends. The Leeds Irish centre was a great place in which to see in the New Year. Their friends had a young baby, and spending a lot of time with them and seeing how they coped, as well as with Lisa's sister and her young daughter, made them reassess their previous typical young professional, middle-class plans. To the extent they had ever really considered the issue of having their own kids, they had both assumed they might wait until in their thirties. That's what people like them seemed to do – become established in the their careers, earn some money to build up savings, have the holidays that DINKYs enjoyed, and then settle down to have babies in a few years. But they had loved spending time with their friends and Lisa's sister with their babies. They had started to feel that although it was nice to have a nice house, car, great wedding and luxury honeymoon, and to be progressing well in their careers, was it really enough? They both had commented that Christmas, although pleasant, did not feel complete somehow. They said that maybe in future, they might work at soup kitchens or something similar, to feel as if they were doing something more over the festive period. They never reached that stage, as nine months later, their first child was born.

Births

People told Cory how incredible it is to see your children being born and particularly how amazing the first one is, as it changes your life forever, but no words can truly describe it. The births of their four children have been the happiest, most positive emotional events of his life. Other events in his life have been great, including marriage, but nothing really compares. One year on from their wedding, after attending NCT classes and trying to comprehend (so innocently, like lambs to the slaughter) the earth-changing event that was about to happen to them, their eldest son was born. Those of you who have been through it know how it just blows your mind. Those of you who have yet to experience these joys, enjoy it when it happens. It is truly amazing. It explains why parents feel so protective of their children forever, even as they go through the traumas of teenage rebellion and hatred for those very parents who love and nurture them, through to adulthood, when they invariably move away and don't stay in touch as much as the parents would like (which is what Cory and Lisa are currently going through with their own kids, as they did to their parents thirty years ago). As parents, you have created and brought into this world these tiny, helpless little bundles of life. Good parents therefore spend most of the next twenty or so years (and forever, in reality) looking after, guiding, helping, advising, and worrying about their offspring.

As this book isn't specifically about Cory and Lisa's marriage, the good and bad and ultimately what went wrong, there won't now be a detailed recounting of their married life. Suffice to say, their lives changed significantly over the next few years as the kids arrived and the family grew. For now, they debated names and Sam was chosen for their new son. He had been born early in the morning, and Lisa stayed in hospital with him for a few days, alongside some of the other mums from the ante-natal group. Cory took holiday/ paternity leave, all still a grey area back in the early 1990s; none of the clarity and extensive time off now permitted by legislation for dads back then. But he fortunately had an understanding employer (unlike the next time, as we will come to shortly). He visited the hospital daily and started bonding with his baby boy, as he got things ready for his homecoming. Two particular memories occur to Cory now, two decades later, about the change to their lives that occurred having their firstborn at home. Firstly, there was the sleep deprivation. No one who has yet to experience it can truly appreciate the horror of this torture – and yes, it is that. You can understand how prisoners are subjected to it to break their spirits. It works! Cory recalled foolishly thinking after the first few nights that if he got an early night that night and slept well, it would be okay, rather like you do when you've partied all night or stayed up for a holiday, New Year's, or (if you are unfortunate enough) to have had to work overnight. Although you are exhausted, you know that if you get an early night and sleep well, you will catch up on some of the missed sleep and start to feel human again. The problem with babies is that they are blissfully unaware of such adult logic. They are like some of the more basic of God's creatures; they function (at that stage) at very simple levels revolving around their own needs to eat, sleep and be comfortable. That's it. Nothing else concerns or occurs to them, certainly not any wider social awareness of the stress they are inflicting on their doting parents, who start out cooing over their offspring and end up crying in despair during those lonely early hours of the morning, when the rest of the world is sleeping and the feeling of isolation is so intense. It is in these bleak hours that every parent, no matter how loving, has begged the baby to stop crying, has craved silence, and dark thoughts have crossed their minds. Obviously most never succumb; sadly, some do. It can be a very cruel and unrelenting period, especially for new parents. Cory recalled that one Saturday evening, he foolishly risked staying up to watch *Match of the Day*, as their own bedtime was gradually getting ever earlier to adapt to Sam's erratic sleeping pattern and guaranteed night-time awakenings. Cory's fuddled brain thought that it shouldn't matter, as he would be able to catch up on his sleep. Huge mistake! He never did. Sam didn't care; he was hungry or needed changing when it suited him not to accommodate his parents' needs.

The second distinct memory was the peace and tranquillity in the house when Sam did sleep; although this did lead them into something of a false sense of security when it came to their second pregnancy, which was shattered by real life intervening as ever, as we will see shortly. This was particularly marked during the day, when Cory and Lisa could actually do other things. This was never the case during the horrific night-time sleepless sessions, as the stress levels are multiplied a hundredfold by the ridiculous early hour of the morning it is. If Sam woke at, say, midnight or 1 a.m., although disruptive, as the exhausted parents would have only had an hour or two's sleep (in the early days, later they learned that 9 p.m. bedtime for them was the solution), they could usually expect to feed and change him, put him back to sleep, and get a few more hours' sleep themselves before daylight. However, if and when he woke at 4 or 5 a.m., that was it. By the time he had been sorted, it was dangerously close to being the start of the day, and often, no more sleep could be achieved, even though that was all they craved. Looking back, Cory can see that babies' sleep patterns appear to go in three- to six-month cycles. The first few months are disruptive, but you somehow cope; after a few months, the baby usually starts sleeping for a bit longer, more regularly, and there is a return to some semblance of normality, or at least not quite the same level of exhaustion. It's as if they deliberately push you to your limits, until you are about to snap, and then suddenly improve for a while. You then get used to a more normal sleeping pattern; then they start to teethe and it's very disruptive again. And so the cycle continues. Just as you are relieved at some normality descending, they crank up the disruptions again. They know! How he envied his posh, rich bosses, who appeared unaffected by their own babies! They hired night nurses to deal with this aspect and generally left all baby-related activities to their wives, nannies, and female family members, as this still sadly was the attitude of many a chap, especially in the City.

Cory bonded with his little mate, his firstborn, his new son. Grandparents helped with the childcare so Lisa could go back to work, and Cory did as much as he could during the week and then spent every weekend playing with and looking after his new little best friend. Apart from the natural joy of being a new proud father, undoubtedly there were also subconscious elements of finally a new, exciting life coming along instead of the pain of the previous two young deaths. Cory was certainly terrified deep down of anything happening to his baby, which he knew was due to having lost Penny and Alfie. He knew that bad things do happen in life. As part of this (over) protectiveness, they had heard of cats potentially causing cot deaths, when seeking warmth by lying next to babies and smothering them. They panicked one day when they found one of their cats in Sam's room while he slept; the cats were re-housed through the cats' protection league. The reality was that they had merely been surrogate kids until Lisa and Cory got the real thing, and isn't that what many pets are to most adults, after all? Sam thrived; he grew from a cute little baby (although every parent thinks their kids are cute, even when they patently aren't) into an even cuter little toddler – and there is naturally no bias whatsoever from the author here! He took his first steps and then started wandering around their house. Apart from bath time and watching Sam sleeping – both of which any parent will tell you are amongst the most amazing experiences you can ever have – one of their cutest memories was when Sam would wander around their room, peeking through the wooden slats at the bottom of their pine bed. They were all very happy and comfortable; they continued to do well at work, and now they had a real purpose and meaning in their lives through their beautiful little toddler. So what do people who have the choice, no medical issues, etc. invariably always do in that situation? They think, 'Isn't this lovely and cute? Shouldn't we add another baby into the mix, to further build our lovely family?' And that's what they did. Shortly after Sam's first birthday, they discovered Lisa was pregnant again. Something seemed different this time though, which they assumed was simply as she was coping with Sam as well being pregnant. The first scan offered a very different explanation. Twins!

Their best laid plans to build their little family had been somewhat accelerated by family genes. Lisa's mum was a twin, but it had never really occurred to them that twins may be an option, certainly after only having Sam the first time round. How naive yet again they had been! There were two little blots on the scan photo, two little heart beats picked up by the sonographer. Lisa and Cory were incredibly excited; this was something new and unexpected. Now instead of going from one to two kids, they would suddenly jump to three. They were still living in their idealistic little bubble, that same one that led otherwise sane and rational people to think adding more kids anyway was sensible without any real thoughts about the practicalities. Real life was about to get in the way of their romantic views of the world. But for then, they didn't have to face reality. Their families were very excited for them too. The only sign from anyone of the harsh reality they would face came from one of Cory's bosses. This lady had twins. She knew! When Cory told her they were expecting twins, she tried to force a smile, but he could see the strain. She tried to say well done and be positive, but actually, she said, 'Good luck and I wish you all the best.' He thought it slightly odd at the time. Looking back, he knows exactly what she meant.

Lisa was pregnant over the winter months and carried on working. Cory took his little toddler buddy Sam out at weekends to play in the park, to jump in puddles, to kick through the leaves, to jump over flower beds, much to the apparent annoyance of old biddies in the park, who dared to challenge them. The hypocrisy as their rat-like little dogs shat everywhere was not lost on Cory, as he told them. He no longer was as tolerant and polite as he had been brought up to be. He was tired and getting older, now approaching thirty. But more than that, being a parent changes all your values and focus. Whereas previously he had generally tolerated people he didn't like or didn't agree with, now he didn't. The social conventions he had been brought up with no longer were his guiding principles. Instead, his focus was purely on his family. He would do everything for them. He would protect them from anyone and anything. He no longer was prepared to be polite when someone offended him. All of this is undoubtedly part of growing up anyway, of going through the growing pains of the teenage years and into your twenties, establishing yourself in the world, settling down in a career, relationship, marriage and becoming a parent. All these momentous and often life-changing events do of course change you, as your views of the world change. You can see why often people who don't do many of these things in their twenties suddenly panic in their thirties and worry that they may miss out. They are all incredible experiences on life's amazing journey – hard work, but so much more rewarding than anything else. Some people say they choose their careers, wealth, and material possessions instead, but are they really happy? To quote the Dalai Lama once more, when asked what surprised him most about humanity, he replies:

> 'Man surprised me most about humanity. Because he sacrifices
> his health in order to make money. Then he sacrifices money to

recuperate his health. And then he is so anxious about the future
that he does not enjoy the present; the result being that he does
not live in the present or the future; he lives as if he is never going
to die, and then dies having never really lived.'

Cory entirely agrees. Although he was a City lawyer, he could see how many he worked with did not have happy home lives; work dominated their lives and that in turn caused issues in their personal lives. Cory didn't want to sacrifice seeing his kids grow up for City wealth. His view of the world and other people started to harden, and he found that made him challenge things he would otherwise previously have tolerated. He didn't necessarily any longer accept the bullshit that surrounds us, both at work and in society generally. Time becomes more important. A balance between doing your best at work and home is suddenly of much greater importance and a higher priority than ever before. As your own views change and harden, so must those around you. Clearly, work and your partner are the main examples of this and these will be explored further as this tale unfolds. But another manifestation of this is how you react to other people. Cory had been brought up to respect his elders, to be polite, and he had noticed his parents were also very deferential to professional people - priests, doctors, etc. Cory's faith had been challenged as a teenager and destroyed by Penny and Alfie's premature deaths. From a religious perspective, he could not comprehend all the platitudes he had been given by all sorts of denominations after both deaths; he was now at least agnostic. But more than that, he had seen how the professionals after his brother's death had been unable to explain it; to offer credible explanations on the effects of the Heminevrin; to say whether the doctor was wrong in prescribing them to an unmonitored alcoholic, and how they had appeared far too ready and willing to accept it as suicide (which had been incredibly painful for the family, for the few days until that theory was disproved). Cory was now himself a professional, a City lawyer approaching thirty years of age, with a wife, mortgage, baby son, and twins on the way. As has so often happened in Cory's adult life, a confluence of personal and professional issues and considerations came together over that period to lead him to make the decisions he did.

This has happened a number of times since. Cory has come to rely on his instincts, his thought process, and his rationalisation of the circumstances he faces that lead him to make the decisions he does. The fermentation of all that had happened to him as he approached thirty, as he truly found his place in the world, had a profound effect. Suddenly, the thought of spending family Christmases away from home, of making long journeys to accommodate relatives' plans and wishes, no longer seemed as important. Cory and Lisa had been good, dutiful young people for a few years. They had travelled around the country to fit everyone in. But now their priorities had changed. They had to put themselves and their own new, growing family first. This led to some awkward conversations with family; Lisa was more concerned about the effect, Cory didn't give a shit - which he believes is typical of the different attitudes men and women have in such situations. They had done their time. It was now their time to do what was right for them. This included the particularly awkward issue of people smoking heavily around kids (as it still was socially acceptable in those days). Lisa's family were heavy smokers; few (if any) of Cory's family were. Lisa smoked; Cory didn't. For years, as they socialised with her family, he had been permanently enveloped in clouds of smoke. It was still socially acceptable; smoking on planes, trains, and buses was still allowed - a different world, but no one appeared to know any better then, rather akin to performers in clubs who didn't smoke dying of lung cancer due to their massive secondary smoke inhalation over many years and those poor miners and other factory workers in confined spaces who suffered with asbestosis and a plethora of other respiratory diseases. However, various studies were increasingly being published about such matters, including the dangers of secondary smoke, particularly to children. This was relevant not only to cot death issues, but also a more general awareness that smoking in itself was extremely harmful and secondary smoke did affect children's health. Against this background, Lisa and Cory had to have a few awkward conversations, particularly with her family and their friends, who wished to puff away merrily around both a pregnant Lisa and then their new-born baby. Cory felt strongly that they should stand up for themselves, even if it was awkward. Subsequent science and the recommendations now about the dangers of smoking (generally and around kids) showed they were right to do so. Just look at the current TV advertising campaigns showing how smoke lingers. But he just felt it was right to do so even then, before society had caught up with the damage it was doing by allowing smokers to pollute everywhere and everyone. He had put up with it for years, out of politeness; maybe he should have been more assertive sooner. But now was the time to stop for his kids' sakes, if not his own. From that point on, he brought the same resolve and determination to every major issue he was to face in his life, for good or bad, for better or worse.

Lisa's pregnancy with the twins was okay for the first trimester and for most of the second trimester, although the effects of carrying twins, still working part-time and having Sam to look after started to take its toll. By the start of the third trimester, matters were starting to cause some concerns. The twins appeared to be competing with each other in her womb, with Twin 1 seemingly taking more of the food and nutrients available from the placenta and depriving Twin 2, who was therefore smaller. Doppler scans and more regular hospital check-ups became the order of the day, and Lisa was told to start taking things much more steadily, to reduce working hours and rest more often. She did all of this, but still concerns persisted, and when attending a now regular Doppler scan at thirty-three weeks into the pregnancy, the medical staff suddenly became very concerned about the state of little Twin 2. This led to medical consultation, discussion, and ultimately they decided to perform an emergency Caesarean that day - the fear was that Twin 2 would not survive if left in the womb. This was all very traumatic, made worse as Cory (who had been to a number of the scans previously) wasn't there. He was at work, in court that day – in the Court of Appeal in London, as part of the legal team involved in the Lloyds agents litigation, listening to some of the country's most pre-eminent QCs submitting points of law and construction to a panel of the top Appeal judges; all very high profile and exciting, and it looked great on his CV to have gained such experience, yet it all meant nothing when one of his colleagues walked into the court room with a message that he should call his boss urgently. He bowed (as you have to) and left the court mid-session and called the office. He was told that his wife was about to have an emergency Caesarean and he should get to the hospital urgently. He ran from the court, got to the train station, jumped on to his train home, and then drove as fast as he could to the hospital. Fortunately, the operation had been slightly delayed, so he made it in time. He was given theatre scrubs to change into and invited to sit next to Lisa once she was taken into theatre. Lisa had been anaesthetised and a screen was put up so that they couldn't see the incision being made. Although it was all very traumatic, Cory was so relieved to be there. There was a lot of activity, both the operating staff and the midwives standing by waiting for both babies to be delivered prematurely.

Both babies were safely removed from Lisa's womb, a minute apart. Twin 1 seemed to resent being pulled from his safe, nourishing environment and had to be encouraged to breathe once out, as he appeared sleepy and had been fine in the womb. There was a horrible moment when he didn't breathe at first and the panic started to rise, but it was only temporary. Although he was premature, he was generally healthy and fine, just grumpy at having been disturbed seven weeks too early from the sanctity of the womb. Twin 2 was however a different story. The concerns about him not surviving in the womb had led to the emergency Caesarean, and he was even smaller than Twin 1. Both were tiny, but he was much more frail. The following weeks with him were incredibly stressful, and indeed Lisa and Cory were told on at least one occasion to expect the worst by the paediatric consultant in charge of the Special Care Unit. Both were boys and were named Billy and Adam. Adam was the sickly one. He had infections, trouble breathing often; he suffered an internal head bleed and had a shunt inserted in his skull. It was truly awful. What made it all far worse was that in the premature baby unit, over the five weeks they were there, Cory and Lisa saw other parents lose their babies. There weren't always happy endings and successful outcomes for these very premature babies. It was heart breaking. Clearly, the medical staff didn't expect Adam to survive on at least one occasion, given the severity of his illnesses. Cory and Lisa made daily visits, sometimes with Sam, to see his baby brothers, sometimes just one of them, the other being at home with him. Cory's heart sank one morning when he walked in to see Adam's special care cot missing. He desperately asked where Adam was. He feared they were about to tell him Adam hadn't made it through the night. But he had. He had been taken to have further tests; he had lumbar punctures and blood transfusions carried out on his tiny body. He was small, weak, jaundiced, and very ill with infections, head bleeds, and was bradycardic (i.e. his heart rate fell dangerously low when he slept and the alarms regularly went off). Cory found it very difficult to leave his cot, as he wanted to spend as much time as possible with both Billy and Adam obviously, but particularly Adam, if this was likely to be the only time they were going to have. This went on for weeks, and on at least one occasion at home at night, Cory collapsed in tears in Lisa's arms, begging God or Fate (or whatever force may control our lives) to save Adam and to take him instead if necessary. He couldn't face another young death. Cory took time off work; his immediate boss was sympathetic and understanding. Sadly, one of the senior partners was much less so, as we shall touch on shortly.

Cory and Lisa went through the whole gamut of emotions over those few weeks, but ultimately, from the depths of despair, sadness, just waiting for the worst, Adam rallied. He started responding to the constant antibiotics being pumped into him. He appeared to survive his cerebral haemorrhage (although they were warned that it could have caused some damage, which wouldn't necessarily become clear until he grew up). Yet another blood transfusion seemed to kick-start him, finally coming through those soul-destroying weeks. He gradually started to gain colour, no longer looking grey or jaundiced and, although there was still a long way to go, was no longer at risk. He and Billy were still tiny and stayed in Special Care for five weeks, until they had caught up to where they should have been if the pregnancy had gone to full term. At thirty-eight weeks, Cory and Lisa were invited to spend a night with Billy and Adam in one of the 'departure lounge' bedrooms attached to the Special Care Unit. It was a relief, but also scary. Now that the medical issues had subsided, the reality of bringing the twin boys home and coping hit them. Of course, they were delighted and words could not describe how relieved they were that Adam was still with them, after such a bleak prognosis only weeks earlier. On a warm summer's day, they brought their new baby twins home. They were happy, relieved and a family. Sam was twenty months old. It was chaotic for many years after; three young boys were a handful. But it was equally incredible to have three such lovely boys, no matter how stressful and tiring it was.

Cory's immediate boss (closer in age and a father of young children himself) understood and was sympathetic. Although he was a workaholic (as was demanded of you) and had missed family holidays to service clients' needs (as was expected of you), he clearly understood the trauma Cory had been through and allowed him time off and also to ease back in to work gradually. All the other staff, office manager, and others were also supportive and sympathetic; so much in fact that when Lisa contacted them and asked if Cory could take extra unpaid leave for his thirtieth birthday (as he had used up his holiday over the Special Care weeks) for a family holiday, they were delighted to help and thought it was a great idea. These were real, normal people, after all. The only one who appeared not to be happy was one of the senior partners, who was an odd character at the best of times. Cory had been given some cases to look after by him, when a more senior lawyer simply left, as he'd had enough of the unremitting grind of life as a City lawyer. There was little guidance, simply an expectation that Cory knew as much as the more senior colleague and should get on with it. Cory's time off and regular visits to Special Care clearly irked the old chap, to the extent he once said that he didn't know why Cory had to visit the hospital so often; he had a wife to do that sort of thing, didn't he? When he went on the week's family holiday (fully approved by everyone else at work who understood the need for it after the traumas of Special Care, Adam's illness, and having premature twins), this senior partner said he supposed Cory and the family needed it, but it wasn't terribly convenient any time over that period. Cory carried on, but doubts were now flooding into his mind about his career. This was exacerbated by their return to chronic sleep deprivation. If they had thought the first few months with Sam had been bad, the next few months almost killed them. Adam and Billy had a habit of alternating when they slept and woke. This was probably for the best, as trying to cope with both at once was a logistical nightmare, but it didn't seem like that at the time. Lisa and Cory therefore had some night-time help from grandparents, but you could tell they found it all far too stressful and tiring to do too regularly. It was pure torture. Relentless. Unending. They devised a pattern, whereby Cory would sort Sam out for bed when he got home from work, while Lisa looked after the twins. Once Sam was in bed, Cory would take over from Lisa looking after Adam and Billy for the next four or five hours, while she had some sleep. At 11 p.m. or midnight, she would then come back and look after the twins, who lived and slept in their small cots in the lounge, allowing Cory to go up to bed for a few hours. At about 5 a.m., he would then return to look after them for a few hours, while she got some more sleep before he had to go to work. Sam was fitted in when he woke up too and was dropped at the child-minder or nursery. This went on for months, though it felt like years. It was soul destroying, but they had to do it. They lived for the weekends, when at least work wasn't part of the equation. The stress of having to help get the boys ready in the mornings before rushing for his train to commute to London was huge. It was all very fraught. The last thing he needed to overhear were snide comments from the young, single colleagues if he was five or ten minutes late (when all they had to do was roll out of bed and trot to work). It made him realise that a lot of people in office environments seem to spend more time moaning and bitching about others than getting on with their own lives. He has often thought that if your average British worker exerted even a fraction of the time and energy on their own jobs that they do on monitoring and complaining about others, our economy could thrive and compete much better with so many others. But much more of such themes in the next planned volume in this series! At work, he was so tired that often he would find himself just staring at the dry legal documents he was reviewing and drifting away (not that they were ever a riveting read at any time!)

There was no real interest from the senior partner; his sole purpose appeared to be cranking the pressure so that everyone worked hard, billed high, so he maintained his millionaire lifestyle with little regard for those around him. That was sadly typical of the attitude of many of that generation of City lawyers in the early to mid-1990s (arguably, it still is in some cases, although many of them have now retired, forgotten as creatures from a different age). As a broad generalisation, they were the white, middle-class men who had been brought up in times when men didn't show affection. They undoubtedly had austere fathers, nannies to look after them, and probably had been to boarding school. They were generally sexist, homophobic misogynists with other equally less-than-enlightened

views of the world. They lived in a narrow, privileged bubble, where
they had made millions over recent years, given the City 'Big Bang'
and all the changes to the more genteel City world they had entered
decades earlier. Some of the friendlier senior partners told stories of
how life even until the 1980s had involved getting the same train
into London, sitting in the same seat, in the same carriage, with
the same people every day (very *Reggie Perrin*). They queued in an
orderly fashion for the Tube and tutted disapprovingly at those who
didn't. They arrived at the office 9.30 a.m. (ish), doing a couple of
hours work, and leaving letters and documents to be typed up by
their secretaries as they went out for client and business lunches (the
good old days of the long, boozy British City lunch), returning hours
later to sign the letters and deal with any matters arising, then off
to the pub for a few pints with colleagues before getting an early
evening train home to the countryside again. A lovely life! No mobile
phones, computers, emails, or any other technology to interrupt their
balanced lives. And then came the technological revolution, Big Bang,
and the City changed. Clients wanted immediate answers from their
advisors, not considered thoughts espoused in a detailed letter a few
days later. All-night working became the order of the day for many
lawyers, especially the macho corporate and finance ones serving
banks and similar clients. The American influence changed the old
school City culture; boozy lunches were frowned upon and longer
working hours arrived with the advent of technological advances,
including computers, mobiles, and twenty-four-hour availability. The
older partners hated it, but the upside to them was that as their firms
and partnerships expanded, they as the senior equity holders now
drew more in profits than ever before. They loved that part. One of
life's great ironies was that they were in an age they didn't understand
and generally refused to accept, yet they were the ones who profited
from it most initially as the senior business owners!

Yet their old-fashioned views still prevailed. Junior lawyers were
akin to their servants to run errands for them, to pick up suits from

dry cleaners, and deliver their cars to required destinations, as well as doing some legal work occasionally. Attractive young female lawyers and secretaries were generally there to be propositioned regularly and invited out for drinks and dinner when inappropriate comments and behaviour could be tested out on them. Some of course welcomed such approaches, being there to work short term with the longer term aim being to nab themselves a rich chap ideally as a husband. The guys didn't always intend things to go that far but would play along for a while to get some form of office relationship with these attractive young women out of it. Cory recalled a former boss telling him sagely how in his secretarial recruitment business, in the bad old days, male bosses demanded secretaries purely with certain physical attributes rather than by reference to their secretarial skills. He also advised how the women would work in the area of London closest to the mainline station they commuted to. So Essex girls tended to congregate in the offices in the east of the City, next to Liverpool Street and Fenchurch Street stations; the glamorous Fulham, Chelsea, Putney and Parsons Green types were more usually found in the wealth of Mayfair offices (private family offices, hedge funds, etc.) allegedly hired more for the way they looked than what they did (on a work level, at least) and so on. These are themes for a later volume in this series rather than detailed consideration now. Cory had seen it for years and began to think that he wasn't sure he could necessarily be part of the world these dinosaurs inhabited long-term. In one of his '360 degree' appraisals, he mentioned some of the issues he had; HR did nothing, but the partner was clearly furious that the comments had been made, the moral clearly being: 'Be very careful what you say.' Sadly not advice Cory particularly subscribes to very often! At least the City has progressed significantly from these old-fashioned days over the past twenty years generally; a few lingering examples of the old City male does still exist, although thankfully he is at least partially extinct now.

All of this caused Cory to reflect on what he wanted from life going forward. He had after all fallen into the law by chance, as he didn't know what else to do over a decade earlier as a bright but naive A level student. He had been on that treadmill many got on ever since – university, law school, training contract, qualification and then progressing up the ranks within a law firm. But now he had three young sons, had seen the attitudes of many he had previously aspired to join, and he no longer was sure that was for him. He wanted to be an active, involved dad more than he wanted a City fortune. He could see no justifiable trade-off for not being involved as his kids grew up instead of being stuck in an office for endless hours, even for the spectacular money that could be achieved. He and Lisa discussed it and she was supportive. She was obviously concerned that he shouldn't throw his legal career away, but agreed with his concerns about the City attitudes and demands on parents preventing them spending real time with their kids. From a practical point of view, it needed both of them, plus grandparents and child-minders, to cope with the boys. They had been forced to move to a much bigger house once the twins settled at home, as five of them in a two-bedroom house just didn't work. His City salary was therefore important, but not more than them being a proper family. They had finally had to accept the realities of life. After Sam was born, they both tried to carry on working full time but soon came to realise that only works if you have a nanny, which they didn't want. Lisa had therefore reduced her working hours and did so a bit more, now they had three young kids to look after. He started looking at in-house jobs and law lecturing, but nothing really grabbed him. Ultimately, he did make a significant move and a change of career direction, which he has never regretted since. Not once, ever. But that is another story entirely in its own right and will be explored and recounted in detail in the next instalment of this tale in due course.

Suffice it to say for present purposes that he thought long and hard about the career change, about getting off that treadmill he had been on, without really ever looking up for the past decade. As soon as he did, he felt a sense of relief, of freedom that he knew meant he had made the right decision. And he has done so in other major life decisions since too; although now looking back, he knows he has at times acted rashly, made wrong and bad decisions, and certainly regrets some of what he has done; to do otherwise wouldn't be honest or human. But he knows that for the really big decisions in his life, he has never taken these lightly, acted rashly, or acted on a whim. In fact, quite the contrary; in every case, he has agonised perhaps for too long about what to do, his head and heart wrestling as to the correct outcome. As an intelligent, inquisitive, argumentative lawyer, Cory assesses and tests all outcomes. He has been told by people he thinks too much, that he is too intense, he pours over everything in detail. But that is how he knows that when he makes life-changing decisions, he is doing the right thing ultimately. He only acts in such significant cases once he has analysed matters to death; once he has factored all rational and emotional ingredients fully and exhaustively. Clearly he doesn't do this with every decision he ever makes, but he certainly does and always has with the big ones. Sometimes he wishes he didn't think so much, but it's the curse of having that kind of brain that never stops (like his Dad, particularly after Alfie's death), that is always mulling things over, always ticking away, awake or asleep, never stopping; unless drunk, which is one of the reasons he does like to just get utterly pissed sometimes, so that he can escape his own constant thoughts and the never-ending whirling of the cogs in his brain! Although his memory and powers of recollection have helped him throughout his career, the fact there is no off switch and that everything is always flying around in his head can be a curse rather than a benefit. That's just the way he is, it is a family trait. It certainly means he has no choice but to think everything through, to fully consider everything, always. Even in his sleep, he finds his dreams are so often extensions of the current thoughts and issues swirling around his brain. At times, they can be so realistic he almost believes them to be true or omens/messages as to what he should do. Against this background, whilst there may well be better ways for Cory to switch off than alcohol, he at least enjoys that one (even if those around him often don't!).

So Cory and Lisa battled on, with some family support and got through those crushingly, relentlessly tiring first six months or so. Quite how they managed it they will never know, but they had two babies and a toddler to take care of, so they had no choice but to do it. The kids were all they had time to focus on, apart from work, and it remained that way for a long time. At the time, they didn't fully appreciate the full extent of the (self-inflicted) strain they were under. But looking back and subsequently watching others go through similar times, it is clear that it was a pretty horrendous period in terms of the impact it had on them and their relationship. But that wasn't their focus at the time; looking after their kids was a full-time job, and somehow they just about juggled everything they could to keep it all together. There is no doubt with the benefit of hindsight that sizeable cracks started appearing in their relationship then, but they were too tired to notice. Or at least too preoccupied looking after the boys to deal with them. If they had been wealthier and able to afford nannies and night nurses (as his bosses had), some of these issues may not have been there. If they were part of the idle rich, without the need to work hard to pay the mortgage to keep the house for their family, to feed and clothe them, life would inevitably have been easier. But they were just a normal, young, professional, middle-class, aspirational couple with a young family, struggling to keep it all afloat. A classic case of the harsh realities of real life getting in the way of the romanticised view of a happy young family growing together. As the saying goes:

> 'Normal is getting dressed in clothes that you buy for work and
> driving through traffic in a car that you are still paying for – in
> order to get to the job you need to pay for the clothes and the car,

and the house you leave vacant all day so you can afford to live
in it' (Ellen Goodman)

There are many other variations on this theme. The short, sad point is that in the modern world, we sometimes lose sight of what is important. Or even if we don't, we are forced to act in a way that makes it seem as if we have. Wouldn't we all be happier if we could have proper time with our kids, especially when they are young? Rather than having to juggle time with them alongside long hours at work to be able to house and provide for them. Isn't life the wrong way round? We spend all our young years trying to juggle everything, sometimes successfully, but often not. Pursuing careers and advancing at work isn't always conducive to a good family life; indeed, the two can often be contradictory and conflict strongly. So one or often both suffer, as we are torn between them. Yet we then reach a stage in our later years when we have more time, money and wisdom, but then far less to do, especially once the kids have left and we miss them. The law has now finally changed to allow parents to share maternity/ paternity leave, but will employers actually accept men taking prolonged periods off work? Are social attitudes yet so advanced and progressive? Cory doubts it.

Cory and Lisa battled on; it was unrelenting. Busy at work and at home. The boys were amazing, great fun, and worth all the pain, but it was tough. Exhaustion doesn't come close to describing it; it was more like being in a slightly detached, parallel universe. They functioned as they had to; they fed, clothed, bathed, and looked after their three young boys; they played with them and kept them busy and amused, a full-time job in itself. Then on top of that, they tried to carry on their legal careers, until Cory reached the point where he couldn't carry on (nor did he want to) and changed his career direction. Lisa reduced her hours. It gradually improved as the boys grew, slept more, went to nursery and child-minders, but those few years are something of a blur. They somehow got through it, mainly by going to bed as soon as the boys were in bed at 7 or 8 p.m. to grab as much sleep as they could. Their lives were very full and busy with their wonderful kids and the rest of life's requirements, such as work, shopping, and other mundane matters. They had no time for each other sadly, and the cracks in their relationship widened. Cory has seen this happen in many (if not all?) relationships, when young parents are struggling to cope with more than one young child, the inherent sleep deprivation and balancing all of this with work and real life. Many couples in these situations reach breaking point. Sometimes, things can be repaired as the kids get older, and some semblance of normality (and sleep) returns; sometimes they can't. Cory and Lisa wanted to make their marriage and relationship work, for themselves and all their plans for life and especially for their children and the beautiful family they had created. But the harsh realities of life wore them down over those years. They lost themselves in their beautiful young boys, their lives revolved around them entirely, and it was amazing to see them grow and develop. Nothing compares to that incredible feeling for any parent, the pride, the love, and the fact you have created these little people. It is true that you can have no comprehension of how you will feel. The unconditional love parents give their children is probably all that keeps everyone going in the very bad years and avoids more child cruelty and inability to cope. But this can come at a price; as you lose yourself in your children, you can lose each other and your relationship. Cory and Lisa certainly aren't alone in this, but it gradually happened to them.

They rallied and battled back at times, knowing that the rough periods would pass. They even had a fourth child (Chaz). He was a natural birth, and the joy at having his three elder brothers come to the hospital a few hours after he had been born to meet him was incredible. A sign of their advanced parenting skills now was that Lisa and Chaz were discharged that same day, and he was home a few hours later. No hanging around in hospital with this young son! They talked about it all to see if they could fix things. There was clearly no going back to the way things had been pre-kids, as their lives had changed irreparably beyond that. But they had to see if there was a way of them rescuing and rebuilding their relationship. The problem was that they were just more like friends than anything else now. They had four amazing children together, a nice home, a comfortable life, and on the surface, all they wanted. But as we all know, what is on the surface is often not real. How many couples who appear so happy in public, who put on a show, no longer have anything with each other in private? Apart from their children, they no longer appeared to have anything in common. They appeared to have grown apart as they had grown through their twenties and into their thirties. They can never know how much each element contributed; but by New Year's Eve 1999, the New Millennium which the world was celebrating, they weren't. As everyone else looked forward with excitement, they didn't. They no longer talked much anymore, spending their evenings in separate rooms at home once the kids were in bed. Cory would often take the boys out at weekends without Lisa. They had talked from time to time about splitting up, having a break, but clung on, as they had been so in love and had their wonderful children. But during the course of 2000, the gap between them seemed wider than ever. Cory would not presume to relate here what Lisa was thinking, but he was unhappy. She seemed to be too. There was a lot of tension between them. It was obvious to his family, who although never saying anything at that stage, gave knowing looks at the atmosphere. Fortunately, the boys were all too young to pick up on it, and that was ultimately what led Cory to make the decision he did. Lisa had a close friend from Uni whose dad was a senior type in industry. This chap had left his wife as soon as his kids all got to school-leaving age, when his youngest went off to the Uni. He moved in with his secretary, who (allegedly) was his long-term mistress. Although Cory only heard and saw most of this second or third hand, he heard the severity of the impact their dad's departure had on the kids. They hated him and felt as if their family life had all been a lie, a fraud; it had never been real and he had simply been biding his time to leave for years. The youngest child refused to speak to him for years after, apparently. Cory and Lisa's child minder was married with two daughters, who were both at secondary school, when it transpired their dad had been having an affair and eventually left their mum to move in with his new girlfriend. There was a similar reaction. Cory factored all of these issues in to his own dilemma, allowing his unrelenting brain to churn it all over endlessly. He and Lisa were no longer happy together. Maybe that would have happened anyway after thirteen years, as they grew up from naive young twenty-somethings to more world-weary mid-thirties adults. Perhaps that's why people sometimes waited to have kids in their thirties. But the combination of them having a lot of young children, along with their own issues and growing apart meant everything was coming to a head.

He loved his children more than anything in the world. Having seen the devastation and resentment caused in the other two families when the respective dads eventually walked out, he knew he couldn't stay long term just for the kids' sake, if he and Lisa had come to the end of their relationship. It wasn't as if they hadn't tried to fix things a number of times. This had been going on for a few years now, and they had subsumed themselves in their kids, to the cost of their relationship; they now appeared to have lost the connection they used to have with each other. They now were connected only through their incredible boys, but that wasn't enough to keep their marriage going. Cory was also approaching his thirty-fifth birthday that year. He was torn. He would never leave his kids, but he had to balance working in London with his life with them anyway. Sometimes, he wouldn't see them on weekdays if he had to leave early to get to London for meetings or if he was delayed coming home before they went to bed. He loved his weekends with them, and they would often traipse around *Legoland*, *Thorpe Park* or similar venues. Or they would play for hours in the park or visit *Toys R Us*, especially on rainy days, just him and his four boys. He now often felt as if he was a single parent anyway. This continued for months up to the summer of 2000. It was all swirling around in his head endlessly. He couldn't stay if he/they weren't happy. They couldn't pretend for the next ten years (or longer) just for the boys. That wouldn't be healthy or realistic, and as the boys got older, they would pick up on it. Whatever the damage of them splitting up, he wondered if it may be better for the boys to get used to it when they were young, so that they grew up with it. Cory agonised over what to do. He and Lisa now no longer discussed anything other than the kids. They were generally civil to each other, but it was as if they both knew they were finished as a couple, but what could they do about it? Their previous and ongoing discussions about trial separations had never got beyond them maybe sleeping in a different room for a few nights. There had never been any discussion about how it might work in reality, about all the practicalities. As they reached the summer of 2000, Cory knew that they had to do something. They were due to go on their annual visit to *CenterParcs* that August, following a stay at a child-friendly, kids-activity hotel with her sister and family. Cory appreciated that if he and Lisa split, all such family things would end. He knew it was sad and had hoped and prayed and tried to convince himself that they should stick it out for the boys, but eventually realised that he was kidding himself. Without the boys around, he and Lisa no longer wanted to be even in the same room as each other. It was a very strange feeling when they had been so close for so many years, had these wonderful kids together, but there was a void between them now. They talked over the summer. Cory also started going out more to after-work drinks, which he had previously tried to limit so that he could get home to his family. Now his view was that he would spend all weekend with his boys, see them most mornings/ evenings, so actually having a social life again in London was better than sitting alone at home in a separate room from Lisa. He was bored and lonely at home. No doubt Lisa felt the same. Not with the kids, but with each other. It was very sad, but that was the reality of their situation and it had been like this, on and off, for a few years now. It couldn't continue. As their holiday approached at the end of the summer, Cory continued to wrestle with his conscience: what should they do?

As mentioned, Cory has been blessed with a certain amount of intelligence and a brain that has helped him to get through countless exams and to be good at his job; the down side is that he can seemingly never switch it off (and resorts to drinking to escape at times). But that means he never makes a major decision in his life lightly; he thinks it all through endlessly, in this case, for a concerted period of months, on top of all the mental and emotional wrangling in his head intermittently over previous years. He wanted a happy marriage to go with his nice home and beautiful kids. But it wasn't. Neither of them were happy and had stopped trying with each other. Cory went to work as normal one summer's morning, all of this whirling around in his head on the commute to London, seeping through his work thoughts. He sat at his desk looking out at the sunshine and thought, 'This has to end. We're not happy together any more. Surely we can still put the boys first and make sure they're okay without being together unhappily.' For no apparent or explicable reason, he came to a decision there and then. It was as if the computer programme in his head had been assimilating all the data, assessing all scenarios, predicting all outcomes, logging all eventualities, for months now; it suddenly had reached the end, the conclusion, the answer. But of course, any major decision like that, no matter how rationally we think we are making it, can never take account of the pure, raw human emotions that will be involved. He is mindful of Einstein's wise words here:

> 'The intellect has little to do on the road to discovery. There comes a leap in consciousness, call it intuition or what you will, and the solution comes to you and you don't know how or why'

He went to see his boss and explained that things weren't great at home; he needed to go home to try to sort things. His boss mentioned that he had sensed things hadn't been good for some time and Cory should go. Cory arrived home at lunchtime. The boys were all out at nurseries and child minders, which was his intention. He and Lisa had to talk, without distraction. She knew that too. They stood in the kitchen and finally talked about things as they hadn't for months, about how their love seemed to have gone, how all they had left were their kids, but nothing between each other anymore. It was a truly sad experience, but also a necessary discussion to have. Their holidays were imminent, so they agreed they would go on those as a family, for the boys' sakes. When they got back, Cory would move out for a while, to give themselves some space to think about what they both wanted. Cory would come round every day to see the boys, either weekday mornings or evenings and have them every weekend. That way, they would both have proper time with the boys, but also their own separate time to socialise and see if they were happier apart permanently. Cory put a deposit down on a small flat just down the road from the family home, and they departed for their final family holiday. The kids kept them busy and preoccupied as usual most of the time; there were a few tense moments where they talked about living separate lives, but generally they were civil, as if a weight had been lifted from their shoulders. This, of course, was the calm before the storm!

The boys enjoyed their holidays and when they got home Cory and Lisa explained that Cory was moving down the road to live in a flat closer to the train station to get to work in London more easily. He would come round to see them every day during the week, either in the mornings or evenings. And they would spend every weekend with him. As the boys were so young, they accepted this and it became the norm for a number of months. It all became very acrimonious the following year, as the realities of no longer being together but still seeing each other almost daily, as Cory maintained his regular time with the boys continued. Divorce followed and it became all-out war for a period then and at times sporadically subsequently (even occasionally still these days, although far less often now thankfully). Cory's firm advice to anyone is to only divorce if you are absolutely sure, as it takes on its own momentum and causes rifts and schisms that it shouldn't. The family courts and divorce lawyers have supposedly moved to exploring mediation and a more conciliatory approach to such matters. But the problem remains that (a) the protagonists emotions are very raw and can hate each other and (b) the English court system remains an adversarial one, where many lawyers see point scoring and winning at all costs (notionally for their client) as more important than anything else. This doesn't lend itself to a harmonious background to such an emotionally fraught situation. Cory was staggered to have even his own lawyers tell him that he was a 'modern dad' and his daily access to his boys was not normal and couldn't continue. It was not what dads usually wanted or expected, and if he pushed it, the courts were likely to side with Lisa's pompous barrister, who suggested fortnightly access at weekends in McDonalds would suffice! Ridiculous. No wonder *Fathers 4 Justice* and similar organisations were forced to go to such extremes to highlight issues, raise public awareness and still valiantly campaign and fight such outdated prejudice. Cory never accepted this and fought for years to prevent anyone stopping him from seeing his boys and being a proper dad to them. The full effect of the divorce on the boys doesn't really fall within the remit of this book but hopefully will be dealt with in a subsequent volume. It is Cory's biggest regret from all of this. It has caused family rifts between the boys and Cory and Lisa at times. As the boys grow up, they have started (and will continue) to form their own views of their parents and what they did or didn't do for, and to them. He just hopes that none of it caused such irreparable damage that the boys can't be happy in their own relationships going forward.

Cory now sat in his small one-bed flat down the road from his family home, alone, contemplating life. He was almost thirty-five, married, with four wonderful children, had a good job, a nice house and car, and yet it wasn't enough. What had he done? What had he thrown away? But he hadn't, had he? He didn't leave on a whim. He didn't have an affair and leave to be with that new person. He left because he and Lisa weren't a real couple anymore; they were simply parents of the same amazing kids. They both deserved personal relationships that made them happy; and they hadn't had that with each other for the last few years in reality, save for a few brief peaks to balance the long troughs. Life was never easy, but it felt as if it was the right thing to do. The kids were still young enough to accept it; he and Lisa were approaching their mid-thirties so had time to move on and find other people to be happy with. As ever, at the back of Cory's mind was his fatalistic view of the world caused by Penny and Alfie's tragic premature young deaths. If we have no idea how long we had on this earth, we had to make the most of it:

> 'Dream as if you'll live forever, live as if you'll die today' (James Dean)

He and Lisa used to be happy; they had many good years together and produced four fantastic sons. Rather than bemoaning the fact that their relationship had faded and died after thirteen years together, maybe they should be thankful for what they had:

> 'Don't cry because it's over, smile because it happened' (Dr Seuss)

He also recalled the perhaps apt Anais Nin quote:

> 'Love never dies a natural death. It dies because we don't know how to replenish its source. It dies of blindness and errors and betrayals. It dies of illness and wound. It dies of weariness, of witherings, of tarnishings'.

Not everyone agreed with these views, and we will explore these shortly. Indeed, many of Cory's colleagues and clients in the City said he was a fool. He should just have affairs and flings at work and in London and then go home to his wife and kids afterwards in the evenings and at weekends, as so many evidently did. Cory did not want that life. He wanted a real relationship, where he had everything with one person, as he and Lisa used to have. That was his benchmark. They had lost their way with each other after over a decade together; but he knew what happiness, closeness and love was and wanted that again; he missed it. He didn't want different bits from different people, as so many seemed to be advising. Maybe he was still young and naive, maybe he wanted too much. Some who offered this advice were older and seemed to be suggesting that you can't have it all with one person; you need different people to offer you different aspects of a relationship. Cory couldn't help feeling though that these were just excuses for these middle-aged men (and some women), who were unhappily married or bored after years together, to sleep around and try to have the best of both worlds. Cory didn't want that. He had found himself increasingly attracted to other women, as he realised that he and Lisa couldn't carry on, but it had never crossed his mind to try and have both. Indeed, a year earlier, a work colleague had made a play for him and made it pretty obvious what she wanted, but Cory did nothing. That wasn't what he wanted. His desire for other women now was because he and Lisa no longer had their old connection that had caused them to fall in love all those years ago. That was the part he missed most. It is one of life's ironies that despite all the sex with many women in all the years since, it has never been just about that for Cory. Rather, it has been about trying to find again that connection, chemistry and love. His primary (if not perpetual) pursuit has been happiness and love again. Has he ever really found it? Let's now explore the amazing, sometimes traumatic, and often chaotic journey he has been on trying to find it!

PART III

Drinking & Dating; Secretaries & Strippers

*'You don't lose friends, because real friends can never be lost.
You lose people masquerading as friends, and you're better for it'*
(Mandy Hale)

Friends & Family

The reaction of family and friends varied. Cory's parents and brother said that they had sensed tension for a long time, so in that sense weren't surprised; but it was very sad after so long together, particularly with a young family. Cory's mum (who is very astute) said that he had been like a caged tiger for too long at home. They said they would do whatever they could to help with the boys, as they were the priority; Cory and Lisa's relationship was none of their business. Her family sadly didn't take the same view. Whether it was an instinctive parental reaction to 'protect' their daughter or they were somehow trying to make up for their own divorce, quite what their (misguided) motivations were wasn't entirely clear, but they took a much more interfering role. This led to wider family divisions that have never healed.

Friends fell into three camps, his, hers and mutual. It was a bit like a Venn diagram though, as there was some overlap, especially with Uni friends who had known them both for over a decade. Most ultimately stuck with their own gender (as tends to happen in these situations), but one of Cory's close friends from Uni was regrettably a casualty of the fallout, as he tried to take both sides – never a wise or easy manoeuvre in the open warfare that is divorce! The other main category of mutual friends, other couples, tended all to gravitate towards Lisa. Socially, most couples' relationships and mutual friends are driven by the woman, through her contacts with other mums and their greater interest in organising dinner parties and social activities. Men follow along dutifully and, if lucky, find something in common with the other male hangers-on, as they drink their way together through social gatherings. Without the women organising these events, it is highly unlikely anything would ever occur, as men don't generally organise such things, the only exception usually being where men organise work-related dinners (with their boss and wife to further their careers, or similar) or social events with their own long-term male friends, with partners in tow occasionally (but not always – boys nights out and boys tours being sacrosanct!). Therefore, when a man is no longer part of that couple's social group, the other men melt away and no longer have contact. They have no interest in the other couple's relationship (as men just don't, unlike women) so aren't particularly taking sides, but they certainly aren't going to challenge their own wives' support of their fellow woman in this scenario. One brave chap did even admit as much to Cory over a beer at a kids' party some time later – he apologised and said he hadn't agreed with the official stance taken. He confirmed that he had no views on (nor interest in) other people's relationships, but that apathy meant that he certainly wasn't going to argue with his own wife over her unflinching support of Lisa. Cory was persona non grata in those social circles; no great hardship particularly, but all rather petty. One of the other mums even took it upon herself publicly to approach Cory in front of his kids and start to castigate him over his failed marriage. Cory was staggered at her crass ignorance and interference and told her as much, very bluntly.

There were similar incidents with Lisa's parents purporting to help but initiating abusive arguments in front of the kids about Cory leaving and physically blocking his access to get to the boys. Not great behaviour from grandparents in front of their own grandchildren. As Cory pointed out, they had damaged their own kids with their behaviour during their divorce, so who were they to judge or opine on anyone else, and they certainly should stop interfering. It was very odd to be enemies with people he had been close to, and even family with for much of the past thirteen years. Although Lisa's mum was a bit mad and could be annoying (which mother-in-law isn't, it just goes with the territory!), he had never had a cross-word with her; Lisa dealt with her when she overstepped the mark at times. Although many years later, Cory's mum, when mentioning the extent of the bile the mother-in-law had poured out during the divorce, said that Cory's dad had always said they should be wary of her and never get too close, as she wasn't to be trusted. Wise and perspicacious as ever. Cory and Lisa's dad had one tense discussion years earlier, when Cory was a junior lawyer at one of the big City firms involved in Thatcher's mass sell-off of all our state assets. He had made multiple share applications and unfortunately had used Cory's name without asking. It was a disciplinary offence for any lawyer involved in the privatisations to buy shares, as potentially there could be insider dealing issues. Cory was furious when he found out and told Lisa's dad as much. Although he was apologetic, it all seemed so greedy and unnecessary and could have landed Cory in deep trouble. The argument with him now, as he blocked Cory getting in to the house to see the boys, was far worse. These were very fraught and tense times. You certainly do find out who your real friends are.

Hedonistic Days

Alongside the stress of the seemingly never-ending divorce and contact issues, there was however a whole new world to explore. Cory was single for the first time in over a decade, and he fully intended to make the most of it. Looking back now, another decade and a half on, he knows that he has. His motto has been:

> 'I'll look back on this and smile because it was life and I decided to live it' (Anonymous).

His priority remained his young sons, and whatever else he did, he always made sure he saw them daily, at least until he was stopped by the divorce lawyers from doing so; he worked harder than ever to make sure they were secure. Just before their final family holiday together in late August 2000, once Cory knew that he and Lisa had reached the end, he found himself having a very brief fling with a work-related colleague. It was never serious and ended the moment he went on holiday with his family. When they got back, he really was single. He felt a freedom he obviously hadn't ever really had (or wanted) in his adult life before – like a kid in a sweet shop! Cory returned to work after their holiday, cycling down the road to see his kids either every morning before work or in the evenings after and then fully every weekend. Indeed, at one point, Lisa raised the prospect of her returning to work full time and Cory staying at home or working less hours to be the primary carer – he agreed immediately. The idea was never pursued.

On his return to work, Cory learned that the secretary in his team had apparently split up with her boyfriend recently, according to office gossip. Susie seemed like a sweet young girl, but Cory had never thought of her in anything other than a professional way until then. That soon changed. They chatted socially at a work drinks do and seemed to get on well, so much so that towards the end of the evening, they ended up going on for another drink together. They found themselves flirting and then kissing in the bar. The steps of the Bank of England were where they consummated their new-found friendship that night. They agreed that they would like to see each other again but that they would keep it a secret at work for the time being. So their working relationship carried on as normal for a couple of months before everyone found out in the office. They saw each other increasingly regularly outside work, as well as fulfilling fantasies about sexual activities in the office too – in meeting rooms, toilet cubicles, on the stairs, and over the desk after hours. As Cory had his kids every weekend, eventually Susie met them and they seemed to like her. They got on well, perhaps because mentally, she was closer to them than to Cory (as he, perhaps cruelly, thought later). But at the time, that didn't matter. Cory was enjoying a great sex life with an attractive young twenty-something, so life seemed good. In retrospect, it was clearly just a rebound relationship from his years of marriage. And that is the main lesson Cory would implore every other man who is having his mid-life crisis to consider, carefully. Do not throw everything away just because you are worried you have lost your mojo, feel old and inadequate, no longer virile and attractive, and all the other extensive reasons men give for their mid-life crises. That obviously was what people had meant when they had told Cory he was a fool to leave his wife and kids. They would have been right if it was just on a whim or to satisfy such usual clichéd mid-life issues. Their specious arguments though about just having affairs were not what he was seeking. A few years later, he had this very discussion with a client who became a good friend, who went through something very similar and was essentially ostracised by some of his senior colleagues. Not because he had an affair, but because he left his wife and kids for a new relationship with his secretary. He was told in no uncertain terms that was not the done thing. He could fuck as many women as he wanted, but he should always return home and stay with his wife and family. Some of these people purported to be very religious too. Bizarre to see how people's moral compass has become so skewed and their beliefs so alien to what most people would find acceptable. Yet here they were, senior lawyers and others in the City, fucking their way through junior members of staff regularly, secretaries and all sorts of other mistresses, but believing it was all somehow okay as they went home to the big house, provided financially, and attended the appropriate religious building with their family in a show of unity at weekends. Cory wouldn't presume to judge these people, nor should they have judged him. The reality appeared to be that like endless politicians who fall from grace through their infidelities being exposed while espousing family values and (false) religious moral standards, these people with power usually believe they are invincible and can have it all. They also are invariably terrified of losing their wealth through divorce. The City is full of many still working when they should have long since retired to now fund both their original family and often the new much younger one too.

One of the most bizarre episodes in these initial few months was Lisa one day realising that Susie was at Cory's flat down the road, out of sight and mind (or so they had hoped). It had somehow come out during yet another argument between them. Lisa stormed off to confront Susie, leaving Cory at the family home with the boys, desperately ringing Susie to warn her that her evening was about to take an unusual turn. The plan had been that Cory would spend time with the boys, put them to bed, then return to the flat for the rest of the night with Susie, who was happily awaiting his return. How naive of Cory to assume that anything would ever be simple in trying to balance everything! Another invaluable life lesson he was to learn harshly over the coming months (and years): apparently, you can't have it all. As Cory later realised, the whole period was fraught, as everyone was still so emotionally raw; it was like living in a tinderbox, where even the slightest inflammatory spark could set the whole thing off in flames; not just a small fire either, rather a powder keg of emotions, so incendiary and packed so tightly that any explosion would be an all-consuming conflagration. As he said at the time, he felt as if he was building a house of cards ('You may well think that, but I couldn't possibly comment', as Francis Urquhart/Usher would say). It was all so flimsy. The slightest waft of air or knock could bring the whole thing crashing down without warning. Anyone leaving a marriage or relationship where children are involved requiring ongoing parental contact should steel themselves for this. Never take apparent civility and acceptance at face value, when pure human emotions inevitably intervene no matter how calm and rational people have agreed to be. Susie's phone was going to voicemail, and the texts went unanswered. Cory could do nothing more but sit and wait, as he clearly couldn't leave the boys. He was told what happened later. Apparently, Lisa had reached Cory's flat and rung the bell, but no answer. Thinking that Susie may be ignoring her, she evidently went around to the back of the flat and shouted up. Susie, who had been in the shower and therefore in blissful ignorance of the unfolding drama, was suddenly confronted by someone screaming outside the bedroom window. She then saw Cory's messages warning her that an angry Lisa was on her way – but she was now there. Initially, the two women had something of a slanging match, which went on for some time and became very personal. Somehow, they then moved from that to agreeing to stop shouting at each other publicly to having a more considered discussion. This followed. By then, the boys were all in bed and asleep, so someone (Cory can't now recall who) suggested that the three of them should have a glass of wine and chat at the family home. Weirdly, they all got on very well, and that was the start of Lisa meeting/talking to Cory's subsequent girlfriends, which continues even now. Cory has repeatedly said he finds it all very odd and feels uncomfortable if (as happened with one subsequent partner) the two women go out for a drink together – as guess what an inevitable topic of conversation will be – yes, him. And that is just odd! He has met one of Lisa's subsequent boyfriends but only briefly in passing. They agreed that if either had a serious partner that the boys would get to know, then the other parent should meet and be comfortable with them. That Cory fully agreed with and understood, but beyond that, no thanks. It just reflects the different approach of men and women to most things in life. Cory's view is that once he has finished a relationship with someone, that's it; it's over, move on. Many women seem to like to stay friends with exes and get to know future partners. None of that has ever appealed to Cory. His view is that if it was a serious relationship, then usually it's too difficult to stay friends, as there is too much baggage. Just leave it behind and move on. And if it wasn't serious, then usually it ends because you realise you don't like the person as much as you thought you did, once the initial excitement and novelty wears off, usually after a few months at most. So why would you want to stay in touch? Cory recently reiterated this to Lisa, when they were having a slightly odd but civilised discussion about life and love at a family meal – the boys certainly found it all very strange. Lisa and Cory have obviously had to maintain contact for the boys; to put their kids' needs first, but if they hadn't, he maintains they would have no further contact, as is the case with all his other exes. Life is just easier that way.

Lisa said she liked Susie and was happy for her to be around the boys, particularly as she could see that they liked her. That meant that rather than Susie never straying far from the train station or beyond Cory's flat, she was now allowed further down the road and into the family home too. She was invited for family meals and stayed over with Cory and the boys there occasionally, when Lisa was away at weekends. Most weekends though, if Lisa was around, the boys would come and stay at Cory's flat. It was cosy. Things carried on like this for a few months, the house of cards seemed to be holding up, occasionally swaying in the wind when there were tensions and disagreements, but generally staying intact. As it turned out, it all was a facade. Just the calm before the storm. Lisa did understandably ask Cory a couple of times if Susie was intelligent enough for him. He made some effort at a plausible response, although not being sure how convincingly. Of course, what he couldn't say to Lisa was that Susie was a nice young girl, but that a lot of their relationship was very sexual. He was happy to not have the intellectual connection he was used to in return for sex on tap with a young hottie! Discretion being the better part of valour won out for once (very unusually for him). The other piece of inspired advice his wise stress counsellor had given him (the second, proper one who got it, not the textbook clichéd first one he never saw again) was that people often unburdened much on their minds seeking peace and tranquillity, believing that telling the truth will somehow set you free. It doesn't always. He maintained that often the act of telling a partner (particularly an ex in a fraught divorce situation especially) about something was actually selfish, done for the protagonist's benefit alone. Rather than clearing the air, it hurts the recipient of the news and causes a whole new raft of anger, resentment and issues. Cory had no doubt he had been guilty of that during the previous months with Lisa. He had undoubtedly fanned the flames at times, but at least not on this occasion. Cory had no idea how long things would last with Susie; he wasn't even thinking like that. He was just enjoying it. Women though think differently to men, almost always about almost everything! He has grown to realise that as an indisputable and universal truth over many years; our conflicts can never be resolved as the way we approach them, think about and analyse them are so alien to each other. It's like two people trying to argue in different languages, each not understanding a word the other says! Or like one person seeking to illustrate their points through complex mathematical formulae, while the other responds with creative poetry and prose. There is no connection, no mutual comprehension, just bewilderment that the other doesn't get it. Our minds are just so different; a world apart, and we simply have to accept it!

Although Susie was nice, she was from one of the rougher parts of the south coast and still had connections down there. She went home fairly regularly, as her parents were ill, but then also partied when there. She admitted to Cory a few months into their relationship that she felt out of her depth with him and especially with the family set-up. Lisa and the kids were great, but maybe he should go back to her, as she felt like an interloper in their family. She even wondered if it was some middle-class game to seduce the working-class girl! She had commented one night when Cory took her to a nice restaurant in London that it was all new to her; that she felt like the Julia Roberts character in *Pretty Woman*. She liked to drink and also use other substances. Cory made it clear from the outset that they wouldn't drink, etc. when he had the kids, as they had plenty of other nights to do that. He was at that stage still virginal as far as the gamut of drugs available was concerned. She accepted that she couldn't be drunk or under the influence around the kids. As he had them every weekend, this was okay initially but started to cause a few issues after a while. She wanted to go out and party at weekends or go home to the south coast. He understood that and made it clear he was happy to party with her any other night of the week, but not when he had the boys every weekend. She liked them and all seemed generally fine. He even went down to meet her parents one weekend, for Sunday lunch. All seemed happy and harmonious, although the highlight of the trip was Cory and Susie's sex in the car overlooking the ocean after. Unfortunately, as they got towards Christmas that year, she was going out more to party sometimes with Cory, sometimes not. She started complaining more. Ultimately, he came to realise that this was often as she was on a downer from her partying elsewhere the night before. She had worked part time in a bar for a few months when still with her ex and got a lot of male attention, as young, attractive barmaids do. She admitted she had slept with one of the guys before she got together with Cory, as he had given her a lot of gear and they had partied and slept together a few times apparently. There was also another guy from the pub who she described as her best friend. Cory met him and just knew the truth. He was a classic unrequited love man. He desperately wanted Susie, but she had no sexual or romantic interest in him. Instead, he had watched her leave her boyfriend, shag a local bad boy, and now end up with a divorcing dad. She had shown no glimmer of interest in him in the way he wanted at any stage, and it was eating him up. Cory could see it clearly. Susie couldn't. She swore they were just close friends, nothing more. Cory warned her that the bloke was obsessed with her. She said it was fine; he knew there was never going to be anything between them and accepted it. He didn't. Cory knew that this bloke was shit stirring in the background, asking her why she was involved with a divorcing bloke with four young kids. Why was she meeting the ex-wife and getting drawn in? He was feeding her doubts, notionally as her 'friend', but clearly in the hope he could step in and woo her away. Matters all came to a head over the next month or so.

It started around the time of Cory's birthday, when they had been out drinking in London. On the late train home, Susie fell asleep. When she woke, Cory said something to her like, 'Are you okay?' and she inexplicably responded by lashing out and punching him in the head. She was wearing a big clunky ring, which connected with Cory's temple and hurt. One of the passengers clearly told the guard who insisted on taking their details (a train company policy apparently, clamping down on violence on late-night trains). Once they were home, they were then disturbed by the doorbell – it was the police following up on the incident. Susie explained that she had woken suddenly on the train from a weird dream, hadn't immediately recognised Cory smiling at her, and lashed out, thinking he was apparently some random aggressor from her dream or pest on the train. Or so her story went. Cory confirmed that although his head hurt, that was all there was to it. There was no question of a fight or pressing charges. The police seemed satisfied and left. Susie never did explain what her dream was, but clearly it was a sign of some kind of troubled mind. If only he'd paid more attention then. But he didn't.

Two more incidents then occurred in fairly quick succession. The first was Cory's thirty-fifth birthday celebrations in London. It was a weekday night, so a few hours in a local bar seemed sufficient with workmates as well as other friends. A good crowd was expected, but as the evening approached, Susie started being funny at work with Cory about attending. She suggested they sneak off to a meeting room, have some fun, then he should go to drinks and she would go home. He didn't understand it, so naturally accepted the first part of her kind offer but then insisted she came to the drinks. A few workmates didn't know about them until that evening, although all their close friends did. Their public shows of affection left the others in no doubt though, that they were together and seemed happy. The evening was great, and as the bar closed, everyone agreed that as they were working the next day, they would go home and not carry on partying. As Cory and Susie walked away from the others towards the bus stop, she started having a go at him, saying she hadn't wanted to come; he had embarrassed her by chatting to other girls and generally just being odd. Whether it was just the drink or something else too, he didn't know. Cory was stunned, as he thought they had a great night. He therefore didn't react as sympathetically as she wanted, and the whole thing suddenly escalated without warning. She grabbed him so forcefully it ripped his black overcoat. He was furious and pushed Susie away, turned and walked off. He was suddenly hit and knocked sideways against a large glass-fronted bar window. Some do-gooder had seen him push Susie, who had fallen over, and decided to be a gallant vigilante, launching himself at Cory. The window they hit suddenly cracked and shattered. That appeared to scare Cory's assailant, who disappeared into the night. Everyone around was bemused. That was more than enough for Cory; he got up and walked away to get his train home, alone. He woke the next day to find a huge bruise across his back and side from the assault but as he had no idea who the bloke was could do nothing about it. Susie was not at work that day, but he still was shocked at her and what had happened, so didn't contact her. It was then the weekend and he relaxed with his boys. By Sunday evening, he hadn't heard from her, so he made contact. She claimed not to remember much about the incident, but then claimed that some guy had offered to let her stay at his place that night in London and she had done so. She said she thought he may have taken advantage of her, so Cory said she should go to the police. She never did. Things were clearly awkward, as they had to work together, but they had no contact other than that for some weeks. Then the work Christmas party arrived. Everyone was in good spirits; the wine, beer, and cocktails flowed. At the meal, after a lot of drinking, Susie was seen kissing one of the other attractive female members of staff, much to all the guys' delight. She then proceeded to crawl under the table to try to make things up to Cory by performing a sexual act (as the Sunday newspapers refer to it) on him. Needless to say, that night, they ended up in bed together again.

Susie was offered the chance to go skiing with friends over Christmas. They agreed it made sense for all concerned, so off she went with her present from Cory. He had Christmas with his family, and she returned on New Year's Eve. Cory met her at Waterloo; they came home and quickly made up for lost time. But then she started drinking and passed out. He couldn't wake her for ages and was due to collect the boys, who were temporarily being looked after by his parents, as Lisa had by then gone up to London to see in the new year. He was consequently later than planned to collect the boys and could see the concern in his parents' faces about his partying with this new young girl, but he told them all was fine. He was headstrong and desperately trying to keep the house of cards from collapsing. It was very stressful, but he was determined to try and do it. He wanted to try and have it all. As usual, he should have listened to his parents. As the well-known motivational quote points out, we can have anything if we work and try hard enough, but we can never have everything.

House of Cards

All was okay for a few days, until the boys went back to Lisa. Susie had come and gone between Cory's and her shared rented flat in south London. There had been some talk of her moving in with Cory after Christmas, and they agreed to go out and talk about everything in the new year. They went out in the local town and had a good time, even surviving with no issues the usual bar sleaze- balls moving in on Susie every time Cory went to the bar or loo. It's one reason Cory trusts no other man, as there is no loyalty. Generally speaking, men are primarily driven by their sex drive and sexual desires. They sometimes temper this inherent, base, natural instinct out of loyalty to wives, girlfriends, partners, and occasionally friends and family. But not always. Most men would fuck everyone they could whenever possible, if they truly believed they could do so with impunity. Many do so anyway. Men certainly do not regard a girl who is with another man as in any way off limits. They sniff around regardless, especially in the bar and club-pulling environments. Cory accepts it as a fact of life, but despises his fellow man for it. He is used to the attractive women he becomes involved with being attractive to others. But he finds other men's lack of class crass in the extreme. Fine to look and admire, but please stay away when you can see a girl is with someone else. Don't pounce as soon as his back is turned. Seriously. What do you really think will happen? She'll be so wowed by you, random bloke, using your standard chat-up lines (as you move from girl to girl around the bar) that she'll immediately dump the guy she's with and run off with you? Get real, boys! Stick to the single girls and stay off another man's patch! Anyway, Susie and Cory had a good evening despite this and then decided to get some late-night food on the way home.

For some reason, Susie got agitated as they waited for their kebabs, and again suddenly things escalated for no apparent reason. She started complaining about his kids, about how much time he spent with them and being rude about them. Cory had no idea where this all came from but told her to shut the fuck up; he'd had enough of her mad rants. She started crying. He went down an alley for a pee and, when he came back, found her talking to policemen. They asked Cory what was going on; he said that nothing was occurring. They were clearly suspicious of everyone in late-night drinking mode and grilled Cory about why Susie was crying; had he assaulted her, physically or sexually? If not, why was she crying? Where had they been? Why had he been down the alley? What was he doing? Was he using drugs? He assured them they'd only been drinking, had got some food, had got ratty with each other while waiting, as they were tired, and had a stupid argument. The police looked unconvinced but let them carry on home. Cory asked Susie what she had said; she started having a go at him again, so he said that was it; he'd then had enough of her weirdness. He walked off and into the flat. She followed but apparently didn't have her key with her. She was therefore buzzing at the door and crying hysterically, which other neighbours heard. Cory let her in and the argument continued. He asked why she was so fucked up, why she kept going like this. If she couldn't accept his kids, she should go and not pretend to like them but then complain increasingly about them. They had both been drinking all evening, which as everyone knows is very often the cause of silly petty arguments exploding out of control. One of his friends had recently ended up in custody, as the most innocuous argument with his then girlfriend over the TV remote control had blown up out of all proportion. That's what happened here.

She was obviously hurt by what he said and told him people were telling her to get out of the relationship (her 'best friend' being one). She was confused. Cory said he liked her, but he had enough shit going on with the divorce and kids, so couldn't give her more than he had so far. He thought it was enough; they had a lot of time and fun together, but if she didn't, he couldn't change anything now. Things grew tenser; insults became more personal; she screamed that she'd fucked other people back home when they'd started seeing each other. Eventually, she smashed a few CDs in her anger and frustration. She then tried to slash him with one of the broken pieces, which led to a bit of a fight. It calmed briefly only for her then to stub a cigarette out on the back of his neck, twice, as he turned away from her. She screamed that he should not ignore her, not to turn his back on her. That was it. The pain was intense, his flesh was burning, and a red mist descended over him. Instinctively, without any rational thought, he turned and lashed out, catching her in the mouth with his fist. She flew across the room and banged her face on a table as she fell. Her teeth had bitten into his hand on impact, leaving two deep wounds. The shock of what had just happened stopped them in their tracks. They both knew they had gone too far. As they sat there bewildered, the doorbell buzzed. It was the police. Neighbours had called them because of the noise. Their timing couldn't have been worse. Had the police arrived earlier, they may have stopped things escalating; had they arrived later, the scene wouldn't have been as bad. But at that point, they walked into what looked like a battle zone. Blood from Cory's injured hand was dripping everywhere, his shirt was ripped open, he had cigarette burns on his neck, and scratches on his face. Susie's mouth was swollen and she had bumps on her head and face. Ambulances were called, she was treated at the scene and he was advised that his hand injuries needed hospital treatment. Given that a domestic incident had occurred, he was arrested. The police said technically they should therefore keep him in handcuffs to, from and at the hospital; but as he seemed reasonable, they wouldn't do so as long as he behaved. He did. He had nothing to hide and told then exactly what had happened. After hours waiting at hospital, where his injuries were eventually treated, he was taken to the local nick, put in a cell for a few hours and then told he would be released on bail while their investigations proceeded.

Susie had gone back to her own flat and was medically okay. They didn't see each other for weeks after, not least as Cory was subsequently admitted to hospital with concerns about the infection spreading in his hand. He was transferred to a specialist hospital in London for an operation and was hooked up to a drip for a few days. The human mouth apparently is one of the most germ-filled places there is, and it had all gone in to Cory's wounded hand, which was very painful indeed. Divine retribution, no doubt! Susie returned to work and faced endless questions about her facial bruising. She went home at weekends and her rough local mates offered to sort Cory out. And of course, it was all too much for her 'best friend', skulking as ever in the background like some Machiavellian character waiting to make his move, to rescue her, and live happily ever after together. Let's call him Perv. He was in his element, telling her that this proved all he'd said, Cory wasn't right for her, she should never go back, and she should press charges. The problem was the police had already told her that if she pressed charges, Cory would too. It was clear that both were equally to blame and responsible for the fight, both had hit the other, and perhaps the evidence even supported the view that she had started and provoked it. She of course knew the truth and no charges were ever pursued. Susie was under pressure from all around her to either tell them what happened or to let them sort Cory out for her. But she didn't want that. After a few weeks, she contacted Cory and told him what was going on. Lisa got involved and talked to Susie too. The house of cards that Cory had exerted such huge energy to try and keep stable, solid, and in place had come crashing down around his ears. He felt as if he could identify too closely with the Michael Douglas character in *Falling Down*.

His hand had become badly infected, particularly the finger where the wound was deepest and he was later told he could have lost it. He had to attend the hospital for regular check-ups and physiotherapy. He took more time off work and eventually told his boss what had happened. He sought out a counsellor to address the stress he was juggling alongside trying to keep all aspects of his life going. The initial one he saw claimed it all stemmed back to his childhood; basic textbook therapy but absolute nonsense. He subsequently moved on to a different one, who got it. Over the following months, he identified that Cory was in a battle for ongoing regular contact with his boys, but felt as if he was like a boxer going in to the ring to fight with his arms tied behind his back, a very appropriate analogy indeed. As always with such matters, though no one can sort it out for you, that is only ever down to you. People can talk, listen, and advise, but only you have the power to change the issues affecting your own life. Or at least how you deal with them. Cory realised that it was all becoming too much; he was running at maximum to juggle everything, trying to have it all. But life is rarely like that and can be very unforgiving. It seemingly was all too much, trying to have a new relationship and keeping his regular contact with his boys; the cracks were beginning to show. The strain of it all had bubbled up and exploded that night. He felt as if his life was a pressure cooker, and whilst he was a strong and resolute character, each event had added to the pressure build-up, to the steam starting to escape. But instead of a gradual release, it had been like a volcanic eruption, all stress-related clearly, and the enforced time out in hospital gave him a vital period of solace, time to reflect and think it all through. As the saying goes:

> '. . something very beautiful happens to people when their world
> has fallen apart: a humility, a nobility, a higher intelligence
> emerges at just the point when our knees hit the floor'
> (Marianne Williamson)

After periods of discussion, Cory made a sideways move to another business, and Susie moved on to be a secretary elsewhere. For some reason that seems bizarre to Cory now, looking back and typing all that happened, they even got back together for a period of time, but of course it wouldn't work out. Susie told him at one point she was pregnant, but he didn't know if that was true; nor even if it was, whether it would be his, given all her claims and their break-ups. Their relationship fizzled out; too much damage had been done. But not before Perv had started sending Cory anonymous threatening text messages. Cory knew it was him, but Susie would not accept that. She finally admitted to Cory at the end that Perv had denied his involvement endlessly; until he had let it slip one night in a drunken call to her, when he had vowed his undying love and that he would do anything for her. She was shocked. Cory was not. He agreed not to do anything, provided Perv disappeared and never repeated his cowardly no-names late-night text threats, some of which even arrived while Susie was back with Cory (and thus scared her too). It was all part of the death of their relationship though, which seemed inevitable after all the shit. What he didn't expect though, was her parting shot, which transpired to be her seducing his recently divorced, senior manager at work (soon to be ex-friend) and fucking him as a final act of revenge. Nice touch.

Fortunately, at the time, the boys were blissfully unaware of all these issues. They simply knew that Cory had hurt his hand and was having it fixed at hospital. They had liked Susie, but got used to her not being around as much and then not at all. Cory hoped it would have no lasting impact on them, just being part of them getting used to different people coming and going from their lives, as they progressed from child minder through nursery to primary school and beyond. He subsequently decided it was time to give up the rented flat and get something more substantial for him and the boys, so he gave notice, started house hunting, and moved in with his parents into their spare room for the summer period while he did so. This was a good temporary solution but unfortunately went on slightly too long, and tempers became frayed in the final weeks, as the house purchase typically dragged on longer than it should have. It meant the boys had Cory and their grandparents around at weekends, had a bit more space and a proper family feel. But it was crowded, and of course, with four young boys, you have to keep them occupied at all times. Cory was still regularly taking them to local parks, swimming, to *Legoland* and *Thorpe Park* almost every weekend in the summer months. Then it came to the summer holiday, and they decided to go back to their favourite *CenterParcs*, Cory, his four boys, and his parents.

Relations with Lisa were now at an all-time low. The previous arrangements that had worked so well for months suddenly no longer suited her. Cory was aware that her friends and family were constantly stirring the cauldron of hate and bile against him, telling Lisa not to let him have it all – to be fucking his young secretary (or whoever) while still seeing his boys. Their advice apparently was that he shouldn't be allowed to see his kids as some kind of punishment! Lisa appeared to resist their venom initially, realising that what was best for the boys mattered most. But the drip-drip effect of their pernicious arguments over many months gradually wore her down. She was dating someone new, and perhaps that also meant she needed the dynamics to change. Like Cory, she was also seeing a counsellor, seeking to find herself again through all the raw emotion of the collapse of their marriage. That's how traumatic it was for both of them; almost the equivalent of a death in terms of grief after so long together, after all they had together but was now gone. It was clear that it couldn't be fixed; it was finished. But they had to still be a large part of each other's lives for the boys; an almost impossible conundrum, as they needed to move on from each other and start afresh but had the constant reminder of seeing and talking to each other regularly because of their young children. The tightrope they were on was almost snapping under the strain of it all. Naturally, she had been shocked at the explosion between Cory and Susie, which Cory entirely understood. He had too. No doubt a combination of all these factors, the passage of time and need to move on, came together at a time lawyers were heavily involved trying to conclude their divorce. They didn't seem to help matters at all. Suddenly, what had been amicable, or at least civilised and as cooperative as possible arrangements were changed overnight. A revised contact schedule couldn't be agreed and tensions were rising between them, both being stubborn lawyers and neither would give way. Matters escalated as the twins' sixth birthday approached, when she unilaterally declared that he was no longer welcome in the family home at all, ever. Her parents blocked the door to prevent him seeing his kids, who he saw staring in dismay at the scene through the dining room window. Both sides called the police, who attended and clearly had no interest in becoming involved in a (non-violent) domestic argument. He wanted just to go in and see his kids; she announced she was now scared of him and didn't want him in the house, all very new after his regular access for the previous eight months. Even when he suggested the police come in as well to counter her (alleged) fear, she refused. It was an impasse. Cory was forced to leave. The divorce turned very bitter and ugly for months after that. The worst part for him was no longer being able to see his kids every day. He didn't particularly care what she said about him, as vicious and vindictive comments are sadly often part of any divorce, but why deprive their boys of their loving dad? While these arguments proceeded through the courts, Cory's contact was reduced. He refused to accept their suggested alternate weekend arrangements; they wouldn't countenance any continuation of his daily visits. His own lawyers even told him that his previous contact was unreasonable, as dads didn't normally want so much contact. How sickeningly unenlightened! Cory was forced to agree to a compromise, whereby he saw the boys a couple of weekday evenings each week and then some convoluted formula about weekend contact, where they stayed over with him two nights one week, and one night the next. All utterly ridiculous.

The simple point was that he would never give up his boys, no matter what. Even with an outdated attitude from the courts and his own lawyers (not to mention her dinosaur barrister's views of minimal contact being acceptable), he swore that he would not give up. He had to agree that he wouldn't attend the house other than on those specified dates and times to collect the boys, and he no longer went inside. This led to a ludicrous situation where he was one day driving past the family home and saw his boys outside; they saw him too and waved and smiled and shouted, 'Daddy!' He obviously stopped, got out, and hugged them at the roadside. They asked when they were seeing him again; he explained that it could only be at the agreed times, which they clearly didn't comprehend. He said he would sort things as soon as he could. It was heart breaking. The next day, his lawyers received a threatening, aggressive urgent fax from hers, stating that if he saw the boys outside the agreed schedule again, they would apply for injunctions and seek other sanctions against him. His protestations of the innocence of the situation fell on deaf ears, even from his own lawyers, which was typical of how the family courts and matrimonial lawyers dealt with matters a decade or so ago. Cory can only hope that a more enlightened view prevails these days, as it is only the kids who suffer from being deprived of both parents. He knows from discussions he had at the time, in the depths of his despair at the iniquity of the situation, that many men lose their kids in these situations. Often dads would gradually, reluctantly just fade from their kids' lives in these scenarios, especially if the mum remarries and a stepdad takes over. He vowed he would never allow that to happen between him and his boys. Was this was just his natural father's instinct, his very stubborn, determined personality, or his innate fear of losing any further loved ones? Probably a combination of all of these, but it made his determination unbreakable that he would never stop being a real dad to his boys. Although he could see how some dads gave up and walked away, feeling they were no longer wanted or loved, he never would. It was no one else's right to interfere and stop his boys seeing their dad – he would fight the legal system all the way to prove this. Whatever issues he and Lisa had, whatever she thought of him, those were different considerations and should have no bearing on the boys needing their dad. And of course, his need for them.

Summer Fun

Cory therefore found himself with a lot more free time during the ensuing months. Susie was long gone; he had moved out of the flat and was living in his parents' spare room. Apart from his prescribed time with his kids, daily commute and work, he suddenly had more time on his hands for the first time in years. He didn't know what to do. Then mass-dating ensued to fill the void. He flirted with and briefly dated the attractive young doctor from the London hospital who had fixed his injured hand, but she decided a man with four young kids was too much for her. Her true calling was overseas aid work, not UK domesticity. A real shame, as they got on very well. There then followed a whole series of random dates, casual shags, one-night stands, girls from work, pick-ups in bars (although never as the clichéd lounge lizard types he hates with their inane, wanky, chat-up lines). There was even one from the queue outside *Tiger Tiger*, which led to a late-night assignation in the office. Sadly, in Cory's efforts to tidy up afterwards, instead of just leaving the debris in the bin, he cleverly (or so he thought!) decided to take the bin bag outside. He was confronted by uproar in the office the next morning, as a used condom had somehow fallen from the bin bag and been found hanging over the edge of one of the internal steps: a delightful sight for those first in that day. He confessed his guilt immediately, as that was just in his nature. Others have told him repeatedly that he is too honest, and that's why he has so much conflict in his life. He should learn to be more circumspect in what he said, to be more secretive and guarded in his personal life. But that is just not the way he is made. He has no shades of grey generally.

The managing director said it had caused some offence but no one had died (i.e. it wasn't a major offence in the grand scheme of life), so they should all move on with their lives. In fact, he and Cory started having a few drinks together from time to time after this, so perhaps there was some grudging male respect or something similar at play. Cory was incorrigible, chatting up every attractive woman he met – from all the local barmaids, to the girl in the tanning shop round the corner from the office, former work colleagues, current work mates, and a trainee policewoman he met in a bar. He was having great fun, but none of it really made him happy or content. The sex was good, he was enjoying all the socialising, but none of them ever turned into anything serious; he realised that this endless fun being single was not what he wanted. It was all a bit shallow. He had known true love for many years with Lisa and he wanted that back again. His wild single lifestyle all came to a head for him when he was mugged in the King's Cross area one evening after a night out in a local bar. Everyone else had headed home, but he wanted some more fun, so went for a wander. He was played superbly by the girl he bumped into. She asked for money; he said no. He was not completely stupid (even when drunk, well, not always!) and suspected if he handed anything over, that would be the last he saw of her. So she played her long game; they talked, got on well, she offered to take him somewhere for a party. Although he knew it was all dodgy, he thought, 'What the fuck!' He was a single man out in London after drinking with mates, not wanting to go home alone. He thought he was being clever not handing money over, but of course, these 'clipper' girls (as he subsequently learned they were called) are professionals; they do this every night, endlessly, and always have another play. There first effort is usually along the lines that if the guy hands some money over, they'll go and party. If he does, she'll run away. If he doesn't, the next stage is to take him to a doorway and tell him that they have to hand the money through the letter box and then be let in. If he does, she disappears inside, and he never sees her again; there are no doubt many variations and his experience was limited. In Cory's (drunken) case, she kept asking if he had enough money. She encouraged him to go to a cashpoint and get some out so they could really party; she could get anything he wanted, etc. Of course, this is all to ensure that he has sufficient cash on him. She announced that she had to make a phone call. Cory knew innately throughout that it was probably a con, but thought he was smart enough so far and she was no street skank. This was an interesting, attractive girl, who kept reassuring him. Well, she would, wouldn't she? So she made her call from a phone box and then said they wanted to talk to Cory. As he said hello, he was roughly pushed forward and banged his head. He was dazed. A male voice behind him said they were the police and what was he doing? Was he consorting with street girls? He was being frisked. Cory soon realised it was a con; he was being mugged, gently, cleverly, but they had his wallet. He said that they could of course take it and its contents, but please not his dead brother's photo and death notice which he kept inside. But they did. They disappeared as quickly as they arrived; it was over. That was enough for Cory. No more.

He craved the emotional closeness that he and Lisa used to have. Having had it previously, he knew what he was looking for. He had become friendly with the MD's PA over recent months, but had been told she was in a long-term relationship. Cory didn't pursue people in relationships; he knew from his own personal experience how traumatic a break-up was and didn't wish that on anyone else. Emma was tall, attractive and good fun. They had good banter; it transpired they were both from Leeds originally and seemed to be forming some sort of friendship and bond. As the MD's PA, she was also aware of the various shit going on in Cory's personal life and was supportive and kind about it all. One day, Cory heard a rumour that she had apparently recently had a brief assignation with one of his workmates; he was intrigued. He found out more from various sources and discovered that she had split with her boyfriend and was now looking for fun. Perfect! He was easily able to change his approach towards her, imperceptibly at first, to move from just being friends into something more flirtatious. He talked to her more in the office and outside too; they watched Leeds' European games together in bars and matters culminated one weekend when he had yet another argument with Lisa about his contact with the boys. He had wanted to take them to *Legoland* for the day, but she had seemingly made other plans to scupper this. He therefore was at something of a loss, as he'd set the whole day aside for them. He started a text conversation with Emma that led to them agreeing to meet in a local town for a drink and chat.

She drove, so didn't drink. Cory however drank and poured his heart out to her about how he missed his boys, how they were all that mattered, and that although all his partying and shagging around was fun, it wasn't what he wanted from life. It was an empty existence. They spent hours together, and then she mentioned she had to make a move. He said it was a shame, as they were getting on so well; she agreed and invited him home with her. He went. And that was the start of what neither of them had expected. She admitted that she had thought he was just a bad boy shagger from reputation and incidents she knew of. She had been amazed to see how much he loved his boys, and to hear him talking about them had changed her view of him completely. Although they weren't seriously involved initially and she was open about others she was seeing, it soon changed over a few weeks into a real relationship. They came to realise that all their prior months of talking just as friends now gave them a huge head start as a couple. It was nice; they liked each other. They had found someone close in each other, whilst so busy looking for it elsewhere in others. Their friendship was now so much more, proof again to Cory that his best relationships, no matter how long they lasted subsequently, grew out of initial friendships. Even if this was unexpected, given her role as the MD's PA, they decided to keep their relationship secret at work and did this very successfully. No one knew. It added a frisson of excitement, especially when the MD was out and he would pop along to the big office, lock the door, and live out more of those office-based sexual fantasises with her. The thrill of potentially being caught really seemed to excite her, and he was happy to go along with anything that fed his sex drive. She remained supportive and understanding about his fight with Lisa over contact with his kids and was happy to see him when he wasn't with them. He spent increasing amounts of his spare time at her house, commuting in with her but without anyone seeing them. They were getting on very well, so decided to have a short holiday together, which was fun and brought them closer. Purely coincidentally, Leeds happened to be on a pre-season tour nearby, so they went to watch them play. Although there were many highlights, the one that sticks in his mind now was her insistence that she gave him a blowjob as he drove their hired car along a scenic country road. It's quite hard to concentrate at the same time on both, he discovered!

Cory was due to be best man at his brother's wedding that summer, with the boys all wearing mini-top hat and tails outfits too. They looked very cute, but now they're all a lot older and bigger, their uncle admits it was probably quite cruel to insist on dressing them like that. It was by no means the simplest logistical exercise, getting all four of them dressed in the morning; ensuring they didn't play for hours and mess it all up; keeping them amused during the church service (during which Chaz, the youngest, spent most of the time sleeping on Cory's shoulder); then a rapid change before the wedding reception so they could be dispatched back to their mum and the outfits safely stored for return to the hire shop. Exhausting! He and the boys spent the night before in a room at the local bed and breakfast his parents and other extended family members were staying at so that they could all get ready together on the morning of the wedding. The boys came to the service, but then left before the wedding reception so that Cory could then switch from being dad and chaperone to being best man properly to his brother. It was agreed that Emma would then join them for the evening reception, when Cory could finally relax and just enjoy himself with her. She was fine with that and as usual seemed fairly pragmatic about such things. Lisa did turn up to pick the boys up, as agreed, but was late and Cory wondered if this was deliberate. It may just have been the vagaries of London transport, but in the emotion of the ongoing divorce, everything is questioned, and often spurious attributes are given to every action, good or bad. He subsequently learned some time after the event that she had rung his brother and sister-in-law (to be) and caused some issue about it all a few days before the wedding, which was not forgiven or forgotten by the women involved (as is their propensity in such matters) for many years. He was blissfully unaware of it all at the time.

Emma was very helpful as he prepared his best man's speech and supportive as ever throughout. The only real issue between them was that by the time she arrived and was keen to party the night away, he was exhausted from the day's stresses and strains and performing all his duties. She wanted to dance; he needed just to slump in his seat and slowly let the alcohol wash his exhaustion and stress of the day away. It was one of the few arguments they ever had. But it was all soon over, and she was great with his family and his brother's friends, both that night and at the post-wedding breakfast in the local hotel they all stayed at the next morning. Indeed, his brother's younger male friends all told her Cory was clearly too old for such a vibrant young girl and she was way too good for him. Nice try, young men! The bigger issue to emerge at the wedding was the unspoken animosities between their elder family members, which had apparently been simmering for years, all exploding to the surface that night. As mentioned, their dad was from a large Catholic family, and there were a collection of aunts, uncles and cousins in attendance. What Cory and his brothers hadn't realised for all the years they had attended big family gatherings as kids were the tensions between those siblings. Their dad and his younger sister appeared to be exempt as the babies of the clan, but there were long-term generally buried problems amongst the elder ones. The eldest brother (something of a cheeky charmer rogue) had apparently taken some family money years ago and never been forgiven for it; the next eldest brother had spent years in the armed forces and was quite an imposing man, who turned quite nasty when he drank (another of the many reasons Cory's mum hates excessive drinking, especially by men); and then there was one of the elder sisters, who was incredibly bossy and domineering and whose husband was the commensurate meek and mild mannered chap. Or so we all thought. Cory didn't see what happened, but apparently it all kicked off between them late at night after a day of drinking at the wedding. Some comment was made that led to the military man being very cutting about his siblings; the bossy sister told him to shut up and that led to some response about her not being so high and mighty when she had an affair with a priest when younger (shock, horror!) and her husband was the archetypical dirty old groper at family dos. He had, for years, apparently touched female family members in a too-familiar manner; had squeezed too tightly when hugging them; had let his hands slip, wander, and linger too long – just like the old uncle in *Bridget Jones* she was forced to endure at every family Christmas gathering. It seems every family really does have one! This was dynamite, shattering their big Catholic family unity and showing that if you scratch beneath the surface, there's all sorts of things going on. It appeared that the catalyst for all of this suddenly bursting out very publicly was that the groping uncle had unfortunately been too affectionate in an embrace with a teenage niece, and the shit had really hit the fan. He was just a bit of a dirty old man, but of course given all the recent revelations about the disgraced Jimmy Saville and his cohorts, you never really know.

Cory was progressing with his house search, and Emma started helping him to find potential homes. She came on some viewings to offer her opinions. He found a suitable one, made an offer, and waited for the interminably slow conveyancing system to go through its slow-moving motions. As well as decrying the English legal system's attitude towards children and father's rights in matrimonial matters, Cory's other major bugbear is the ridiculously antiquated and inefficient nature of our conveyancing system in this country. It is shockingly bad and adds so much stress to an already emotionally fraught period in people's lives (just like in divorces). Rant over! He moved in just after the kids went back to school at the end of the summer holidays. Things with Emma were great; he had even met her dad when he was down visiting and they had got on well over lunch (there was no sign of her mum though, as apparently they had little contact). Emma had briefly met the boys over the summer but was seeing more of them at the house. She struggled to cope, understandably. She was a girl in her early twenties, with a limited family life and no real experience of kids. While she had accepted Cory's time with the boys previously, he'd also had enough time for her completely separate from them too. Now they had their own home again; even when they weren't there, it was still very much their home, and it was evidently not what she had expected. There had been talk over the summer about her possibly moving in once Cory had the house, but that seemed further away than ever as things stood. It seemed that the harsh realities of life had suddenly come home to roost. She had enjoyed their carefree time together over the summer months mainly at her house, when he was free. But now the balance had shifted, and he was going to be based at his new home much more, with his boys there more regularly. Negotiations with Lisa seemed to be progressing well, marking a pleasant change from their previous animosity. Both had calmed down; they were now less antagonistic towards each other and both knew that they had to get on for the boys' sakes. They had worked through some of the inevitable pain and emotion of the divorce, which clearly had to be vented, as it's just human nature to do so (and like any grief, it can't be suppressed; it has to come out and be gone through, no matter how painfully); though arguably a pair of equally stubborn, stroppy divorcing lawyers (both carrying thirteen years' emotional baggage with each other) made it far worse!

Yet now tensions arose between Emma and Cory that had never previously been there, and they gradually saw each other less and less. This also coincided with the business being affected by huge fears and uncertainties in the City, post-9/11, which had just occurred; various cuts and restructurings took place, leading to people being systematically released over the following months. Cory was one of them. His and Emma's relationship just faded away over this period. She subsequently admitted that a house full of young kids had just scared her and was not what she wanted. Cory was therefore looking for a new job in a tough economic climate. He had his new home for him and the boys but was now relying on credit cards to survive. He had given Lisa his share of the family home as part of the divorce settlement and had voluntarily been giving her half his income too. Times were tough, but as always, he was determined to fight through and improve things. It just went to prove that eternal theory that rarely do all aspects of your life ever go well at the same time, or as Helen Fielding so succinctly put it in her *Bridget Jones* diaries:

> *'It is a truth universally acknowledged that when one part of your life starts going okay, another falls spectacularly to pieces.'*

That was certainly true in his case here. He had previously been without a home, with less contact with his boys for too long. Now, just as he bought his house in order to spend more time with his kids again, he lost his girlfriend and then his job! Cory wondered whether he was being punished for leaving Lisa, as it had certainly been a roller-coaster past year since he had. But as the quote from Paulo Coelho has it:

> *'Life is too short to wake up with regrets. So love the people who treat you right. Forget about those who don't. Believe everything happens for a reason. If you get a chance, take it. If it changes your life, let it. Nobody said life would be easy, they just promised it would most likely be worth it.'*

Cory certainly subscribes to this viewpoint; he did then in the bleak days and has ever since. We get one life, we have no idea when it may end and when we may lose it all. So live life to the full and enjoy it, particularly the things that matter most to you. Cory has always lived his life by this philosophy.

He attended endless interviews, but businesses generally weren't hiring. He no longer had the money to go out partying, drinking, and womanising, so what was he to do with all his spare time? Then he had a brainwave; he would buy a home PC with one of his credit cards. Genius! Emma had even unexpectedly turned up one weekend to check he was okay (which was nice of her) and ended up helping him install the PC, as she knew about such things, well certainly far more than did the Luddite that Cory was. This proved to be an inspired purchase, as obviously he was not currently working, had limited money post-divorce and redundancy, had just bought a house with a mortgage to pay, and had four young sons to feed and clothe. Not only was the PC invaluable for his numerous work applications, he also now felt less isolated from the world as he sat at home. He could connect with the outside world again, to fill his endless hours when the boys weren't with him. And that's how he discovered online dating.

Online Dating

Back in the early 2000s, online dating was relatively new and still not necessarily as widely socially accepted as it is now. But it seemed much more genuine and straightforward than it does these days. Cory had a look recently and was bemused by the endless number of options and cost. He even signed up briefly on one (having had a lot of success the first time round) but found that people appeared to be not genuine or profiles copied across multiple sites caused confusion and the whole thing just seemed far less appealing than the last time. Of course, he is also almost fifteen years older than last time, so that could have a bearing! Sites for older, often wealthy men to buy young brides or girlfriends isn't really what he is looking for, despite people telling him that's all he is doing in his pursuit of younger women generally anyway! The reality is that none of these online sites can guarantee that you will meet anyone you like and with whom you may have that elusive chemistry any more than randomly meeting someone at work, in the pub, and in all normal walks of real life. Just because people are on there, all apparently looking for love or at least some kind of connection (whether emotional or purely physical), it is inevitably as random finding 'the one' for you on there as it is in the real world. But that wouldn't be the greatest sell, would it? Yes, of course, people meet and get on online. But not with everyone they meet, and you have to plough through a lot of unsuitables, time wasters and just plain weirdos. If people devoted as much time as they do online to going out and meeting people socially, who's to say they wouldn't have the same success? But in this online-obsessed world, somehow online connections, introduction and dating sites are deemed to be a better use of people's time when they are lonely and looking for someone to fill some void in their lives. Work colleagues, family connections, friends of friends, and other mutual social introductions still remain a far easier way of meeting potentially suitable partners. No doubt we all know people who have met through these routes. Look also at all the relationships and affairs that spring in the work environment, where people spend more hours daily with each other than at home with their partners. Some become genuine romances that last, some just lustful encounters to break the tedium of most people's dull working lives. They add a touch of excitement and a thrill to otherwise normal lives. Anyway, back to Cory's online dating successes back in the day; as one of the girls he met online quite openly said to him, her firm view was that all the girls on dating sites in those days were damaged. She said it was akin to going to Battersea Dogs home. They may look good and seem okay, but they were all there for a reason, and usually, it was that they had been badly treated or abandoned previously. If only Cory had paid more attention to that at the time. But he didn't. His view remained that life is for living and learning from your mistakes, finding out for yourself so that afterwards, you can look back and say, 'Yes, that was entirely accurate!'

So Cory launched his online search for love, or whatever may come from it. As he was now spending increasing time online at home (a new experience for him), he also joined Friends Re-United – which the older readers will recall as the UK precursor to the Facebook phenomenon; younger readers will have no comprehension of a world not dominated by Mr Zuckerberg's ever-expanding empire, as it increasingly infiltrates every aspect of our ever-more social media-reliant lives! He reconnected with a couple of women he had worked with years earlier but nothing had ever happened at the time. Now it did. What a great new world, where you could find people from your past and go back to complete unfinished business! He also used that old male chat-up methodology adapted by many a man on a night out looking for female fun – the numbers game. There were a few aspects to this. Real womanisers in any walk of life, in the office, at a bar, online, etc. will simply chat every woman up, knowing that many will say no. But on the law of percentages, some will be interested. It's a shotgun, splatter approach, but it works for some people apparently. And then there is the graduated scale of chatting up women. This can work online and in other aspects of life too, but is most often observed as an interesting anthropological study of male (attempted) mating patterns in clubs and bars. It is well known that as the night progresses, men move through the different levels of target quarry. If they have the confidence, they start with the stunners, who may well be out of their league. These beauties, who are constantly inundated by male attention, will usually decline, either politely or mockingly, depending on their level of disdain for your efforts, appearance, etc. Men then move through the subsequent categories of attractive women. But bearing in mind their aim is also invariably to drink themselves stupid as the night progresses, beer goggles can come into play. As they become increasingly drunk and desperate, wanting to make sure they don't go home alone and miss end-of-night action, they move on to those dismissed at the start of the night, their belief being that they are very gallant gents and that these girls will be flattered, oblivious to the fact the message they are really sending out is much more that any port in a storm will do. Sometimes it works though!

With the online sites, the starting point for Cory would always be the photo, and if he was attracted to someone, he would then initiate dialogue. He had been on a few blind dates and dates through dating agencies that weren't (then) online. These hadn't worked though, as he found that many a woman's description of herself didn't quite accord with how he would have described them. He had been on one classically embarrassing date, where he had left after one drink, having even considered climbing out of the toilet window to escape! When he relayed this story to the lady he was with on another blind date, she evidently thought he was going to do the same every time he went to the loo. Cory therefore made it a policy to (perhaps shallowly) filter by photos first and then to move on to personality. This seemed to work at that time, as he ended up quite quickly meeting Vanessa for a drink in a London pub. She was attractive and sexy, not as young as his recent secretarial conquests had been, recently split from a long-term relationship, owned her own flat, car etc., and generally seemed to have her 'shit together' a bit more than the younger women had. They flirted, talked on the phone and online, and got on well. This carried on when they met; they had fun and agreed to see each other again a few days later; she would come to his house. Of course, one can never presume or take anything for granted, but things are much more likely to happen when a woman agrees to come home with you. This was excellent for a second date, and Cory was excited that someone who seemed great was almost in his clutches so quickly. However, things never are as simple as they seem or go as smoothly as they should; the most inexplicable hitch arose.

Emma had emailed Cory to ask how he was and to let him know she was seeing someone else; she hoped he was okay and just wanted him to know. He wasn't quite sure why she had emailed him that. Instead of just saying thanks and congratulations, which he has found subsequently always to be the best approach if exes ever contact you and start talking about their new love interests and particularly asking about yours, he foolishly engaged in a discussion with Emma. Fatal. It seemed a bloke she had mentioned to Cory when they had been together, someone who tried to chat her up regularly, had pounced just at the time she and Cory were drifting apart. She was sorry and admitted it had made her think Cory and his kids were too much for her, as the other guy was an easier option. Unfortunately for him however, he had failed to factor her feminine emotions into the equation, and she had evidently grown to resent him for pressurising her into choosing him over Cory. This reinforced Cory's long-held view that he didn't need to know any of this shit, and that once a relationship ends, it is best just to move on and not look back. Get on with your own new lives without each other; don't stay in touch, don't talk about your new relationships, especially if there was an overlap between yours ending and the new one starting! It serves no purpose other than to piss people off, but it is another of those huge differences between men and women, their emotions, and how they like to address life. That was the effect here. Cory said he didn't want or need to know any of that; Emma apologised and said she felt she should tell him.

Women over-analyse and reflect on everything. Men deal with what they have to at the time and then move on. A classic example of this, away from the complicating emotions of relationships, occurred very recently at Cory's youngest son's Sunday football game. Chaz's team was holding their own in a tough, physical game against a south London team. There was the usual pushing and shoving, with teenage hormones on display, but it was all generally under control. Suddenly, yet another collision between two of the more feisty boys on either team led to a lot more as half-time approached. Pushing, swearing, name-calling, and a kick off the ball led to a pitch invasion by the opposition coaches (a far cry from the FA's charter and guidelines for grassroots football!). They claimed it was to stop anything escalating, but of course, it had the opposite effect and merely inflamed the situation further. Once all calmed down, they were insisting that our player, who had aimed the kick, deserved to be sent off. The problem was that they were still on the pitch intimidating the young referee. He sensibly decided just to book our player but not theirs for his provocation and immediately bring the first half to an end. The issue was discussed at half-time, and everyone was told to just play football. Our team went on to lose. All the mums on the touchline discussed this at some length together throughout the second half and decided that the incident had emotionally upset our boys so that they hadn't performed as well in the second half. They mentioned this to a few of the dads, who looked blankly back at them. There was no emotional trauma causing our boys to lose. The other team were just stronger and our boys had done well to hold them for most of the first half, but as the game progressed and they tired, the gap between them became more evident. That was it. Nothing else. The boys hadn't brooded on the issue at all. It struck Cory that it perfectly illustrated the chasm between the way men and women think about everything. Men are simple beasts and don't generally over-think anything. Women, on the other hand, can't help but analyse everything, always looking for hidden meanings and deeper emotions that often simply aren't there in the average male brain. As the saying goes:

> 'Women spend more time thinking about what men are thinking,
> than men actually spend time thinking at all' (Anonymous)

No wonder men and women struggle to have relationships. We're completely incompatible in so many ways, especially emotionally. The one common theme Cory has worked out over many years, though, is that we share one facet of human nature. People stay in relationships often because they are simply too scared to leave. All financial and practical considerations aside – although these are naturally major considerations to many people – human nature means that emotionally, we rarely leave one relationship without believing we have the prospect of another available. That's not to say that everyone who leaves already is having an affair or has the next partner immediately lined up. But there will have been someone who has turned their head or at least made them wonder what it may be like. And this applies to both sexes. So in all the years Cory has heard that marriages or long-term relationships have ended; that someone needed space, or time alone, or other such sentiments; he has never been surprised when subsequently, it has emerged that actually there was an alternative waiting to step in. Often, the new relationship may possibly have begun (even if not physically, then emotionally) before the end of the previous one, giving the leaver the confidence that they wouldn't throw it all away for nothing. They wouldn't be alone. Cory would invite everyone to reflect on this; he has no doubt that many people will know of some scenario where a split was said to be amicable, no blame, people growing apart at the time, only for it to emerge later that the leaver is now with someone who was there all the time. It happens so often. We are all just weak humans after all. We crave love, affection, comfort, sex, intimacy and the whole gamut of human emotional needs that make us all fatally flawed.

Back to the story. Cory replied to Emma that it was all irrelevant and didn't matter now, as he had met someone new. Clearly, this wasn't what she wanted to hear. Cory has learned a lot through these classic mistakes over many years, particularly that replying openly and honestly to what you think a woman is asking you is just plain stupid! You have to work out what they are really asking you, trying to somehow understand the female brain, her logic, and thought process. Now this is almost impossible for men who have a perfunctory way of dealing with such things. Male functional logic lacks any of the inexorable intuitive emotional intelligence women show in abundance. Cory's response thus caused the conversation to take an unexpected turn. Emma asked what Vanessa looked like and to see a photo. This is also something Cory has come to learn about the fairer sex over the years, that no matter how critical of men they are and how baffling we find their behaviour towards us, that has nothing on how judgemental they are of each other. The bitchiness can be unreal. The way they check each other out, jealous of anything the other girl has better than them (whether bodily or clothing, accessories and possessions); smug and sneering about anything that's not as good, is truly scary to behold. Cory has seen it first hand from one of his most recent love interests, a truly beautiful girl who faces little competition from others, and yet over all the years they have known each other, she has always found something to criticise about any other woman he has ever shown any interest in. It just seems to be in her genes; it is an instinctive reaction, part of the law of the jungle that is the female emotional mind! It's no wonder many women, especially very attractive ones, often say they get on better with men than with other women. They tend to have more male than female friends (but seriously, girls, please ask yourself what are those male friends' real motivations). What a complex and fragile web of human emotion we all weave and somehow have to deal with, not only our own, but those of our partners, families, workmates, and everyone else we encounter in the world. Sometimes we cope, but most of us just plod on with life hoping that somehow it will all work out along the way. It's certainly enough to drive you to drink!

Cory foolishly sent Emma a photo of Vanessa during their increasingly heated exchange, when he should just have retired from the conversation and whole situation gracefully. But he didn't. Another important life lesson for men: just don't get drawn in to these emotional discussions and situations. We are wholly out of our depth. We have no idea what is going on in the female mind. We are completely unsuited to trying to deal with it. Any efforts by us to rationalise, explain, lighten the mood with humour, etc. are utterly stupid tactics. But by far the worst error is to argue back. Cory had done so here. And he paid for it. The next thing he knew, when he contacted Vanessa the next day to check all was still okay for their date, she ignored him. He found this all extremely perturbing and frustrating, so he pursued her for a response. Eventually, she said she wasn't interested in dating a man who still was involved with his ex. This was all news to Cory, and when he asked for clarification was staggered to hear Emma had emailed Vanessa to say that Cory was still with her, or pursuing her, or something along those lines! Cory was astounded and naturally denied it all. He explained that he had stupidly sent her photo to Emma naively as requested and perhaps slightly boastfully to show he had moved on to someone better. This had caused Emma's jealousy, but it seemed to assuage Vanessa's fears and she saw it just as a jealous ex shit-stirring. She did want to know though why he had been talking to Emma. Why was he still talking to his ex at all? Did he still care about her and so much more! Cory let rip at Emma asking what the fuck she was playing at. She had moved on, he was doing so now as well, so what was the problem? Emma apologised and admitted she had been jealous when she saw the photo, as her new guy wasn't working out as planned. Cory wondered subsequently if she had got back in touch to maybe try and get back together. This simply hadn't occurred to him at the time. If he ever did that, trying to get back with an ex, he always made his intentions plain at the outset. But he was a simple man with a straightforward approach to life; no match ever for the cunning female brain he has spent so long struggling to comprehend. He now accepts that he will never really understand it.

Emma had somehow got the email address from what Cory had forwarded. She was very friendly with the head of IT systems and networks at their office and had sought his help to decode and find the source. All of this meant nothing to Cory. But he knew the guy in question, that he had a major crush on Emma and would do anything for her. She just had to flutter her eyelashes and he was putty in her hands. He wanted to be so much more. Yet another one of those 'just good male friends'. Unless they are gay, men cannot be just good friends with women. Sexual desires will always be present and ultimately get in the way. Hence, many women have best male friends who are indeed gay, as they can be normal with each other without fear of him misreading the situation and trying something on. This guy was quite a sad character, as the nature of his job may suggest. And not blessed by nature with looks either. Yet he and Emma were friends and would often sneak out of the office together when the MD was away. They would go and watch the latest film releases or to view venues for Christmas and summer parties, which turned into all-day shopping and lunching trips. He had even taken her on holiday to Disneyland in Paris, paying fully for her. They had shared a room, with separate single beds, and she admitted after she did feel slightly uncomfortable a few times, as he seemed to be getting too friendly. He had never liked Cory, as Emma was in his view clearly with the wrong man.

Vanessa finally turned up at Cory's house for their second date, after a few days' delay as they resolved the (non-existent) Emma issue. It had taught Cory another of life's vital lessons in how to deal with women, both exes and current ones. He has never made the mistake again of discussing new girlfriends with immediate exes and vice versa (as that is a whole new can of worms just waiting to be opened – just don't go there, brothers, you can never win!). He was now wise to the female approach, at least to this aspect, even if he still struggles to understand so much else about women! Vanessa had driven to his house, so he immediately said she was welcome to stay the night if she wanted to, so that she could relax and have some drinks. She initially said no, as good girls do, playing the game, worrying what men will think if they say yes too soon. All very silly. Cory has often thought that life, which is already hard and complicated enough in so many ways, would be so much easier if everyone was just honest about their feelings and desires and we didn't all have to play these games, especially when dating someone new. Suffice to say, she relented, as he plied her with alcohol (a lifelong skill he adopts with every woman he has ever met). They had a great night, the first of many to follow. Christmas was approaching and Cory was invited to meet her family. What a shock that was! Vanessa was a smart, slick, well-presented, attractive woman who worked in sales. Although she lived in the same area as her whole family, she was the successful one, living in the nice part. The rest of them weren't so lucky. Her parents and sisters were lovely normal people living on a council estate, but it was her sisters' partners that shocked him: real geezers, proper duckers and divers. They invited Cory to join in some of their ventures; he politely declined. This was a whole new world to him, mixing with slightly scary people in a rough part of London. But he liked Vanessa; they were getting on very well, so he thought little of it. Cory was invited to bring his boys up to a local pub for Sunday lunch one weekend with all her family. Apart from his ongoing issue of having very little money (as he was still looking for a job, no one hiring around Christmas) and that soul-sinking moment when he went to the cashpoint and there was nothing to withdraw, he thought he should make the effort. The pub was awful. It had sounded great, a big carvery-style place with indoor ball pit and slides for the kids to play in. Sadly, it was in the middle of a horrible area and inhabited by truly terrifying people – and that was mainly just the loud mothers and their poor little verbally abused kids. The men all looked scarily dodgy but were largely congregated at the bar, leaving their women to scream incessantly at the kids to control them. Strangely, swearing very loudly at their youngsters didn't necessarily seem to make them behave any better!

Cory huddled his kids around Vanessa and made his excuses as soon as they politely could, claiming one of them was ill so they could escape. It was an experience but not one he would ever repeat. Despite his career working in the City and partying there and in the

West End, he had no real exposure to these much less salubrious parts of town, nor did he want to. It is very instructive to reflect on the disparity of wealth across a few miles in London, which seems to be getting ever greater now, as only wealthy foreigners can afford prime London residential properties; not a great social model, and you can see perhaps why we had riots a few years ago; the burning sense of injustice and desperation in the poorer parts are as palpable as is the ostentatious display of wealth in Mayfair and similar areas. What a society we have created! Cory regards himself as somewhere in the middle (as one might suspect of a solid middle-class chap), wishing he could do more to help redistribute wealth across society. Apart from his social conscience prompting him initially to support the SDP (pre-Lib.Dems), then to vote for Tony Blair's new Labour; his efforts were limited to various charitable donations and to paying a lot of tax when he was earning good money. He had wondered about entering politics at one stage but found the falseness and bullshit (if not downright lies) from many a politician too much to stomach. He hardly wanted to leave the City, inhabited by many stereotypes he didn't like, merely to enter the political world where they may be even worse. He also reflected that his personal life may be an issue. Or rather, not so much what he did, but the fact that he was open about it – after all, many politicians did all he had and often far worse, but just denied it and pretended to be God-fearing, family-orientated, morally upstanding citizens. It will be very interesting to see how the impending UK General Election plays out. Wider society's faith in politicians was almost completely destroyed during the expenses scandal, as it seemed merely to reinforce the public's long-held view that too many MPs were only in it for themselves; had no understanding of real life and normal people's struggles or issues and were completely out of touch. This sentiment has seen antipathy increase towards politicians generally, apathy in the younger generations and many older ones too, who no longer have any faith in the traditional mainstream parties, who are losing support to previously minor parties. These parties may well come to hold the balance of power in Parliament post-May. Watch this space!

As New Year's Eve approached, Cory and Lisa had as usual worked out a convoluted formula for the boys spending some of Christmas Day with each of them, then a few days with each before rotating again and alternate New Year's eves each year. The boys were with Cory on New Year's Eve, which he planned just to spend at home chilling out with them. Vanessa was aware of this; he had invited her round if she wanted to come but said he would obviously understand if she would rather be out partying or with her family. Apart obviously from his commitment to his boys and wanting to be with them, Cory was now in his mid-thirties and had enjoyed over twenty years' worth of drunken New Year's Eve parties (and even a few sober ones when younger too!). He had learned that they can be great if you have something specific to do; but if you chase a fun night for the sake of it, as people often do on this night in particular, it can be a damp squib all too often. And very expensive. It wasn't as if he hadn't been partying a lot over the past year, so he felt no hardship. In fact, he was quite looking forward to a chilled night in with the boys. Vanessa said she would love to join them; she and Cory agreed to have a quiet night in, so he bought champagne, smoked salmon, steak and a few other nice items; they planned a civilised, romantic evening once the boys either went to bed or zoned out on the sofas watching TV, if they were determined to stay up to see in the new year. Just before Vanessa was due to arrive, she called him saying that her family had asked them both to another family party and had invited the boys too. Cory said that was very kind, but the boys wanted to be at home that night. Somehow, as the conversation unfolded, he heard himself offering to host everyone at his house! He had a decent-sized house, with four bedrooms, two large reception rooms, and an open plan kitchen space and it had suddenly seemed like a good idea. His eldest son was unhappy at having all these 'pikeys' descending on their house and disturbing their evening; the other boys thought it was great that they were having a party and other kids were coming over.

It ended up with something like eight adults, all drinking, and at least as many more kids scattered all over the house for the next eighteen hours. It was fun but not quite what had been planned. Her family loved it and approved of Cory, her posher boyfriend with the nice house. His boys went back on the agreed rotation to Lisa, and Vanessa was due back at work, so he went up to stay at Vanessa's flat for a few days. It was agreed that he would also bring the boys up the following weekend. That was a shock to Vanessa's system, to have four young boys all camped out in her lounge and waking up early on Sunday morning, which was normally sacrosanct to her as her time to sleep in until midday: another clear sign to Cory of how so many of these women told him how great and adorable it was that he loved his boys so much and had them so often, until that impacted on them and reality hit home. But Cory and Vanessa were fine and carried on for a few more months, until he returned to work full time in the City, when his free time to spend with her diminished hugely. His weekends always had some chunk taken up with the boys, so they had much less time together. They had reached that point, as he had with the previous two relationships as well, where it's all very wild and exciting for the first few months, but then you start to wonder where it's all going and how it will develop from there. The previous two hadn't and Cory suddenly realised that although they got on well, rarely argued, and had a lot of fun together (especially in bed), it wasn't really enough. She was a lovely woman, but could he really see himself with her long term? The sad truth was probably not. His primary quest was to find love again, and he didn't think he would with her. Now he was back in the City full time, apart from time constraints, the slightly snobbish side of him realised he couldn't see himself associating with her family much more either. It again reinforced Cory's view that many relationships could thrive and prosper if they were all we had to focus on and worry about.

But when you have to factor in real life, work, kids, families, and everything else we juggle in our normal daily lives, it all chips away at the good stuff in every relationship. The key is to find a balance or to find a relationship strong enough to withstand all this other erosive external stuff. Much as he liked Vanessa and as well as they got on, he just couldn't see it developing into anything more with her. He told her as much and she was very upset. In fact, she even made up a dating profile and contacted him pretending to be someone new, to find out if he had met anyone else. He missed her companionship and especially their sex life but knew she wasn't what he was looking for long term unfortunately. He felt bad, as there was nothing at all wrong with her or their relationship; in fact, she was great, but just not 'the one' for him. He knew that he had to be honest about what he wanted and felt it better to end it now than drag it on. He therefore returned to his quest to find true love again; his crusade through life which seemed to be proving as successful as searching for the Holy Grail! He returned to his online dating and met a handful of other women, most of whom talked of wanting relationships but seemingly were really after sex. He was happy to oblige. Then he met Zara. Online she called herself Pippa, but once they agreed to meet, he established her real name. We will explore Cory and Zara's relationship further shortly, but before we do, there is another part of Cory's life that needs to be addressed: his increasingly regular visits to strip clubs.

Strip Clubs

Where to begin? Cory had been to a strip club for the first time at the end of his marriage. It had never been a part of his life previously, and then suddenly he was taken to a couple in one night as an almost thirty-five-year-old by a couple of real City twats on a stag do for a mutual friend. These guys were just not his types and in fact managed to be so obnoxious, sexist and generally arrogant and unpleasant (i.e. typical City stereotypes) that they proceeded to have the whole group thrown out of both clubs. But not before Cory stared in awe at the array of scantily clad, sexy women on display; he was truly a kid in a candy store, as he melted into the ambient sexuality of the venue and the girls. It was to him the equivalent of walking into 'Old Town' in Frank Miller's Sin City films and beholding all the beauties around him. Why had he never known of such amazing places before? He had returned a few times to the clubs with other workmates subsequently, but was still a bit naive in such environs. That is until, purely by chance, he discovered a club that he was to go on to frequent on and off for the next decade.

He had been out for a few drinks one evening in London with his old boss, catching up on work and personal lives, the latter more easily as the beer flowed, as is always the case with men! As the bar closed, the other chap announced he was off home to his wife and cats – which he had affectionately named Bogey and Snot (the cats, that is!). Cory was in one of his single-man, party phases and decided to follow the music and find a club or party to go to. Weirdly, he discovered something right beneath the office he had worked in until only months earlier, for well over a year, but had never known was there. He followed the party music downstairs and attempted his best party-blag entrance approach – he was a friend of Joe's (everyone knows a Joe, don't they?) and had been invited along. The woman at the door smiled knowingly and said the entry fee was £20 and he was most welcome. Cory paid, walked in to where the lively music was blaring, and thought he had died and gone to heaven. Whereas the other strip clubs he had previously been in were big and ornate, all very nice but quite impersonal, this was the complete opposite. Small and intimate, no stages, all on one level and packed with immediately accessible semi-naked beauties. The inane smile on his face was clearly visible to everyone, as he was told how happy he looked. And why wouldn't he? He was about to become acquainted with a club that intermittently formed a major part of his life over the next decade, on both work and personal levels. Various girls approached him, chatted, offered dances (and more) and explained prices, but he was simply happy sitting, drinking and looking, drowning in the mass of semi-naked girls surrounding him. He may have had a few dances; he can't now remember, but then he saw her across the room, walking away from him: the dark hair down to her waist, the lithe sexy body, and the most spectacular, long, shapely legs in black thigh-length boots, leading to such a cute bum. He then knew that he was most definitely in heaven. She was a vision. She eventually came back towards him; he asked her to sit down and they started chatting, drinking, and so much more. This was the start of a great friendship with Debbie that taught him a huge amount about that fantasy world, which has stood him in great stead ever since.

Debbie was from the same part of the Home Counties as Cory's parents had moved to, so they actually had things to talk about. And she genuinely was, as he checked that she knew the area and could volunteer facts. He had already learned from his brief other visits to such clubs that many girls will simply latch on to what the often very drunk bloke is talking about and play along with it. The whole world is a fantasy one after all. These girls are dressed sexily and provocatively, as they are working and performing. When you see them after work, as they leave the club (as he came to over the years), they are just normal girls, dressed down in tracksuits, keen to blend in after a night on display. They are there to make money for themselves through dancing and VIP sessions with the guys and for the club through the various drink and bottle-purchase requirements. As many of the girls have told him over the years, it's no different to going to Mayfair nightclubs and having a minimum spend on the best VIP tables. He sees their point, and in fact, a number of the most attractive ones alternate their working lives between the two different kinds of clubs, acting as greeters or hostesses in normal clubs as well as dancing in strip clubs. The best ones, who earn most money, aren't just the best looking (although that certainly helps); they are the ones with the most engaging personalities, who men are happy to sit and talk to for hours, paying the requisite amounts for the girls' time, dances etc. along the way. Cory has only met a few like that in the fifteen years since he first entered a strip club and has grown close to them, as we shall see.

Cory obviously fancied Debbie, as she knew. That was the base line of her job, for men to find her very attractive and to lust after her. The next stage, beyond initial dances, was then to befriend the men and make money. He understood that but told her how he had been so disappointed recently by a girl in another club; he thought something might develop with her, until she told him categorically that it was work only. She liked him but only in the club. Her view, one shared by most girls, is that a man is in the club to spend money, so he may as well spend it on her rather than other girls. She will therefore encourage him to spend as much as, and often more than, he can afford. She is there to tempt, tease, and cajole – that's her job. As long as men understand that, there's no issue. If they want free chats with women, they are in the wrong clubs. Though Cory would query whether there is really any such thing, as don't men often end up paying one way or another wherever they meet women they like? The other issue to always factor in is how unscrupulous some clubs can be in getting increasingly drunk punters to endlessly charge dances, drinks, tips, and VIP time to their almost maxed-out credit cards. It was a valuable lesson for Cory to learn so early in his visits, and it has enabled him so many times to cut through the shit subsequently and to find out if there is any stronger connection with any girl he meets there. Although he and Debbie are no longer in contact, he counts another girl he met in that club a decade ago (Anna) still as a good friend; and he has been fortunate enough to have had a few proper relationships with girls he met in such clubs in the real outside world too (as we will come to). Cory's view was that he had spent over a year in all the normal bars in London, between his relationships, and wanted something new and exciting; this certainly fulfilled everything on his wish list. His friends told him he was a mug and the girls and clubs were ripping him off.

However, at least one of those friends was an alcoholic with a gambling addiction. He pontificated that his West End casinos were infinitely better, as they offered him and friends complimentary meals and wine regularly. Er, no – they gave him meals and wine (a) to encourage him to go there a lot, especially with his lawyer friends and (b) it was all more than paid for out of the tens of thousands he had lost over the years. Cory's view was that we all have vices, proclivities, and deep desires that we like to pursue, and each should be allowed to pursue his own. He was happy to spend a certain amount on a dancer in her club, but then if nothing progressed outside, he would move on. This approach has worked for him for a number of years. It is of course not everyone's choice of lifestyle, nor is it the best venue necessarily to try and find a girlfriend; but that is how Cory came to view the clubs. Without that element, he agrees it would be sad, empty, and pointless; having sated that desire and fulfilled that fantasy, he now only occasionally goes back to the few clubs he knows very well for a drink and to catch up with all the staff and management he has got to know well over the years. He could never hope to replicate again what he found there over these years, nor would he want to. He has been told recently by a current lady he has been in flirtation and discussion with that he obviously has that *Pretty Woman*-type penchant going on, hoping to save strippers and rescue them from that world; all very deep and psychological, but maybe there is something in it, as Debbie did remind him of the Julia Roberts character who he lusted after in that film. This new friend has also commented more generally that he seems to have had a whole series of relationships since his marriage ended with damaged women (or 'fucked up' actually, to use her words). Maybe he is attracted to them and they to him, given the own damage Penny and Alfie's deaths have caused to his psyche. Or maybe it's simpler than that; everyone is damaged to some degree, but he is just more open and honest than most about his, in clubs, when he meets someone he likes, and now in this book.

Cory and Debbie partied a lot, in her club and outside. They became close, but there was a problem, as she had a girlfriend. Like a number of girls he has met in these clubs over the years, they enjoy relations with both sexes. It just adds to the attraction and fantasy to Cory, as to many men. She passed Cory off to her partner as just a punter, but there was more to it, at least for a while. It was just not enough for her to leave her girlfriend for Cory at that time. It was another classic case of the right people meeting at the wrong time; a few years later, they got back in touch. Debbie admitted she had been tempted, but it just wasn't the right point in her life. She was at that later stage now living with a guy who had kids from a previous relationship. She had given up dancing, as many do, either having made enough money to retire or just because they've had enough of it and are burnt out. Debbie was one of the latter. She lived life to the full, drinking and taking all sorts of other shit almost daily. She was a fun girl to be around in party mode. They had some wild times, especially impromptu all-night parties in local hotels, often with other girls, who Debbie clearly liked joining them. She told Cory all the tricks girls played to get more money from punters and to maximise their earnings for minimal effort. It was a valuable education and insight for him to this new fantasy world. They had a great time for a few months, but he told her a few times that he needed and wanted more. Despite them being close and spending a lot of great time together outside the club, doing everything imaginable, it wasn't enough on its own long term. As always, Cory was chasing that elusive dream of reconnecting and being with someone fully, properly again. Debbie was only part time, due to her own relationship, sadly. Despite her protestations about Cory only being a punter to her girlfriend, she sensed it may be more and started sending Cory threatening messages, saying he would get what was coming to him if he didn't back off and leave Debbie alone. Another of life's invaluable lessons: jealousy is a powerful enemy! Although they had fun, Cory told Debbie eventually that he was going to find a new girlfriend, as it was clearly not going to be her. She said she was fine with this and understood, until it actually happened. Then she went weird and fucked up their friendship over it. So that brings us back to Zara.

Zara was initially one of a number of attractive women Cory approached online. He was in dialogue with a few of them, but he immediately knew there was something about her personality, about their conversations that drew him to her more than the others. She was more challenging, more intelligent, and he was drawn deeper into their exchanges. That's not to say he didn't also enjoy his chats with others, which were more straightforward and quickly progressed to sexual badinage, online and over the phone and indeed then meeting up for sex. She wasn't like that though. Her online photo was consistent with how she came across in many ways, attractive but a bit posh and perhaps too proper and polite for such behaviour. They eventually met for an initial drink and got on extremely well. She was tall, leggy, sexy, had a great body, and much more attractive in person than in her photo. But she remained a bit posh and slightly diffident, it seemed. They spent hours together talking about all sorts of personal things, quite deep for a first date, but more an extension of some of their online discussions. There was a connection; she was articulate, engaging, and intelligent. All essential components to excite Cory intellectually and mentally, which is often more of a turn on for him longer-term than the purely physical. They played pool at Cory's suggestion, mainly just so that he could watch her leaning over the table. He was smitten. He felt the chemistry and sensed she did too. The evening came to an end, and as they lived an hour apart, they had met in the middle and now both had to go in opposite directions. When home, they had a text exchange reviewing the evening, agreeing they liked each other and would arrange another date soon. For some weird reason though, that seemed to become problematic over the following weeks, as they both appeared to be busy at conflicting times. In the end, Cory said that maybe they should just leave it and be friends for online chats, etc. If it was so difficult to see each other, it didn't bode well. Of course he wanted to see her again and develop things much further, but it was proving difficult.

He did wonder if she was just playing hard to get, as women often do for some inexplicable reason. He therefore utilised that classic sales technique of making your interest clear (to avoid any doubt), but then removing it when it looks as if things aren't progressing. It's the surest way to test the other party's resolve. If they really aren't interested, you are bringing an end to their prevarication and procrastination; if they are, you are calling their bluff. It worked; she was suddenly a lot keener to fix a date and was even annoyed when the first date she suggested was declined by Cory, as he had an important long-standing work commitment. Her view was that she should be a priority now that she had given him a date; such is the view of attractive women! They did however agree to meet a few days later. As she lived an hour's drive away, Cory said she was more than welcome to stay over. She said she would consider it, but only sleeping on the couch; nothing was going to happen if she stayed. She actually arrived slightly early, and Cory was still on the train on the way back from London when she called him to say she was there. She waited in her car outside his house until he made it home. A good sign. No prima donna tantrum or flouncing off. They had a few drinks and she revealed a bag of weed she had brought, which she enjoyed as a smoker. Cory still struggled, but for the greater good, he joined in. He (like any man) was thinking, 'I have this fit bird I fancy in my house. She's now too over the limit to drive home, so she's staying. How to now manoeuvre her from her protestations that she would only be on the sofa and nothing would happen into what he wanted?' So they agreed she was staying, on the basis she had repeatedly stressed throughout. Cory therefore kept pouring the wine and the conversation flowed. They definitely had an intellectual connection;

the question was could he now convert that into a physical one? As the evening wore on, the wine flowed ever more and he at one point leant towards her, then stopped and pulled back. He apologised to her and said she was so beautiful and sexy, they got on so well, he really wanted to kiss her but had promised her nothing would happen, so had stopped himself in order to respect her wishes. That old reverse psychology again. It worked. It was done. She was his. Shortly after, he leant in again, and this time they did kiss. Their passion exploded and they were all over the lounge floor. However, he stopped again and said he wouldn't do anything she didn't want, as promised. He went up to bed and said she could sleep on the sofa as she had insisted or was naturally more than welcome to join him upstairs. Five minutes later, she appeared at his bedroom door and they had a great night. The next day, she said she had only slept with him so early (on only their second date) as he lived so far from her community, where she was much in demand but known to be difficult for the boys chasing her to actually get with. She guarded her reputation jealously. But as the saying goes:

> 'Seduction isn't making someone do what they don't want to do.
> It is enticing someone into doing what they secretly want to do
> already' (Anonymous).

They met up again that weekend and carried on connecting, in every way. This continued and he could sense that she was increasingly relaxing and becoming more comfortable with him, particularly sexually; although there was a lot of passion, she was reserved. She started coming to meet him in London in the evenings after work, where they would have great nights out together, often meeting his workmates and other friends. The latter, knowing of Cory's recent penchant for sexy, leggy strippers, thought she was one of them initially. She wasn't, but had that look. She initially feigned annoyance and that she was insulted by the suggestion, but secretly she was pleased. His workmates fawned over her too. One night, they had been at a works drinks do that had gone on late, so they decided to get a hotel room in London. Cory knew a few in the area from his 'dates' with Debbie and mentioned this to Zara. She knew all about Debbie and all the partying from their hours of conversations over the first few months. Indeed, she even said that during their initial dialogue she had thought Cory was nice but probably too normal and boring for her, as he was a lawyer and a divorced dad with four young kids. It was only when he had admitted his late-night antics to her that she had suddenly decided he may be interesting and exciting enough for her! Zara asked if Debbie would be around, as she was interested in meeting her and maybe partying with her. Perhaps if Cory had been sober, he would have seen the pitfalls – going back to that lifelong lesson every man needs to learn, that you never take at face value what a woman says. But as he was by now drunk and in a party mood, he thought it was a great idea! They booked into one of the hotels he knew, having let Debbie know they would be there all night and she could join them at any stage. Cory even started to play out fantasises in his mind about what the three of them might do together that night, again naively thinking as a man does purely through his sex drive and sexual appendages; whereas the girls clearly had ulterior motives to check each other out, having each heard a good deal about the other.

Debbie eventually turned up with the requisite party powder to go along with the booze Cory and Zara had brought and the party began. The problem was that whereas Cory wanted action, the girls just wanted to talk – and as people will know, in those circumstances, people can chat for hours, incessantly. He even foolishly, in his excitement, told them he loved both of them at one point. Doh! At the time, in his fuddled brain, it seemed the right thing to say to reassure both of his feelings for each of them. Naturally, it had completely the opposite effect and put both their backs up. Zara was jealous of what Cory and Debbie had enjoyed together before she

arrived on the scene and wondered now whether Cory still wanted
Debbie rather than her. Debbie was pissed off that Cory had now
moved on and met someone else who was at least on a par with her
in every way. After what seemed like an eternity of the girls chatting
and probing to find out more about each other, Debbie announced
she had to leave. Cory's fantasies were dashed. But as soon as she
had gone, after a bit of a bollocking from Zara about him saying he
still loved Debbie too and Cory having to grovel and placate her
with endless reassurances, she suddenly pounced on him. All her
inhibitions were gone and they had an incredible few hours together.
Later, she admitted that she wasn't sure if they would ever see each
other again after the night's events, so had let loose, not worrying
about what he might think of her any more. Cory had to go straight
to work, and even though he downed endless ProPlus and strong
black coffees, by that afternoon, he was dozing off at his desk, as he
hadn't slept. He just about got through the day and managed to talk
her round over the next few days. They carried on seeing each other
but with even more abandon and pushing the boundaries all the
time. Cory has always been the adventurous type and had enjoyed
hugely the eroticism of the Kim Basinger film *Nine and a Half Weeks*
(and others of that genre), Madonna's *Sex* book and similar ones, a lot
of which he had played out in his own encounters over the years. He
now added to his previous experiences with a new partner in crime. It
was the start of an amazing few years together, doing everything they
possibly could. From regular *Torture Garden* and similar parties, to
strip clubs and threesums, exploring everything they could together,
and growing ever closer through every experience, publicly and
privately. At the outset, they had discussed that whilst fulfilling their
fantasies was exciting, there was a very fine line between enjoyment
and jealousy, insecurity and downright anger. They were conscious
of this all the time, as occasionally one of them would start flirting
with someone else and could sense uneasiness in the other. It was no
open relationship, and most of the time, they actually did very little

with others, certainly at the public events, just being excited at the thought they were in an environment where they could if they wanted to. It was the intellectual and emotional excitement much more than the physical that they sought, craved and enjoyed together. It was a huge aphrodisiac for them, which meant they had an amazing time together, sometimes publicly, but usually privately. Cory's view very quickly was that you were better off going to these events with just a good friend, a fuck buddy, or even someone you just agreed to go with for the night so you could both do what you wanted. It is a minefield of conflicting emotions if you go with someone you are seriously involved with. They met a few couples but never felt comfortable or excited enough to do anything other than just party with them, but did enjoy inviting another person to join them at times for threesums. They were very close, very secure with each other (within these boundaries), and having great fun together too. They got on extremely well by day as well as night, and in Cory's mind, it all felt almost too good to be true. But it is a universal truth that if it seems too good to be true, then it probably is. Cory thought that even if that were true, he was having great fun with someone he got on extremely well with, and they seemed very compatible in so many ways. He hoped it would last a long time, but if not, he should enjoy it while he could. So he made sure he did.

Zara had one son of a similar age to Cory's boys, who lived with his dad. Cory thought nothing of this, as his boys lived half the time with him; Zara said although she wished she had a similar arrangement, her son wanted to live full time with his dad currently. She brought him over to see his boys regularly at weekends and they appeared to get on well. They went on trips to *Legoland* together and even started talking about Zara and son coming to *Center Parcs* that summer with Cory and his boys. Unfortunately, that never happened, as they made the mistake of agreeing to meet Debbie for a drink in a Mayfair bar one evening. She had suggested it would be great for them all to get together and was sorry she had rushed off the first

time from the hotel room. They should hang out and be friends. Cory
and Zara agreed to go and to meet near his office after work first,
before heading over to the bar together to meet Debbie. Zara was
late and told Cory he should go over without her and meet Debbie;
she would then follow on. She subsequently admitted it was a classic
female test to see how keen he would be to spend time alone with his
ex – why do women do that? It's playing with fire, and you often get
burnt, then complain about what was happened, even though you
suggested it and the men wouldn't have done it without your say-so!
Fortunately, he thought that would be odd, so declined and went to
the pub with workmates while he waited. Zara eventually showed up,
late as usual. Seriously, ladies, why do you always have to be so late,
nearly every time? Is it a test to see how long men will wait, how much
we want to see you?! Fucking annoying! They went and met Debbie,
who of course was also late. That annoying habit aside, the girls then
proceeded to do the next most annoying thing women always do in a
bar. As soon as they arrive, once their drink is ordered, they feel the
need to disappear to the toilets for hours (forgive the hyperbole) to
check they look okay, fix their make-up etc. That can be tolerable if
you are with a group, but if you leave one sad lonely bloke sitting on
his own like a lemon for ages, then tensions rise. That sadly happened
here.

The girls could sense that when they returned and Debbie went
to town; she said they had been kissing each other in the toilet, and
Cory looked like he was angry and wound up. She basically started
shit-stirring and trying to provoke him. Clearly her reason for meeting
was to try and cause trouble and maybe even split Cory and Zara
up. Hell hath no fury like a woman scorned! Although she hadn't
been scorned, she had declined to leave her girlfriend to be with Cory
before he met Zara. But such rational points were irrelevant to her;
troublemaking and mischief appeared to be firmly on her agenda.
Cory was shocked, as she had been his friend and they had been
close. But her mad, vindictive side was coming out now. She went off

to the toilets again, alone this time. Zara, who had been very quiet throughout, said it was all very bizarre, as Debbie was clearly already very coked up, agitated, and taking loads more shit when they went to the toilet together (and no doubt even more now). Zara said that she had given some to her and then insisted that they should pretend to have kissed to wind Cory up and make him jealous. Cory asked why Zara had played along with this; she admitted she could have spoken up but was a bit shocked by it all. She said she would go to the toilet now and talk to Debbie. Cory wasn't sure that was the best idea and was pissed off again to be left alone for ages. Of course, Zara wanted more gear herself, which had been her primary motivation for going to the loo again. By the time they returned, what seemed an eternity later, Cory had had enough. Debbie was still being obnoxious, but now Zara was giggling along with her; the gear had obviously kicked in. He stood up and stormed out, telling them to have fun together. He hailed a black cab and climbed in. Zara suddenly appeared at the cab door, telling Cory to come back inside. He said it was pointless, as he was sick of sitting alone while they partied together in the toilets. Zara got in the cab; Cory got out of the other side, walked down the road, and hailed another one. Once home, he texted Zara and said he hoped she had fun with her new friend. She eventually turned up at his house and they had a huge argument. He conceded Debbie had been his friend, ex, whatever, and she had been set on causing trouble that night, but Zara shouldn't have played into her hands, going to the toilet with her, etc. They didn't see each other for a couple of weeks after that, as he was away with his kids on holiday. They talked and texted and eventually sorted things out (for now). In retrospect, Cory should have realised that Zara appeared to prioritise getting gear and having her own fun ahead of them. But they had been getting on so well and having so much fun he didn't really want to contemplate it ending yet. He put it down to Debbie's malicious plotting to damage them and didn't want to give her the satisfaction, so got back together with Zara after his holiday.

All generally went well for the next few months, and Cory was delighted that he had finally surpassed the usual three-to-six-month time limit of his previous three relationships. This one seemed to have more substance. They carried on as before, either meeting in London for nights out after work or her generally coming down to his house. Their sexual exploration continued apace, inside, outdoors, in cars, on trains, in clubs, on street corners and river banks, in fields, on Clapham Common and anywhere else they could find. He would go up to her area from time to time, when he didn't have the boys, but as she had more time than him, it was agreed that her coming to him generally worked best. She had become well known to his workmates and friends, so was a regular at group drinks now and they had further wild nights after a number of these. As Christmas approached, it was announced at work that due to the economic downturn after the dotcom bubble had burst, there would be no big office Christmas party that year. Instead, each team would have a Christmas lunch and then could go on at their own expense to party if they wished. Cory invited Zara to join them that evening in London and she said she would come. As the day progressed, however, and the festive spirits flowed at the lunch, she went very quiet. He called her repeatedly during the evening to ask where she was, and eventually, she said she had decided to go straight to his house and not come to London. That all seemed very odd and pissed Cory off, as they had planned another big night out, which he had been building up towards and looking forward to. He carried on drinking with work colleagues until they all reached the point where they simply couldn't consume any more. He stumbled to his train and somehow found his way home. It is one of the mysteries of life that Cory (like many other City boys, much as he hates to use that epithet for himself) always seemed to find his way back home. Rather like a homing pigeon, he just seemed instinctively to know the way. Fortunately, he has never featured on those hilarious online newspaper or YouTube clips of the drunken office chap falling up and down escalators, down steps, staggering along the street; but he so easily could have. People did often say it was incredible nothing bad ever happened to him, but maybe his fatalistic view of the world meant that he thought 'whatever will be, will be'. He was in the hands of fate, so whether he was drunk or sober made no difference. A great excuse clearly!

As he got home, all was okay between him and Zara to begin with, but they ended up arguing about why she hadn't come along, particularly as she had agreed, knew everyone and it had messed up their planned night out. She didn't seem to care and was very non-committal in her vague responses. The tension escalated between them, he wanted to know why she was being so evasive, which led to a screaming match and some pushing and shoving each way. They fell into the Christmas tree together. She jumped up and ran out of the house and banged on the neighbour's door, asking to come in. The bemused neighbours opened the door and invited her in. Cory got up and followed suit. However, when he banged on the door, he wasn't met with the same welcoming reception and merrily invited in! Instead, his macho little Italian neighbour started shouting and swearing at him in Italian. Cory told him to fuck off and tried to push past him to talk to Zara. The neighbour pushed Cory, and he fell backwards out of the front door, which was then slammed shut. Cory got up and banged on the door some more. The next thing he knew, flashing blue lights appeared behind him; the police had been called and he was arrested for being drunk and disorderly. A night in the cells followed while he sobered up. He was released without charge the next day. Zara had gone home but came back a few days later, and they moved on with things, leaving what had happened as a stupid Christmas drink-fuelled incident. He never did find out why she hadn't turned up in London as planned. If only he had. It was a sign of things to come. But he didn't. They had a good first Christmas together, some of it alone together and some with his family.

There was something strange about Zara though. It intrigued Cory but also worried him. He put it down to her being shy or not being used to family life. When she had first met him and then his friends, she had asked a lot of questions. People liked that, as it seemed to show an interest. Many women prefer just to talk about themselves; she didn't. But therein lay the issue; she was too secretive, too closed about things in her life. Cory gradually got her to open up, and it began to emerge that she had a rough life since her early happy childhood living in the most desirable parts of West London, going to the poshest schools and having wealthy parents. This was all consistent with her poise, demeanour, attitude and accent. She clearly was from a good background. Cory had assumed when he first met her that she now lived in the Home Counties, as her family were out there, but that's where her story became tragically sad. Cory doubts he ever fully knew all that happened or that she ever told him the whole truth, and certainly there were variations in her stories often. But the gist of it was heart breaking and went along the following lines: she and her younger sister were indeed posh young things, well schooled and looked after. They lived in a very desirable area of London, enjoyed a great lifestyle, and seemed to have everything they could want. Their dad was involved in the city ship-brokering world and travelled extensively. They had a nanny to help their mum look after them, as apparently she wasn't terribly maternal. They holidayed on cruise ships and in all sorts of exotic locations and were regulars in all the best London hotels and restaurants. And then came the financial crash of the 1970s and their dad lost a lot of his money. Apparently, the cracks of a more austere life started to spread through all aspects of their previously privileged world. Their parents evidently had affairs and drank a lot, as was the norm for the London social set they belonged to. The story was that their mum left their dad to be with one of her lovers and the girls stayed with their dad. He however sank into an alcohol-fuelled depression as his world crumbled around his ears, losing his money, wife, and much of his business in a short period of time. The girls tried to cope, but with their mum elsewhere and dad often spending days in bed, it couldn't continue. Although Zara never went into detail, the girls ended up in care. She said that her parents proceeded to drink themselves to death (although she told one of Cory's kids that they had been killed in a car crash). Whatever really happened, the sad truth was that these lovely young girls rapidly lost their comfortable life of privilege and comfort; but much more importantly and tragically, both their parents died in quick succession.

They struggled in care, as of course, they were now mixing with very different people to those they had previously. Sadly but inevitably, they rebelled or were led astray, as they were introduced to a whole new world. Years later, Cory realised the full extent of the damage caused and particularly their introduction to drugs. At this early stage of their relationship though, as always, he was asking questions, learning from the answers (both what was said and what was not said) and generally just getting to know Zara. In subsequent years, future girlfriends would tell Cory that he was too demanding of them, particularly in terms of what he wanted to know. He was told more than once that just because he had his shit together, knew who he was, and was therefore happy to reveal everything, many people weren't. Many found it difficult to address their pasts, to face their demons, and preferred to leave it all locked away. He was told he was like an emotional vampire, draining girls with his intense questioning, demanding to know all about them. The point now though was that Zara was a mysterious, clearly damaged, yet seemingly lovely, beautiful woman who needed to be loved. Cory was happy to oblige. He fell for her, head over heels, completely, intimately, passionately; he hoped and believed he had found his new soulmate. He had once again found that connection and chemistry he and Lisa used to have but had lost. He therefore ignored the odd times Zara wouldn't be in touch or when she seemed a touch unreliable or erratic. He just put in down to her feminine wiles. She met his family but always seemed reluctant to fully join in family occasions such as family meals, Christmas gatherings and similar events. She appeared to be shy and uncomfortable at times in company, which struck Cory as odd for someone who certainly looked the part. She was tall, attractive, elegant, intelligent, well spoken and educated, but something was just not right, but he couldn't put his finger on it. This became more apparent as Zara started bringing her own son over to Cory's house to play with his boys. Although he fully understood the difference between her having only one child and him having four, he still found her lack of maternal skills frustrating. He would often end up looking after all five boys, playing with them, feeding them, sorting out the inevitable squabbles, while she was aloof and appeared completely uninterested. He even once found her poor little son just standing in the hallway of his house one day when he got back after an hour or so out taking his boys back to Lisa. When asked what he was doing, the poor sod said he was waiting for his mummy. When Cory checked, she was asleep upstairs and the kid was doing nothing, not even watching TV and just standing there waiting forlornly for her to come back down. She talked more about how her ex had taken her son away from her, but as her son had said he wanted to live with his dad, she didn't want to upset him. Cory suggested that now they were in a stable and hopefully long-term relationship, they should explore her having custody, or at least more regular contact if that was what she wanted. They were a family and these things were important to him. She gave the impression that they were to her too. As so often though, she would say one thing, but then never follow up on it. Actions really do speak louder than words, and she was a classic case in point. But then no one is perfect. Nor is any relationship. We are all human and all fatally flawed in our own unique ways. The trick, Cory had by now worked out through his life experiences, was to stick with something as long as the good outweighed the bad, but then to end it when it no longer did.

Here he was for the first time since leaving Lisa, in a relationship that had lasted longer than a few months, where all the good bits were fantastic and the bad bits were concerns over her quirkiness (which of course was also part of her attraction), rather than anything concrete at this stage at least. She was the creative, arty, ephemeral type, and he liked that. Cory was (and remains) generally a very rational person, constantly thinking, questioning, analysing everything, a product of the way his brain works incessantly and his legal training. He is however also an emotional man and loves to let his heart rule his head, even when he knows he shouldn't. His view then, and now, is that his life would have been very boring had he always done the rational thing. The emotional side of him is the wild side he loves to give free reign to whenever he can; hence, the excessive drinking and partying at times, to escape the confines of his own rationality. He only needs to point out how dull so many lawyers are to show the dangers of allowing one's spark and personality to be subsumed to one's rational self. This can lead to an apparent conflict though, and the dichotomy can best be explained by:

> 'My brain has no heart. My heart has no brain. That's why when
> I speak my mind I seem heartless and when I do what's in my
> heart I seem thoughtless' (Anonymous)

In Zara, he had found someone he loved, adored, lusted after, had an amazing connection with, had a great adventurous sex and party lifestyle with, and who was by that stage his best friend too. All he wanted and needed, emotionally, intellectually and physically, so life was good, so much so that he asked her to move in with him. They had been together for well over a year, and apart from a few blips, all was proceeding very well. They liked each other and had great fun together but, more importantly, had that elusive spark and chemistry (both mental and physical) that is essential for any real relationship to work – certainly for Cory. They were happy but still lived an hour's drive apart, which wasn't ideal. Their kids liked each other and got on, so why wouldn't they take the next logical step and move in together? But Zara was concerned. She said she wanted to, but was worried that if it didn't work, she would have given up her (rented) home in her area and, without family to fall back on, could find herself homeless. Cory understood and promised that if it came to that situation, he would pay her rent for somewhere else for six months to allow her to get back on her feet. Of course, he stressed that he couldn't foresee that eventuality, as everything was going so well between them. She understood but explained that her insecurities arising from her life being ripped apart as a child had a big bearing on such a decision. After prolonged discussions about it all, she announced that she had come up with a solution: they should get married! Cory was shocked. They were in love and got on well, but in his mind, they needed to live together first to make sure that continued before they made the big decision to marry. They continued debating the matter, but inevitably no matter how rationally Cory set out his views, no matter how emotionally he expressed his love for and commitment to Zara, her female logic was simple – if he meant it all, he would prove it by marrying her. No matter what he said or did, he couldn't move her from that view. Cory now realises, with the benefit of hindsight and many more years' experience of women, he was never going to win. Nevertheless, then (and still now), he still argues his case, as he can't help himself. He is stubborn and can be argumentative, particularly when he feels someone is being irrational. It is perhaps clear in that one sentence why Cory's relationships aren't always as smooth as they might otherwise be! He may always lose the argument ultimately and have to back down, but he needs to try. Many women have told him he does himself no favours by doing so, but that's one of life's burdens he has to bear; he just can't help himself!

Cory was torn. He loved Zara, was happier than he had been for years, and finally seemed to be in a secure long-term relationship again. That is not to say he wasn't happy with Susie, Emma, and Vanessa, but not beyond the initial honeymoon period, which is why they ended. He wanted to build on it all with Zara, but he wasn't ready to remarry. He was still involved in intermittent battles with Lisa over contact with the boys and had told them he wasn't going to get remarried any time soon. But Zara had now decided it was crucial. Cory obviously had to back down and acquiesce in the end, but it didn't feel right. Arrangements were made with the local registry office, as Zara said she didn't want a big ceremony. A Christmas wedding was planned, as is all the rage in all the soap operas these days -they were ahead of their time, clearly. Cory remained uncomfortable that it was premature but felt he had to go along with it. That was until Zara announced that her sister with latest new boyfriend and two young daughters were now coming to the wedding, having previously said that no one from her side would be coming. The sisters were apparently talking about the girls being bridesmaids. Originally, they had agreed that if Cory would agree to the marriage, despite his reservations, they would just go off and do it with no family involvement (as Cory felt it was too soon for his boys to deal with). But Zara's sister was quite pushy and had now decided she wanted to be there, with her girls as bridesmaids. This changed the whole dynamic of the occasion in Cory's mind. Unfortunately, Zara decided to raise all of these problematic issues over a meal one night in a local restaurant. The previously relaxed, enjoyable atmosphere was suddenly thrown off course, along with all their wedding plans by this news. Cory was upset. He felt that if Zara's nieces were going to be there, he couldn't really not involve his boys. And if her sister (and unrelated current boyfriend) were attending, his parents and brother with family should be there too. This was typical of Zara. It seemed she had been waiting for the right time to broach the subject and had chosen badly. But more importantly, she failed to seem to appreciate how this changed things hugely. Her glib solution was simply to invite all Cory's family too, but that ignored all of Cory's concerns over it being too soon for his kids. She seemed either completely oblivious to this or not to care. This seemed peculiar, when she had appeared to understand his concerns during all previous discussions. They had a fractious discussion in the restaurant about it, which continued at home. They had reached an impasse and Cory was annoyed both by Zara's attitude and by her sister trying to dictate matters (she was very bossy). She of course fell back to the emotional female argument that if he wanted to marry her, he would and these issues shouldn't become so important. And therein lay the crux of the problem. He knew deep down it was too early to marry her, for all the reasons mentioned above. He had mentioned to his parents and brother what they had planned, and his dad quite rightly questioned whether he would regret not involving his boys. Wise advice as ever, old man. Cory now felt he couldn't remarry without them knowing and being involved but resolutely felt it was too soon. He told Zara this again. But now Cory was no longer prepared to back down. He asked to defer the wedding. She was devastated and ran away. He explained that he would marry her the following year, but not now. He wanted them to be together longer and wanted his boys involved. Cory moved the wedding date to the following summer. He spent that Christmas with his family, not with Zara. They had texted but nothing more. She came back on New Year's Eve and they carried on together again.

Cory that year had another of his epiphanies, when all the stars in his personal and professional life appeared (as they occasionally do) to align and lead him to another of his major life decisions. He was working long hours and commuting daily, squashed on to the packed commuter trains into and out of London with all the other miserable travellers. As many a miserable commuter has incisively pointed out, the laws relating to the treatment of cattle travelling to slaughter appeared to be more favourable at times. Cory at one stage sought to deal with this by enquiring about the cost of first class travel. Initially, the differential wasn't as great as one would have thought, though this has gradually changed over the years, as the train companies have obviously realised many people would pay more for the greater likelihood of a seat they can fit into and the increased comfort afforded. This though presented another of those eternal male dilemmas, a comfy seat in first class, but with all the old fuddy-duddies, or a squashed seat at best (more usually standing all journey) in standard class. But as one of Cory's (womanising) mates pointed out, that's where all the younger, fit birds were, so why deprive yourself? To use a particularly horrible phrase he came up with, it's a choice between *comfort or clunge* (using that unpleasant slang word coined by hormonal teenagers in *The Inbetweeners*).

Thus, his contact with the boys on weekdays was limited. He had been paying half his salary to Lisa as maintenance too. This struck him as ludicrous; he was working hard and effectively paying a lot to not see his own kids for most of the week! Relations with Lisa were amicable at times, hostile at others – at one stage, she had applied for an attachment of earnings order against his salary when he had started at his new job – never a great start in a new company, and his bosses therefore knew what he was dealing with. They allowed him some flexibility with time off for court dates in relation to the ongoing contact arguments and financial claims, and also to leave early one evening a week to see his kids. In fact, as he said at the time he left, as friends and compassionate employers during his tricky personal times, they were incredible. The best. Sadly, their promises on a professional level were less impressive, and Cory found himself simply servicing his own client base without any of the promised synergies and cross-marketing that had encouraged him to join them originally. There were bigger issues at play across the business, with the high-profile owner allegedly suffering a mutiny and being ousted by a coalition of convenience by investors and his right-hand men on the board. All very destabilising (but that's business) and it meant that everyone was living in fear. This led to one of Cory's major US clients being told by management that unless they paid a new retainer or a cancellation fee, Cory and the business could not act for them anymore. This was absurdly short-sighted, especially with such a huge US client, but the bean counters were in charge and long-term relationships were seemingly irrelevant, if they could not be monetised immediately. The client told Cory that they would move their work elsewhere, as they would not be treated like that. They did.

Cory looked at the whole scenario, discussed it with a couple of close friends and Zara, mentioned it to Lisa, and then thought, 'Fuck it!' He resigned and immediately set up his own business, knowing nothing about running a business, company rules, accounts, VAT, and all the other drudgery involved. But he did know that he was good at his job, clients liked him, and he was being thwarted by his employer. More importantly, as his own boss, he would have the freedom to balance his complicated work and personal life to ensure he saw more of his boys and could attend things like sports days and assemblies without it being a major issue. The added upside was that if it worked, he would keep any profits for himself. He started his new business working from home at first and then from a tiny office in serviced office space in central London. Zara helped him with aspects and there was talk of her becoming fully involved in the core business, but the discipline required for that was never her forte. She preferred to drift in and out, ad hoc, as she saw fit. She wasn't an office-based worker naturally, and Cory fairly quickly concluded it would be too stressful for them to try to work together, when she had so much to learn, as well as maintaining their relationship. He therefore gradually joined up with a few other colleagues, most of whom he knew or had worked with previously. One exception was someone recommended by a friend and what a mistake that turned out to be, but more of that later! Although the first year was very tough and money very tight – credit cards and a secured PPI loaded loan (but taken out pre-legislation, so no way of getting back the mis-sold elements, as Cory has now discovered) kept him afloat. And then, just as things looked very bleak, as money and credit was rapidly running out, one of the huge long-term projects he was working on for that very US client whose poor treatment had been the catalyst for him going solo finally paid off. And how! He was cash rich, able to clear his debts, and even to buy a new bigger house. Incredible timing. He could so easily have lost it all, as he was on the brink. Fate.

Interwoven with all of this new-found business owner responsibility, he was still with Zara and talking of marriage; now in a much better place with the boys, seeing them much more often again. Peace once more broke out between him and Lisa. They agreed that the boys would now basically split their time each week between both parents; that each would pay for the boys when with them; and contribute equally to other expenses, such as school trips etc. There was no further need for maintenance, as the boys now had two proper homes and spent equal time with each parent. It was without doubt the best decision Cory has ever made in his life, and he has no doubt that will never change. He had changed from being a stressed, absentee dad paying maintenance for his stressed ex-wife to try and cope with four young boys, while he was forced to work long hours in London for people who didn't really understand his market or clients. Now he was the man with it all, or so it seemed. He was his own boss, and whilst that brought its own pressures, he now had his boys back properly. He has told them often as they have grown up how that was the main thing he wanted in life. They were all still young, but growing up and progressing through school and life. He didn't want to be like so many other men in the City (and elsewhere) who missed their own kids' childhoods as they were too busy pursuing their careers. Of course, money is nice (even important) but never simply for its own sake. He wanted enough to take care of his family and to enjoy time with them; that was paramount to Cory. He knows that he could have made more money over the past twenty years had he remained a lawyer, or if he had put the pursuit of money ahead of everything else. But being a real dad to his boys as they grew up was worth more than any amount of money to him. Whatever the issues of the divorce, he hopes (and believes) that he did the right thing and now is privileged to be the father of four fine young men who are starting to leave home and make their own way in the world. That said, the complexity of being a parent then takes on a whole new layer of worry and concern now. They move out and often miles away from you, they start travelling abroad a lot more without you, and they live their lives as they see fit. You still worry and want to help and support them, but you have to let them go and find their own way, hoping they will come back. As the Dalai Lama says:

> 'Give the ones you love wings to fly, roots to come back, and reasons to stay'

Having survived all their numerous childhood injuries, hospital visits and operations; parties (helped by London bouncers being hired for the Prom after-parties at their house!), and all their drunken teenage antics; now the Magaluf boys' party holidays, trips to Amsterdam, Berlin, and the Brighton party scene all cause fresh concern. Similarly, when they fly off to Ghana to work with orphans for the summer, you admire them but worry – especially when they admit once home the anti-malaria course of pills wasn't completed and they suffered badly with it for a few weeks. Added to which this coincided with the rapid spread (or at least Western acknowledgement) of the dreaded Ebola virus, which led to an early flight home a week earlier than planned! Or worst of all, when you receive the late-night phone call every parent dreads from the new driver teenage son (of course, all the more poignant to Cory). Fortunately, it was only the car in this case that was damaged; all the occupants were fine. Although Cory's naturally fatalistic view of the world made him think of Shakespeare's:

> 'The sins of the father are to be laid upon the children.'

You can never get that time back and Cory regrets not one minute of it; of everything he did to make sure he didn't lose his boys; to be fully and actively involved in all aspects of their lives as they grew from children, through the teenage years, and now gradually into fine young adults. That, to Cory, is the true meaning of life. Nothing else can compare to it. Now that they are grown and leaving home, he can see so clearly how important being with them throughout their childhood properly was. People sometimes lose sight of that at the time, when the kids are young and careers and jobs are demanding. But he would implore you: Just Don't! People change jobs and careers. People fall in and out of love and change partners. These are facts of life, certainly in the modern world, where almost everything is disposable and replaceable. But your children are different. You have created them. You brought them into this world. You are obligated to them. You should give your all for them (while trying to have your own happiness too, but often that has to be second to their needs). You get one chance with them. You can never get back any time you miss. You can never wind the clock back and start again. Indeed, as many older divorced dads with second families and young children attest, the joy of having more time and money to enjoy the new kids still never makes up for missing out the first time around. Cory just knew that; whether instinctively or because life had taken others he loved away from him prematurely. It doesn't matter why. What matters is that despite all the issues of the divorce, he and Lisa have given their boys their unconditional love always. Even during the dark days when the boys as teenagers started taking sides, their parental love never wavered. Nor will it ever. Although they haven't been able to give the boys the ideal, perfect life they would have liked to, they have had two loving homes, backed by wider extended families so that the boys have always felt loved. No amount of money can buy that. And it certainly cannot replace it. As discussed, most people with more than the usual amounts of issues as adults often have come from homes or domestic backgrounds where they didn't have that enviable blanket of security and love. Broken homes can of course cause this, and no doubt the boys do bear some scars from the divorce, but hopefully not as many as could have been the case, as they never lost either parent nor had any reason to doubt how much they are loved. He plans to explore much further the effects of the divorce on the boys in one of the subsequent planned volumes in this series (probably to be entitled *Family, Love & Relationships*).

Remarriage

Cory made allowances for Zara's slightly weird behaviour, as she had lost her parents when young and been thrown into care. He felt hugely sorry for her and couldn't imagine how traumatic and life-changing it must have been. But he also admired her massively, because whatever damage it had done (and it must have), she hid it well and seemed generally well adjusted, just a bit quirky. Appearances can be deceptive however, as Cory was to learn. He loved her and she loved him. They had now been together a couple of years, had a lot of fun, and had grown incredibly close. They had an amazing connection, spark, and chemistry and had survived all the blips so far. Cory therefore kept his promise and told his boys that he wanted to marry Zara. They were fine and accepted it without question. Lisa had to be told; but Cory wasn't sure what the etiquette was for telling your ex-wife that you are about to remarry. He didn't want any long discussions about it and couldn't face another bust-up, so he simply dropped it into a text exchange about Christmas holiday arrangements for the boys that year. Coward! So just before Christmas, Cory remarried (a year after the original date they had planned) at the local registry office, with his parents, his boys, and brother and family in attendance. There was no sign of Zara's sister this year or her son. Even her best friend, who was apparently supposed to be her maid of honour, missed the ceremony and only turned up at the hotel for the small family reception after. All very bizarre indeed!

They had debated whether to invite other friends, particularly Cory's from London, as they all now knew Zara well. But Cory knew that if they did, it would turn into an all-night party with them, and that didn't seem in keeping with the small, intimate nature of the event. They therefore had a meal shortly before in London for close friends and work colleagues and had an excellent night there instead, which seemed much more appropriate. The wedding day was lovely. Zara looked stunning and, in keeping with the quirky side of her character, decided to wear a tight-fitting bright red dress. As they walked from the hotel to their car to drive to the registry office, she certainly attracted many an appreciative look, wolf whistle, and comment from many a male passer-by. She seemed flattered. Cory was very proud. The service went without a hitch, the gathering was small and intimate as they wanted, but Zara still seemed very nervous. After a few photos afterwards, they retreated back to the hotel, where drinks and canapés were served and her best friend finally turned up and then proceeded to leave again very quickly – all very odd, but that was Zara and her life. After an hour or so, Cory's parents took the boys down the road to get burgers and real food (canapés having limited appeal to them) and then home. Cory's brother and family headed off too, leaving Cory and Zara to relax, exactly as they had planned. After the requisite newlyweds visit to their bedroom, they had dinner at one of their favourite local restaurants, a place they had been many times before but now as husband and wife. It was all incredibly nice and felt very personal and romantic. They partied a bit more later that night and then faced the pre-Christmas shopping crowds in town the next day. Cory bought Zara a couple of new dresses and various other gifts. Life was good. They enjoyed a couple of days together, then Christmas and family time. Unfortunately, when it came to Boxing Day, they were all due at Cory's parents, but Zara suddenly announced that she didn't feel up to it and wasn't coming. Cory was offended and said he understood she hadn't enjoyed such family gatherings previously, but now they were married, surely she could make the effort? She maintained she felt unwell and then played her trump card – she was missing her son and wanted to go and see him. Cory, of course, could not argue with that and took her apologies with him to his parents. Later that day, news spread of the Asian Tsunami, which devastated the region and killed hundreds of thousands of people. They had discussed honeymooning out there and could so easily have been there at the time but had fortuitously agreed to defer the honeymoon until after Christmas. Fate.

Clearly in view of the devastation across the region, they had to change honeymoon destination and settled on the Caribbean. Cory felt slightly odd about going back there for his second honeymoon too, which is why they had originally agreed on somewhere in the Indian Ocean. They nevertheless had a great time in Antigua and generally got on very well, apart from Zara seeming to pick up some chest infection midway through, not helped by her smoking (but then, most women Cory had ever been involved with seemed to smoke, so he was used to it). She wasn't in the greatest of party spirits therefore at times, and the very loud American guests at the resort clearly irritated her, as did some of the other female passengers on the flight on the way back. Cory dismissed it as a combination of illness and female hormones. They had agreed that she would gradually move in over the coming weeks once they returned from honeymoon, and when they landed, Cory fully expected that to happen. How naive he was. Zara went back to her area, ostensibly to sort out terminating her tenancy and making arrangements to fully move in with Cory; she was spending half the week with him anyway and (as girls do) had huge amounts of shoes and clothes at his house already. Things seemed to drag though, and Cory sensed her reluctance to actually move in full time, which was of concern, as that had been her entire premise for them having to get married! She almost seemed happy to keep things as they were, living separately but spending half the week with Cory and with her bolt hole to escape to. Cory became increasingly agitated and told her that if that was what she wanted, why then had they bothered getting married at all? That was supposedly down to her need for security when they lived together. But if that wasn't going to happen, it all seemed pointless.

She admitted she was scared and was worried, now that reality was hitting home, that the house wasn't big enough for all her stuff to add in to Cory's and the boys' possessions. They therefore started looking for a bigger house, although Cory was concerned at some of the viewings at the disproportionate amount of space she seemed to want to herself: the largest living rooms etc., evidently wanting to squash the boys into the smaller space. Cory could have understood this from a younger woman and one who didn't have a child of her own (albeit living with his dad) or even if Zara hadn't been with him now for two and a half years and known how fundamental a part of his life his boys were and how important having a suitable home for them was. Cory had agreed that they should get a bigger house so that they could live properly as a family, not with the house partitioned off between the kids and adult zones, as Zara seemed to want. He had four sons; she knew that, so there was no question of her having disproportionate amounts of rooms to herself. This meant that a lot of houses they looked at weren't suitable, or they couldn't agree how to divide up the available space. And then they found their dream home. After months of looking, they attended an open day and the house was clearly very popular. They immediately offered the full asking price. Fortunately, this all coincided with Cory's business suddenly taking off. That initial year- plus of hard work and toil with minimal financial return, all now being worthwhile. Their offer was originally accepted and they were delighted; but their joy was short lived as they were gazumped by one of the other bidding parties. Cory's house was up for sale and was attracting interest, but his prospective purchasers started delaying and seemed to be playing games. They were told that even if they matched or slightly bid above the gazumpers, given the uncertainty over Cory's sale, it wouldn't be enough. Zara was devastated, as she loved the new house. It was a three-storey, five-bedroom, three-reception room town house, with huge rooms, high ceilings, and plenty of space to amalgamate their respective homes and to accommodate Cory, Zara, his four boys, and her son too, when he came to visit. It was also very close to town and the train station, which made it ideal for Cory to commute (his previous house being at least a twenty-minute walk) and for general family life. They looked at a few others but had their hearts set on that house, as they told the agents. Fortuitously, they were introduced to an excellent mortgage broker, who understood their predicament and was confident he could help. He proposed that Cory bought the new house anyway; taking out a new mortgage for the requisite amount on the basis it would be short-term bridging finance until he could sell his existing house and then port the more favourable existing mortgage he had over. As this all coincided with a lot of money coming into Cory's business, so the money-people were satisfied that it was viable and all was put in place. Zara therefore went back to the agents and blew the gazumpers out of the water with a significantly higher offer. The agents then spoke to the broker, who they knew and who was delighted to confirm that Cory had the money, and the bridging finance was secured. Win-win! The agents were able to go back to the vendor with a massively increased offer, verifying that it was no longer dependent on Cory selling his own existing house and that Cory and Zara were therefore ready, willing, and able to proceed as soon as the vendor wished to do so. The deal was done. Money talks, as always. Although Cory subsequently reduced the offer substantially to reflect the work required to update the house (as is often the case with these huge Edwardian homes), he still paid significantly above the original asking price and gazumpers' offer. Everyone was happy. It was worth it, as he had secured the near-perfect home for him, Zara, and the boys. Or so he thought. But life is never as simple as it should be, is it?

Cory believed almost incredulously that maybe he had achieved the impossible. After all the years of emotional pain, failed relationships, incredible stress, almost losing the boys, and various work issues too, things all seemed to be sorted. He owned and ran a successful business; he had a new wife with whom he had found true love and that amazing connection again (long since missing from his life, since he and Lisa had lost theirs years earlier), a big family home, and his boys back full time with him (well, half of each week, but that's full time enough for a single parent with four of them!). It was as if the past few years' balancing act he had undertaken, juggling all the aspects of his life precariously as he crossed the tightrope of life without a safety net (and often slipping, but never quite completely falling off) had been worth it. Was it really feasible to think he now finally had it all? Of course he didn't; it was sadly built on foundations of sand. Is it really conceivable that you can ever have it all? Perhaps that is the main lesson he has learned from life over his half century in this world. We spend so long striving for better (if not perfect) lives, always chasing our dreams, working harder, acquiring bigger houses, more possessions, ever more materialistic wealth, aspiring to have better jobs, more kids, as well as great sex, fun, excitement and danger. Yet the dream we chase is a mirage; the closer we get to having it all, the further it seems to grow in the distance; almost there but never quite in our grasp, an illusion we are led to believe we can achieve if only we pursue it. We can achieve and acquire much of what we want, but can we ever really have it all? Is anyone ever so utterly happy and content with their lives that they wouldn't change a single thing? Maybe that is the curse of being human and our ultimate fatal flaw. We want it all, we believe we can have it, but always fall just short. That is just life!

So Cory and the boys moved into their new home and all sorts of works (that would carry on for the next few years, on and off) started: immediately replacing the antiquated boiler and pipework, upgrading all three bathrooms, showers, putting in skylights on the third floor to give more natural light, redecorating and carpeting throughout, new wooden flooring downstairs, new pine furniture, beds, wardrobes etc. throughout to fill the huge rooms, not to mention clearing the old-fashioned garden and re-landscaping it to include a new Jacuzzi to catch the sun, which became Cory's summer home office for years after (and a great place to party!). It was a big undertaking, expensive, and meant that there always seemed to be some work going on for their first few summers there. It's amazing that even all of that effort and expense wasn't enough, as when Cory recently sold the house, as he no longer needed all the space now his boys were going to Uni and leaving home, the new owners have decided to start all over and replace and remodel much of the home for their own young family. It just seems to be one of the homes, a fantastic family home, superbly located for commuting to London, walking to schools and town, which everyone falls in love with and imagines the potential for their respective young families. But then families grow and leave, and all the space that was so essential is now excessive. Cory had bought it from a divorced lady whose kids had just left home when his were young, and now in turn, as his were leaving, he had sold it on to a lovely young couple with young twins and at least one more on the way. It was a great home, but one of the neighbours, rather drunk at the welcome barbeque Cory threw when he moved in, queried whether it was somehow cursed, as both it and the neighbouring houses had a history of divorces. Cory desperately hoped he wouldn't end up as a second-time divorcee. But his start with Zara didn't auger well.

Zara had finally given notice on her rented property and had arranged a removal service to move her down. Although she had originally agreed to contribute to the mortgage on the new home, she had yet to do so. She was an aspiring photographer, and Cory had systematically bought her new cameras, lenses, a website etc. to help her business. She, in turn, helped with technical and design aspects in his, which was hugely helpful, but for which she was well paid.

Yet apparently, she had no money, so Cory was constantly subsidising her and now had to pay for her removal, as well as both mortgages. Fortunately, business was good, so he was able to afford it, but it wasn't the most auspicious start to all they had discussed and planned for their new marriage, by now seven months old and she was only just moving in with him! They agreed that apart from their main bedroom with en suite, the four boys would have the two bedrooms on the top floor and the one at the back of the house. The three eldest boys would have one each, and Chaz (the youngest) still didn't need his own room so would share with his brothers for the first year or so, changing rooms every few months. That allowed Zara to have the largest bedroom next door to their main one as a changing room, office for her work, and general private and storage area too. Similarly, downstairs, there were two equally large lounges, so one would become an adult lounge for Zara and Cory and the other the kids lounge for the boys. Added to the separate kitchen and dining room, it meant, in theory at least, there should be enough space for everyone. In theory, but not in practice, it seemed. Zara appeared not to cope well with suddenly living with the family. She seemed to want the boys to stay in defined areas, inside and out, and for there to be no sign of them wherever possible. Cory was bemused. This all seemed unnecessarily awkward and as if she was somehow trying to assert herself. Perhaps it was merely her female nesting instinct, but he suspected it was something more worrying than that. It looked to him as if she would tolerate his boys, but not really embrace what he had hoped would be their new life together. After all, if that was not what she had wanted, why bother marrying him at all? It wasn't as if the boys were not going to be there – and they were only there for half the week, so they still had plenty of time just as a couple. The tension grew and led to arguments over the most ridiculous issues, like a small football goal and mini-trampoline being in the garden. Hardly unusual in a family garden! Cory felt he had bent over backwards with Zara, finding an ideal house to accommodate her, all her stuff, and the boys; spending a lot of money on the house, on her, on her photography equipment, and making sure she had a pretty good lifestyle as his wife. They had a joint bank account and she now took out various credit cards, which she used heavily. One of Cory's (now ex) friends drunkenly said that it was curious how she had married Cory just as his business had started to flourish. Cory knew that she had suggested they marry a year earlier, when he had no money, as the business was struggling to get going in its infancy, so dismissed the comments as slightly bitchy and jealous. Indeed, years later, their friendship ended when this same friend one night, when under the influence of alcohol and God-knows what else, proceeded to shit-stir hugely to Zara about Cory. They had argued earlier in the week, and after some evening drinks with friends one Friday, Cory had gone home and switched his phone to silent mode as he slept. Zara had apparently turned up in London very late that night trying to find Cory. She tracked the friend down to a club, where he spouted complete nonsense about Cory having gone off to see some other woman. Zara was devastated. The next day, Cory woke to find endless hysterical calls and messages from her. Where had he been? Who was he with? How could he betray her like this? He was confused. What was she talking about? She told him what the friend had said. He was furious. He asked his 'friend' what the fuck he was playing at and got some incoherent waffle about men should stick together, Cory was too under her thumb, she was no good for him, a gold digger etc. The following Monday morning, when that friend arrived at their shared office and still refused to apologise or admit all he'd said and the damage he had caused, Cory kicked him out for good. Cory suspects that he either had no idea what he had said, as he was off his head, or was too embarrassed to admit it. That was bad enough, but his intransigence and refusal to apologise was too much. Although years later, they bumped into each other at a social function and agreed to have a beer and try to repair things, they never have been able to. It destroyed their friendship.

Zara was now notionally living with Cory full time, but would often disappear when the boys came to stay. They were still having a great social and sex life generally, but the family life he had naively believed their marriage would bring was not there. She got on well with his boys and they liked their new stepmum, but too often she seemed overly irritated by their presence or even by their things. He started to find some of their stuff mysteriously disappearing or being damaged. He confronted her about it and she naturally denied it all. She however let her true feelings show one evening when she grabbed a picture of the boys and screamed that they were everywhere; there was no escape from them. Cory was shocked. It wasn't as if he had kept them a secret from her before their marriage! It wasn't as if she didn't know how hard he had battled not to be pushed out of their lives and how important it was for him (and them) to be with him half of each week. She had been supportive of all of this over the previous three years, but now appeared to be struggling to cope with the reality of living with it. It was as if she wanted Cory and the lifestyle but without the kids. That was never an option; it was a package. All or nothing. Cory understood it was tough for her, not even living with her own son, but grew to resent her constant criticisms of him and his kids. If they were there all the time, he could understand it being overwhelming, but they weren't. He had no problem with her going out and socialising when he had the boys, but when she didn't come back and stayed away for days, that was too fucked up. That was not a marriage, not what he had agreed to marry her and bought the bigger house for. That was not why he subsidised her lifestyle and in fact now seemed to be fully paying for it. He confronted her when she returned from one of her absences. She admitted she was finding it hard to cope when the boys were there; she felt overwhelmed and excluded. Cory said he appreciated what she said and would do what he could to address it, but she needed to become more involved with the boys if she wanted to make it work properly and be part of the family. And this went on for months.

Sometimes it seemed things were getting better, and then she would disappear again. Cory was sympathetic to all she had said, but grew increasingly concerned at her absences. He didn't believe she was having an affair or anything sexual elsewhere (everything was still great between them there – indeed the make-up sex was better than ever, with all the added feelings thrown in to the emotional turmoil), but he knew something was not right. So one evening when the boys had gone to bed and she was again nowhere to be seen, he started looking through her things, all of which were now in his house, to try to work out what was going on. He had never done this before, as his view was (and remains strongly to this day) that if you don't trust someone, you shouldn't be with them. If you have doubts and suspicions, they need to be addressed and dealt with. They cannot be allowed to fester and grow. He had tried talking to her, accepted that she found it tough when the boys were there and preferred to be out. He had no problem with that, but not her disappearances for days. He was nevertheless shocked by what he discovered.

First, her birth certificate, not necessarily a major issue *per se*, but she had claimed this was lost when they were doing all the legal formalities with the registrar before they married. She had, as every girl seemingly does, lied about her age initially and knocked a few years off, just as they habitually knock many off the true figure if the discussion ever gets to how many people they've had sex with! (Or more often, they have the bloke answer first and then make sure their answer is a suitably small fraction of his!). Yet here was the certificate in all her paperwork, not lost at all. Why then had she lied about having lost it? It seemed to be because she told everyone her name was Zara Jane, and although Cory and most people he knew called her Zara, it seemed that wasn't actually her name at all. She was just Jane, which would explain why her sister called her that. It seemed at some point in her life, she had added in the Zara bit, but never admitted it wasn't real. Cory didn't understand why she hadn't just said that; it was a bit odd, maybe a bit of a girl thing, but really not an issue. Her explanation when he confronted her was along the lines that she liked the name and had decided in her adult life many years ago she wanted to be known as Zara, and it was only really her sister who called her by her real name. All part of her escaping her past, it seemed. But the lies worried him.

Second, and much worse, were her bank and credit card statements. This was truly shocking. She was completely fucked financially. Overdrawn in her personal account, she had used all the money from their new joint account and had already maxed out all her new credit cards to the tune of about thirteen grand! He understood that every girl has shopping trips; that's just a fact of life we men have to accept, especially if we want our women to look good – even if the number of shoes, dresses etc. is always way too excessive in our minds. But that again is never an argument men can win! There were regular large cash withdrawals, often all over London, particularly when she disappeared. Cory was furious. When he confronted her, she told him she had been so unhappy since she had belatedly moved in with him and so unable to cope when the boys were there that she had started using drugs a lot more than just socially. She knew she had a real problem but just felt so lost and unhappy. Cory didn't know what to do. He loved her and wanted to make things work, but he knew that historically, she'd had a real issue with drugs. He had come to realise when they were out socially together, that was all she wanted. She wasn't a big drinker particularly, but loved all forms of other illicit substances. It had slowly dawned on him over time, as she was invariably under the influence when she turned up to meet him in London, which was okay if it was just the two of them; less so if with other friends and just plain embarrassing if with clients (who could tell, as London is awash with it, so people know the signs). On one occasion, they had gone to Oxford Crematorium so he could look at his brother's commemorative plaque; she had left him to his own thoughts and returned to their car. How sweet and considerate, he thought. That was until as he walked back to the car some time later; he saw her hoovering up lines in the car! Was she a kindred spirit with Alfie? Maybe this was a fitting tribute to him, which he would have found hilarious!

He had never imagined though that her addiction was so overwhelming. He offered to pay for her to go to rehab, but she said there was no point, as she had been when she was younger and knew it was up to her to deal with it. She also made another admission to him now. About a year earlier, shortly before they married, he had one day noticed a brown bottle in her handbag when she had arrived from her then home. He had looked at the label and seen that it was methadone. He obviously confronted her about it immediately, and she had told him a very convincing story. She had admitted to him in their first year together that she had been heavily into drugs during her teenage years and early twenties, primarily when in care and then when she had lived with an older guy in Earls Court who had got her on to heroin. She had told Cory she had come off it years ago, was now clean, and had never done it since and had been prescribed methadone as part of that. However, due to her opiate and drug tolerance levels being high, when she was in pain, she was now prescribed methadone, as she needed something stronger than normal pain relief. Her pain was due to a leg injury that had required a series of skin grafts over recent years. She told Cory that the leg injury had been caused by a horse kicking her. He knew that out in the country she did ride and look after horses and had broken her collarbone in a riding accident, so it all seemed credible. He of course googled methadone and found that although it's primary use was as a heroin substitute when weaning addicts off the drug, it could also be used as pain relief. Clever girl, she had covered her tracks well. This time, at least. But Cory said he couldn't have her around the boys if she was in such a state and using so much. They agreed that she needed to move out and sort herself out. She repeatedly refused his regular offers for her to go into rehab and said that if she moved back up to her area, she could go back to a drug counsellor she knew who had helped her before. Cory knew he had to agree, as things self-evidently weren't working as they were. He couldn't have her around his kids when she was like this, and their only hope was for her to sort herself out to see if they could try again. So he paid off her debts, but got her to cancel the cards and paid her rent for six months in advance on a house she found back up in her area. They agreed to review things regularly and see how she was progressing. Although he was angry and felt let down very badly by her, he also felt very sorry and protective towards her. Part of him felt as if they should divorce or have the marriage annulled, as she had never really lived with him properly for any concerted period and now he knew why. But then equally, he didn't want to give up on her and the good parts of what they had. Although the marriage had so far been a disaster; not at all what he expected from a second marriage, even accepting that it would be different, he felt that adding to their current issues by divorcing seemed premature and cruel. He still wanted a relationship with her, even if their marriage was patently not working.

Zara moved out. She took a lodger in her house for some income, said she was still trying with her photography business (not that there had been much sign of that previously), and claimed she was also apparently working in a local designer's boutique. Cory agreed to hire a van to drive some of her furniture back up to her new home, which was partially furnished, so there was no great urgency. Eventually, she announced that one of her friends had offered to drive the van for her. Cory pointed out that was fine if they hired one, but if he hired it, he was responsible for it and the insured driver. The friend didn't want to actually pay for the van. This raised Cory's suspicions; who was this friend? When he had first met Zara, she had talked of various male friends, all of whom gradually seemed to disappear as they had become more serious over the years, so he knew full well they were the usual 'male friends', all besotted with her, but in her mind just lovely, helpful, kind friends, and nothing more. Why are women so naive? Or are they? Is it just a way of manipulating men, being friends, knowing that these boys are all desperately hoping for more to develop and getting all the girl wants from them in the meantime, as they wait like dutiful puppies? The classic was a bloke she swore was just a good friend, who it transpired had taken topless photos of her as part of their photography work together (obviously!), which his girlfriend had then found and banned him from ever contacting her again. But this one seemed to be new. Cory gradually gleaned from her that it was one of the photographers she knew who happened to live in Cory's area. There had been one such chap he had met when they first started seeing each other years earlier, a tall gangly awkward type, who was clearly in lust with Zara but was so lacking in social skills and had done nothing about it and then suddenly told her so very bluntly once he heard Cory was on the scene. She had tried to stay friends with him, but he had gone off in a huff when it was clear nothing was ever going to happen between them. This new guy ran a website through which he had got to know Zara and started flirting with her. His girlfriend had recently just left one day, moving out of his house and saying it was over without further explanation. It seemed his infatuation with Zara had increased commensurately, and he had been delighted to hear that she had moved out of Cory's house. He was professing his undying love, bombarding her with calls, Valentine's cards (which Zara had told Cory was from her son when he saw it!), and generally offering to help her get away from Cory for good, and to no doubt run into his arms. Again, she claimed he was just a friend and someone to talk to about all their issues. Cory made it plain that the guy had clearly been after her for months, even when they were still living together; if she was now involved with someone else, they were over. End of! (to use the vernacular so favoured by many 'sarf London' and Essex girls). Zara finally admitted she knew the guy had become too obsessed with her but claimed nothing had happened. Cory told her to prove it by giving him the guy's number. She did. Cory rang him and told him in no uncertain terms he was a loser whose own girlfriend had left him and he should butt out of their marriage. Things were hugely complicated and they didn't need his pathetic pining for her complicating things. If she had been interested in him, something would have happened but it hadn't, so whether their marriage worked or not, if he didn't fuck off, Cory would make him.

Apparently, the bloke was so upset that Zara had told Cory everything and betrayed what he thought they had that he stropped off for months. Although Cory then did drive Zara's furniture up to her new home, he ended up staying the night and they talked for hours. This led to them having a great night together, so they decided that what they had was too good to lose, even if they couldn't have a normal marriage where she lived with him and his boys. Although they were technically married, it wasn't a proper marriage. They didn't live together; she came and went, sometimes regularly, but too often sporadically. They even tried marriage guidance counselling briefly, but she just complained about his kids, so it got nowhere. He was a single dad of four young sons, with whom she had no more interaction than brief conversations if her visits coincided with theirs, depending on her mood. She didn't seem to want to be part of his family, so the mystery remained as to why she had insisted on marrying him. He took the boys to all their activities, from horse riding and judo, swimming etc. as younger kids through to regular football training and Sunday games for years as they grew. Whatever relationship (and other) issues Cory has ever had, his unconditional love for his boys has always kept him sane and grounded. He has always thought (and still does) that it would of course be nice to have real love again, as having experienced it a few times he knows how amazing it is. But never at the cost of his time and relationship with his boys; there are so many stories of second marriages and relationships having issues between step-parents and the original kids, which then leads to problems in the adult relationship too, that it's seemingly a very tough path to follow. It's not as if he doesn't have a lot of love in his life already with his immediate family, for which he is eternally grateful. Clearly his closeness to his boys has affected most of his subsequent relationships; but frankly, given the choice, he knows that he can always find a new relationship, so has no regrets.

Lost Souls

This pattern with Zara carried on for another few years. They still loved each other, but had to reluctantly accept that she couldn't live with him while his boys were there. They still had great times together, out partying and still had the spark and chemistry others said was incredible. Too many nights to record here, but one that sticks in his mind was a night in Camden, when she had introduced 'K' into their activities. Their naivety as to its strength and hallucinogenic qualities left them at one stage stranded on a street corner, he believing that his legs had turned to concrete and merged into the pavement, unable to move them, while she tried to usher him back to the safety of his office until it wore off and they could continue home. He recalled seeing a police car drive by them, but luckily it didn't stop. Another memorable occasion was the night England won the 2005 Ashes. Cory and friends had watched the final victorious overs in a local bar, drinking heavily to support and cheer England on. Zara had joined them, looking very sexy and mischievous (as she often did), and performed a sex act on him in her car parked down the road to set the tone for the night. They had ended up in a club, where they met a lovely young lady who came back to a hotel with them and they partied the night away. They sadly missed the team victory procession the next day consequently, but it was worth it!

A year or so later after a work night out, Cory returned home to carry on partying with Zara (the boys not being there), and she told him the photographer guy with a crush had been back in touch. Cory (alcohol-fuelled) rang the bloke and said why didn't he come round to party with them. He was there within ten minutes! As the night's party unfolded, a threesum ensued, and the guy kept whispering to Zara that she was all he had ever wanted. Cory made it clear through all they did that Zara was with him and would remain so (perhaps cruelly, but assertively). Once the guy left, she told Cory she had found it all too creepy; he was too clingy, and although the sexual bit had been fun, it was ruined for her by his obsession with her. Any future escapades they had were with random people, never again with anyone they knew who had a crush. Feelings just got in the way of the fun. But for all of these nights of fun, for every peak, there was an equivalent trough. There were still arguments about why it all hadn't worked, how shit it all turned out to be, and was it really worth it. They started to grow apart, perhaps inevitably, and had a number of break-ups where they didn't see each other for weeks initially and then months. After a period, they started to date and see other people. One of Cory's friends nervously once told him he had seen her profile on a dating site on one occasion; and they talked of divorce a number of times. But eventually, they would inexorably come back together, as when it worked their connection was still there. They were still told by many who encountered them that they were lucky to have such a strong chemistry together; few people did. It held them together for perhaps longer than it should have.

On one occasion, they hadn't seen each other for weeks and Cory was getting on with his life as usual. One very cold Sunday morning, he was somewhere in the deep south with one of his sons' football teams. His plan was to watch this game, then rush up the A3 to see another of his sons playing elsewhere – the logistical nightmare he constantly faced of having two or three sons all playing Sunday morning football at the same time! He noticed at half-time that he had a missed call on his mobile from a number he didn't recognise and assumed it must be a work call, which could wait. Eventually, when he later listened to the voicemail, he heard a woman explaining that he didn't know her, but she was ringing on behalf of Zara who had been in an accident and was being taken to the local A&E. He immediately called Zara's phone, but it went straight to voicemail; similarly, so did the number of the woman who had left the message. She rang back shortly after and explained she had come across Zara in her overturned car in a roadside ditch on one of the country lanes up in her rural area. An ambulance had been called and taken her to hospital. Cory had to deliver his son at home, arrange for his other son to be returned from his game, then dashed up the motorway to see Zara. She was in traction and apparently had cracked her vertebrae as the car overturned as she swerved around a corner and lost control that cold winter's morning. The medical staff were concerned about potential damage to her spinal cord, and she was under strict orders not to move. This naturally put their latest arguments and separation in focus and they were reunited. As ever though, there was an unusual twist. Cory stayed in the area for a few nights, but had to book into local bed and breakfasts and hotels rather than staying at Zara's house. Years later, she admitted that this was because there was a lot of paraphernalia and debris lying around which she hadn't wanted him to see, as the full extent of it was all still her deep dark secret at that stage.

His mum very sensibly asked him why he seemed to end up with such troublesome women. He answered that he liked mad women; they were more interesting and exciting! The truth, of course, being that Cory has a mad, wild side that terrifies many people, particularly nice normal ladies. He seeks and craves those who share his 'Live Fast, Love Hard, Die Young' (Faron Young) thirst for life, largely because of their own damaged backgrounds. It is a mutual need and attraction. Of course he didn't ever really want the last bit (although it may have seemed like it during the very bad times), like James Dean, Amy Winehouse, and so many others, but enjoys partying and so much more with people with a similar psyche to his own. So he is inevitably drawn to people like him who have been hurt, whose hearts have been broken, but not just in the normal course of everyday life and love (that is too common and mundane);

who have had some major seismic loss in their lives that has skewed their approach to life, sometimes even their moral compass. These people want more than just normality in all aspects of their lives, nice dinner parties and idle social interactions. They have a burning desire for more. If people do not fall into this category, they can never understand those who do. Those in this group (whether knowingly or not) are drawn to each other like vampires in the night, seeking solace and seclusion with each other from the rest of the world as daylight dawns in the real world, from which (emotionally at least) they are slightly detached. Mutual attraction, need, and knowledge of a true understanding of each other's pain (whenever it happened, it never fully goes away) are powerful emotions that fuel the chemistry required in any relationship. They are drawn to each other like moths to a flame, and as we know, that doesn't always end well! Sometimes the mutual pain, suffering and baggage can implode and become too much, too destructive for the people involved. Perhaps too many of Cory's relationships have been like this, but those are the women he is attracted to, spiritually and emotionally. And they to him, it seems. So add in the essential physical and intellectual attraction elements too, and it is a complex, highly charged, volatile package; as his relationship history and issues probably illustrate!

But such people do generally have to live in the real world too; they have to conform to some extent (although they generally hate it) and seek their escape often in their nocturnal activities, real life again interfering with the true emotional happiness we all crave. The turmoil this can cause in their lives, relationships, friendships, work, social life and every aspect of their existence should never be underestimated, but only like-minded tortured souls will truly understand. The normal people will just dismiss them as different, mad, eccentric and weird, believing that they don't give a shit, are rebels and non-conformists; all so wrong. They care about much deeper issues than the things society deems important. Normal people can have no comprehension until something life-changing happens to them, at which point they become one of the lost souls and can never return to their normal lives properly again. All very profound, but sadly true. As the sayings powerfully convey (along with many other variations on the theme):

> 'Don't judge me. You can't handle half of what I've dealt with. There's a reason I do the things I do, there's a reason I am who I am' (Anonymous), and

> 'Don't judge me unless you have looked through my eyes and experienced what I have and cried as many tears as me. Until then, back off, 'cause you have no idea' (Anonymous)

Divorce

As with anything in life, the more strain you put on it, although it may stretch and bend for a while, eventually it will break. Their reunions were great, and although they lasted for a while, things always went wrong again. Over the ensuing years, they had more Caribbean holidays, Barbados becoming a firm favourite during the good times; that is, apart from the night they were asked to leave one very posh, but dull, hotel full of very old people, as a result of one too many of their many loud arguments! He took her to Paris, staying at the George V, dining in the Eiffel Tower restaurant and watching an amazing show at the Moulin Rouge for her fortieth birthday. He bought her a Tiffany diamond and paid for her increasingly regular Harley Street visits for endless cosmetic injections. They holidayed at the Sandals Royal Bahamian Resort and had endless weekends away and short breaks in places like Capri, Amsterdam, Brighton, London, and enjoyed life when they were together. Fine dining in top restaurants, clubbing and partying, regular shopping trips for her, and yet it was never enough. Issues constantly arose. The worst included her using his credit cards (hers having been cancelled) without asking too regularly when she wasn't with him. Her promises to drive over

as agreed once he bought her a new car, then making all sorts of
excuses as to why she couldn't, only for him then to discover that
she was diligently driving to London to get her gear and party. Both
he and even the cleaners, at times, finding needles hidden around
the house, which she claimed were to do with her leg injury, but
turned out to be something far worse; awful arguments about all of
their issues and problems, which occasionally and very regrettably
became too physical, even violent on both sides; her stealing money
from his eldest son's debit card when they were all out one day; her
involving his elderly parents unnecessarily in an argument by going
round to their home nearby and presenting a very one-sided version of
events; her calling the police too often as some kind of silly game and
power trip, usually resulting in them doing nothing and ultimately
threatening to arrest both of them for wasting police time if called
again. She even tipped a bowl of noodles over her own head on one
occasion, falsely claiming Cory had done it, and made up all sorts
of other nonsense far too often. She once locked Cory out and then
panicked when he broke a window to get in, so called the police.
They told her that as it was his house, he was entitled to do so. She
regularly threatened to contact his clients to cause damage, posted a
damaging video clip of him on YouTube until he had it removed and
then sent it to lawyers acting for a former business colleague of Cory's
(in an ongoing business dispute during the recession). A culmination
of all of these things (and so much more) finally killed what they
had. The divorce was on and off over a few years, each taking it in
turns to push it forward, then stop, but eventually, Cory insisted they
finalised it, as the good bits no longer outweighed the bad and their
periods apart had become too extensive. It was very sad, but again it
wasn't as if they hadn't tried time after time for many years. It couldn't
be fixed; there had been too much shit. It was over. It had been so
prophetic when she had told him a decade earlier when they had
first met online that all girls on dating sites were damaged and it was
like selecting a dog from Battersea Dogs Home. They may scrub up

well and look good with a bit of love again, but you can never repair
the damage previously caused to them. Zara was a classic example of
this, sadly. She was an attractive, intelligent, charming, sweet, loving
girl who could never escape her past; her own demons and inability
now to properly interrelate with others, all because her life had been
ripped apart as a teenager. She fronted up well, superficially appearing
as a normal functioning member of society, but was sadly lost in her
own world, apparently unable to cope in the real world without her
crutch. Cory can only hope she has somehow sorted herself out now,
although he isn't convinced, as their very rare communications now
still focus on her view that he treated her very badly during their
marriage with no acknowledgement of her own issues. Of course, he
reacted very badly far too often, and their mutual madness, that had
brought them together and kept their bond so strong for so many
years, ultimately was what destroyed them too. Truly sad; Cory had
loved her and wanted it to work so much for so long. But it didn't.

More Clubs and Parties

Zara had, during the course of their relationship, become quite
a fan of strip clubs. She had asked Cory a lot about them, and her
interest grew as he told her all his tales. She had got to know Debbie
too briefly and wanted to know more about them. This was all
part of their sexual exploration and wild party nights so fitted well.
They started one night by following dinner at The Ivy (a favourite
of theirs) with a visit to Stringfellows. It didn't start well though, as
the doorman initially wouldn't let her in, apparently believing her to
be a stripper herself from another club rather than a genuine guest.
Fortunately, he went on a break, and Cory was more successful
at persuading the next guy to let them in. She said she enjoyed it,
but found it all a bit big, impersonal and mercenary. Cory wasn't
sure if that was just because it was her first time in such a club,
whether it was because the doorman had initially refused her entry

and put a damper on the evening, or whether as a woman, she felt uncomfortable in that environment. They stayed for a while, both had a few dances and enjoyed the atmosphere (Cory more than her), and then left. In subsequent discussions, she said she was keen to see the smaller club Debbie had worked in, so they made that their next visit. As Cory knew the management and some of the girls there, she seemed to settle more easily and enjoyed it more. They became regulars and she became well known to the management there, so much so that during one of their extended periods apart some time later, Cory received a very odd call from his office to say some guy had turned up looking for him and had left a mysterious message. When Cory called back, the chap explained he was an associate of the club's manager and needed to meet to talk. All very ominous. They did so in a coffee bar, as Cory knew from TV shows that you always meet slightly sinister people in public! It transpired that during one of her nights out in London, Zara had gone to the club and told them Cory had been arrested and charged with possession. She claimed that he had told the police he got the stuff in the club. The club obviously were shitting themselves. Cory was bewildered. None of it was true. Not a single word. The chap was aghast. He referred to Zara in the most graphic of Anglo-Saxon terms – hell hath no fury, indeed! Cory went in to the club that night and reassured the management that Zara had made it all up, obviously in her paranoid state trying to cause trouble for Cory. There was huge relief all round and reassurance that Cory was always welcome in the club, but Zara no longer was. She was too embarrassed to ever try to return, in any event.

This was a shame, as she had generally enjoyed her time there, both having dances herself and watching girls dancing for Cory. She even was flattered a number of times to be asked to dance for other customers, as she had the right look, even if wearing her normal street clothes (as opposed to the scantily clad nature of the real girls working there). Usually she said no, but a few times after consultation with Cory, she would dance for one or two guys in front of Cory. It was all part of that whole sexual exploration period they were going through, the excitement versus jealousy bit that can be such a turn-on, as long as nothing goes too far. They experienced this too at other clubs such as *Torture Garden* and others of that ilk, where they enjoyed a bit of exhibitionism, but ultimately preferred only to be with each other rather than joining in with others publicly in that environment. Zara admitted she liked to watch girls dancing for Cory but hated it when he talked privately to them. She got upset with one particular stunning Latino/Hispanic blonde, who Cory spotted and really liked and had dance for both of them. This was Anna. The fine line between jealousy and excitement had clearly been crossed. Cory understood why, as Anna was beautiful; she had the most amazing body and looks and appeared to be a pretty nice person too. She was indeed. Cory has now known Anna for almost a decade and they remain good friends, long after Zara has gone. In fact, a year or so ago, Cory took a group of work colleagues to the club, and one of his female colleagues (whose background included years in the fashion industry) described Anna as the most beautiful girl she had ever seen, with a supermodel's body to die for. Anna was certainly happy to put on a show for the group and to show them how close she and Cory were, having been friends for years. It was one hell of a show that led every man to ask how they could get to know her better and every girl to say their boyfriends and partners were allowed nowhere near her! They had dated a few times years earlier, but sadly never progressed during one of his latter prolonged splits from Zara towards the end, enjoying football at the Emirates and Madonna at the O2 (Madonna being his long-term crush, so this being the third time he had seen her, the previous ones with Lisa at Wembley Stadium many years earlier and with Zara at Wembley Arena more recently). Anna was also his dream girl, not only beautiful in looks, but personality too and what could be better than such a gorgeous girl loving football?

She and a friend joined Cory and one of his mates in their Club Level seats at the Emirates for an Arsenal v. Liverpool match. Cory's mate was something of a local playboy, but out where they lived, not on a London scale. He admitted he was blown away by how beautiful Anna and her friend were, but said he quickly realised they were way out of his league when they started talking about which of the players on the pitch they had dated, and even in one case, one of the world's top players. This was something Cory was to come to realise as his relationship with Zara died and he was back out on the party scene in London. The very sexy, beautiful younger women he liked were not only all very popular with every other man generally (he was used to that with Zara), but particularly with every footballer, gangster, playboy and any other player in town. A whole new league of opponents for him! Cory felt no sympathy for his mate though, as he knew what a snake he was; in fact, in one of their typical blokes' discussions when out one night over too many beers, the friend had admitted he found Zara attractive, and if they were no longer together, he might make a play for her. Cory relayed this to Zara the next time they reunited; she didn't appear to be overly flattered. Nor was he particularly impressed by his friend's comments. It simply reinforced his firm view that men generally only think with their dicks around attractive women and cannot be trusted. Cory and this mate had some good nights out together though. It all started on their sons' football tour to a tournament in Holland. The boys were hosted by the families of the local players in a lovely Dutch village, leaving the dads collectively to stay in a local hotel. Fatal! The first night, after they had safely arrived and dispatched all the boys to their respective host families, it was agreed that the sixteen or so dads would have a civilised meal in the hotel together. Famous last words! The Dutch beer flowed, followed by too much wine, then shots and raiding the mini-bars in the rooms when the main bar closed for the night. A lot of the dads were out of their depth drinking so heavily, but Cory and Daz were in their element; a strong friendship was born, based largely on their mutual proclivities – a strong interest in alcohol and women! Perfect, what more does a male friendship need? Of course, it has evolved over the years and they have both settled down (at times), but one or other of those core principles has remained intact at the heart of their friendship. This led to a number of nights out in their local town being curtailed by them being asked to leave bars and clubs, as they enjoyed themselves too much. Thankfully, those nights have diminished over recent years, as they are growing older, slightly less disgracefully now than before.

As Cory said to one of his sons as he drove him back down to the south coast recently, he no longer has any burning need to go out and party, having done it fairly consistently for at least the past fifteen years now. He is enjoying his current self-imposed exile from the City, the drinking culture, and all that flows from that. After in excess of thirty years' pretty solid and continuous drinking, his body needs a break, and writing this book in his semi-rural idyllic seclusion is the perfect excuse. Without the book, he would be bored shitless (and would have no excuse not to currently be properly working for a living!). It is not only therapeutic; cathartic, an emotional outpouring, at times an introspective search into his soul, to see why he did all he did and where it has led him now; but hopefully, it is also very good for his health too! He has had time to pause and reflect in a way he has not been afforded previously, to take stock and to decide where this wonderful adventure that is life may take him next. But for now, here are some more highlights of those wild, hedonistic party days and long all-nighters in London.

One of the features of some strip clubs a decade and more ago (much less now, as the licencing laws for such venues are ever more restrictive) was that depending on venue, girl, and customer, anything could go. Cory discovered that all sorts of party enhancers could be acquired if you knew the right people inside or outside certain clubs. The girls certainly all had contacts too. Debbie had told him early on that as well as the clubs and girls encouraging punters to drink ever more (thus losing their inhibitions and spending even more money), some girls even popped stuff in punters drinks to help them along. And then there were the girls who left with punters to go to local hotels and who were all very keen on party powder too – which often would mean that the guy was all revved up, but the cumulative effect of all he had ingested led to the mind being willing, but his body not so much. Easy money for the girls then (these days, the more widely available blue pills are one way of seeking to counter such effects, apparently). But much of this has changed now, as clubs are much more tightly regulated, and many have been closed down, had their licences revoked, or faced battles to have them renewed. But back then, you could even (if capable) have sexual activity in certain clubs with some (not all) of the girls. Then of course as you left the clubs, there was an array of drivers waiting to take you on to local apartments for even more fun. Some of these were run by people connected to the clubs, some completely separate, but they were very popular with many a man who staggers out drunk in the early hours, frustrated from an evening of sexual provocation in the clubs and goes on to finish off the party fully at one of these establishments. Cory has certainly had many an extended party in such places over the years when single. They cater for every taste – the Brazilians being the most adventurous and uninhibited people he has ever encountered, closely followed by a whole range of eastern and central Europeans and all sorts of others too. As always, some were just one-night encounters, others led to an exchange of numbers and further interactions subsequently. Cory has recently watched the excellent Sky Arts series *Matrioshki*, which has caused him to reflect properly though on potential issues involved, which he should perhaps have thought of at the time. But he didn't.

The point to Cory of all these nights out and parties was that he was a divorced dad looking for fun. At the start of his time as a regular strip club visitor, one of the management at the first club he visited talked to him about it all. He said that amongst all the City types, professionals, hedge fund chaps, dodgy geezers, and so many more that made up their clientele, divorced men were always amongst the most regular. These chaps would find themselves alone and not wanting to go home to an empty home at night, so they would stay out partying. They were not always looking for sex necessarily, but rather for fun and companionship. Sometimes, they may even occasionally find some connection (bearing in mind however the skill of many girls at playing guys like a Stradivarius). Cory certainly identified with much of that. Although nights out with mates were always a precursor for him (he has still never entered a strip club sober, which is probably very telling over the fifteen years of his visits), when they would all go home to their wives and girlfriends, Cory couldn't face another lonely night. Nightclubs are great if your mates come with you, but you just look sad if you go alone. Strip clubs however are the ideal bolt hole for men flying solo. Even if you go in as a group, the girls are very skilled at persuading you all to go off in different directions, divide and conquer being the true art of war in that environment. It is their law of the jungle: split the men up, take away their safety-in-numbers mentality, and the girls can then work their feminine wiles more successfully on them. But Cory was having fun.

A perk of running his own business was also having a central London office available to go back to and carry on partying too, rather than always in hotels etc. A number of girls seemed to have a thing about offices, and many a wild party ensued over the years. Sometimes, the debris caused a bit of offence the next day (apart from the obvious, broken fingernails, hair extensions and the like were found), but it was worth it for the fun at the time. There are far too many similar stories to relate over too many years here; suffice to say, his boys told him, as they sat and watched *Two and a Half Men* regularly together, that he seemed to aspire to be a poor man's (non-Hollywood) Charlie Sheen in the way he lived his life! Cory was never sure whether to take that as a compliment or insult. Here is one example that epitomises the whole lifestyle at that stage.

Cory and a colleague took a client out for lunch at *Scott's* in Mayfair. It turned into a very boozy occasion, as they still did sometimes back then, in the good old days pre-recession. The long lunch was followed by cocktails at *Claridges* and drinks at whichever Mayfair bars they were allowed into. In one, they were asked to leave when, as the three of them sat on the bar stools in the plush lounge bar area, Cory's colleague slowly just toppled sideways and on to the floor. They got their coats and moved on. The next bar was showing England's final ill-fated qualification game for Euro 2008 – the infamous 'Wally with the brolly' game. By now, the terrible trio were too drunk to pay proper attention and were asked to leave the bar, as they were cheering too much. The issue apparently wasn't their cheering *per se*, more that every England pass, throw-in, and most trivial detail was deemed worthy of increasingly loud cheers. Too much evidently! After stumbling around in the London rain, trying to get into various other bars and being rejected by many a doorman (no idea why!), they found a pub showing the game. Sadly by then, they were too confused to even follow the score or work out whether England had qualified (falsely believing until the next day that they had). After the game, they managed then to lose each other, as all wandered off drunkenly in different directions; as men often tend to. Cory ended up talking to a couple in the pub. The girl was very flirtatious and touchy feely. It wasn't immediately clear to Cory whether the guy was her boyfriend or just a friend who clearly wanted more (yes, another one of those). From the girl's behaviour, he suspected the latter. This was confirmed when the girl went to the toilet, and the bloke, who had previously stood by smiling as Cory reciprocated the flirtation with the girl, suddenly turned to Cory, his face contorted with anger, and told Cory to fuck off and leave them alone. Cory asked the guy why he hadn't said anything in front of the girl. He said he obviously couldn't; she wasn't his girlfriend. Oh dear.

Fortunately, Cory decided discretion was the better part of valour and left. He had encountered this issue at other times in normal bars and clubs over the years. Flirtatious girls would respond well, only then for a glowering male friend to loom into view, chasing away any male opposition. At least you never faced this issue in strip clubs, so he stumbled off to one of his regular haunts. He met up with one of the girls he knew well and ended up afterwards back in his office, carrying on the party with her alone initially, then back at her house, where her flatmates joined in too. One hell of a night!

Cory is pleased to say this was one of many such nights he has enjoyed over the years. He wouldn't say that his appetite is yet sated, but he has certainly had his share of fun. This though presents something of a dilemma for him now. Since he and Lisa split up fifteen years ago, he has pretty much bounced from one relationship to the next, with plenty of wild nights as a single man squeezed in-between. Never quite on Jordan Belfort's *Wolf of Wall Street* scale, but that will at least give you an idea of some of the antics. He has therefore experienced pretty much everything that he, as a normal bloke, ever wanted to (and probably some things he didn't!); he has had a huge amount of fun; endless partying, a lot of sex, in all sorts of places, and met a lot of lovely women along the way. However, all of this has merely reinforced what he has always known: that it is true love he is really searching for. He had it with Lisa for many years and with Zara (at least during the good times). No amount of wild times with other women, although incredible fun, and experiences he is delighted to have had can replace that. There have been others he hoped he might find love with, but they came and went. Anna remains the one current friend he had hoped more could develop with, but they have never been able (so far) to move from just being very close friends. Always the wrong time, wrong place, or just too many other things going on in their respective lives at different times over the years; perhaps they may be able to in the future?

More Dating

Other notable girls from this period to mention include Layla
and Ceri. Layla became one of his best mates for a while, mainly
through her sheer force of personality. She was a petite, cute, very
sexy, mouthy Essex girl, who became his favourite (apart from Anna
always, obviously) in the original club where he had met Debbie (after
the latter had left). Layla was a breath of fresh air in that world and
they just clicked. She understood why Cory went to the clubs, what
he wanted, and especially what irritated him. She would often watch
in amusement as other girls tried and failed with him, as he argued
with waiters about trying to overcharge him and anyone who tried
to 'mug him off'. She just got it – he was happy to pay the going rate
to anyone worthwhile who didn't try to rip him off. She was also
disarmingly honest. She said that she knew she wasn't his usual leggy
blonde type, but she assured him that she was worth getting to know.
She was right. They became good friends for a number of years, and
she told him how she had a plan to make enough money while she
was young enough to then get out and start her own business. She
did. She also hated drugs, as she had an ex 'bad boy' boyfriend, who
was addicted and used to treat her very badly. She was just naturally
high on life. She told him she loved sex and was even appearing in
porn movies. Not surprisingly, she was a very popular girl, in and out
of the club, with a huge range of men, including many well-known
international footballers. Yet she was so grounded, so upfront and
honest, with no airs or pretensions; you just couldn't help liking her.
She was clearly a very savvy, street smart young woman too, making a
lot of money and not frittering it away on the lifestyle, as many girls
in that industry do. In the years Cory knew her, she drove a series of
top of the range Mercs, Alfas, and similar cars. Their friendship grew
in the club and then progressed outside. She was one who particularly
loved to meet after hours in his office; she said it appealed to the
bad side in her (in fact, it was her false fingernail that was found

the next day on the floor); those were great nights. There was one classic night where they met for a drink and she decided to take him to a normal nightclub, where she danced provocatively all night for him. He was the envy of every other man there! Another time, their drink meeting quickly ended up with them rushing back to his office, before she was due at her club. Cory had planned to go home, but they were having such fun that he went with her into the club. The antics continued; she was an insatiable girl! You couldn't do that these days; at one point, he had Layla sitting on one leg being very dirty and sexual, with Anna on the other. Bliss! Layla even suggested a threesum, but Anna sadly declined. Still a great night, nevertheless. She was amazing fun.

Similarly, a girl Cory randomly met in a bar one evening, or more particularly in the side doorway outside it, turned out to be another great girl to know for a while. Ceri was Irish and very hot. He has always had a thing for the female Irish accent, which he finds very sexy. He first noticed her legs as he walked past the doorway; she was wearing a tight miniskirt and high heels – perfection. He stopped to chat, and they immediately seemed to hit it off (she could have just as easily told him to fuck off – it just shows, you never know unless you ask). They had a drink and got to know each other better. It turned out she had been out for dinner with an older married City guy, who she was the mistress of, and was dressed that way at his request. The chap had left to go home or back to work, and she was at a loose end, so they chatted for some time. She explained she had recently gone through a bad split from her boyfriend, with whom she had a kid, and was now doing all sorts of stuff to both make money and enjoy her new-found freedom. This apparently also included porn movies and dating older guys for gifts (as was all the rage apparently on a number of dedicated web sites for such things, which was all a revelation to Cory). They became friends and a bit more briefly, but her life was too busy and complicated for her to get involved exclusively with any one man at that stage, so it faded sadly. As that very astute woman Cory has recently got to know has said, when admitting her own damaged background, Cory seems to be drawn to fallen women, or rather to emotionally damaged (or fucked up, as she eloquently put it) girls, who he seems to want to save. The *Pretty Woman* scenario again, which coincidentally (or perhaps not) was one of Cory's favourite films, and didn't Julia Roberts look so good in it, especially in those boots?!

Cory also met and dated girls in the real world too, but his more recent brief visits to dating sites haven't inspired him. Not only are there now far more, along with some doubt as to the authenticity of many of the profiles, even women he has engaged with have all talked immediately of wanting babies or looking for 'the love of their life'. The problem is that Cory has been in love, married, has four wonderful sons, and doesn't necessarily need all that again. Of course he wants love again – it's a basic human need. But he's in no rush anymore; he no longer feels the need to be in a relationship or perpetually looking for love. Whereas many women (and some men, at least the ones not just looking for sex) on these dating sites are there precisely because they are worried life is passing them by and want to meet 'the one', settle down, get married, and have kids. All entirely understandable, but not in alignment with Cory's needs. One of the many reasons the quirky and slightly different women he meets appeal to him more is because they are less focused on mapping their lives out in that normal way. Deeper emotional connectivity and wilder lives are more their thing. In Cory's experience generally, the madder the women, the wilder sexually they are too –which is great, as long as there is some degree of normality to balance it all out as well. Finally, to state the bleeding obvious, the best strippers are mega-fit (in all senses), super-hot, stunning women who know how to use their lithe, supple, athletic, toned bodies to maximum effect in the throes of passion (wow, time for a cold shower to calm down and get back to the narrative!).

A case in point on the normal woman front was an attractive Czech girl he met online, who lived locally near him and worked as a social worker in his area. They met, got on well and stared dating briefly. Or rather, they did after they got over his initial jokey comment that she did not react well to, that the only other girls he'd ever met from that area of Europe were in strip clubs! Men and women's senses of humour can often be miles apart, and that was so then. She was grossly insulted and launched into a tirade about the evils of strip clubs, pornography and such things. Cory sensed she was not for him long term, but thought there was no harm exploring a bit further and having some short-term fun. This was bolstered when she sent him her lingerie photos; a man always knows that a girl is interested when she sends such personal photos – and they had some fun together briefly. But apart from insisting repeatedly that she could only date a man with a degree (Cory fulfilled this, obviously), which seemed slightly weird, she then dropped her bombshell. Whilst she saw no need to rush into marriage, as she was approaching thirty years old she wanted a baby. Cory suggested surrogacy, which wasn't appreciated. He had no particular desire to father another child and certainly not with someone he had only just met. She moved on and had her child within a year. She then evidently was signed off work on a long-term basis due to stress. So being slightly facetious, Cory wonders if maybe it doesn't really matter where you meet women, it's always like a lucky dip as to what mental and emotional state you get! This one had certainly been a lucky escape.

Cory had that same conversation so many times, with so many different women in the late twenties to mid-thirties age range, all desperately looking for 'Mr Right' to settle down with, with a checklist of attributes the man must possess to qualify. Luckily for Cory, as a divorced dad with four teenage sons, he is automatically crossed off their lists. That suits him. All his relationships have been built on more than simply satisfying someone's checklist. They arise from a real connection, some spark and chemistry, physical attraction, yes of course that is required, but there has to be more for Cory too. Perhaps he's old fashioned, but in his view, there is no such thing as your ideal partner. You can meet anyone in any circumstance and have that elusive chemistry and connection, which is partly physical but much more down to personality and emotional synergies. If you preclude people on artificial criteria, you may never find that real connection and true love. Each to their own and it's clearly a matter of personal choice, but Cory has learned from all his efforts at finding love and having relationships over thirty-plus years now, that you can't force love. You can't create a connection where there is none. You can't fake that chemistry; it's either there or it's not. If there's no spark, it's unlikely there ever will be. These are innate feelings. They can grow over time, of course, as you get to know the person better, their personality, and character, but not merely from a superficial checklist. The following sums up quite well his current views:

> 'I'm not desperate for a relationship, but I do miss the feeling of having someone that can make me smile and feel appreciated. Someone that will make calling and texting me the first and last thing they do every day. Someone that will be there to hold me when I feel vulnerable. Someone that will look past my defects and love me for who I am. Someone that will give me butterflies in my stomach every time we're together. Someone that I can call mine' (Anonymous)

That's not to say everyone thinks love is the priority; many people think that other attributes matter more. The classic case was the beautiful Anglo-Indian 'princess' Cory worked with years ago. She was beautiful and knew it. She played and manipulated men, coquettishly, apparently innocently and naively, but you could see her love of the power and control her looks gave her. Men were putty in her hands. Yet she married a bit of a knob, a posh boy whose parents were landed gentry in some remote part of the United Kingdom. She admitted once when a bit tipsy (very unusual for her, as she was very controlled, rarely let go, and was always in the gym to maintain her perfect figure) that her mother's advice had been to never marry for love. That was stupid and naive. You could always learn to love someone, but what mattered more was money, social position and the security that brought to life. But that led in turn, it seemed to Cory, to those endless loveless marriages, where the bored beautiful trophy wife at home is shagging her personal trainer, tennis coach, pool attendant, stable hand etc., while the Hooray-Henry husband is either getting his with his secretary at work or with his true love, who is another member of the gentry (sounds rather like a royal family issue we had, doesn't it?). Isn't that the same reason why so many rebellious teenage girls date older bad boys, with their cars and money – at least until the novelty wears off, and the girls realise they are just dicks? And so many strippers he has met over so many years have all, at some stage, fallen for the dodgy geezers and gangsters who frequent (if not run or own, allegedly to launder their ill-gotten gains) the clubs. They offer cars, gear, cash, gifts, shopping trips, luxury holidays to buy the girls; the excitement and social standing afforded is attractive for a while, but many girls leave once they realise they are just another possession to these men. They are owned and expected to do as they are told, whatever it is. The men use them as eye candy, have them as another beautiful possession to go with their Rolexes, luxury cars, and other materialistic possessions. The beautiful sexy young girl on their arm is just another trapping of their success, another trophy to show off, just another status symbol. They feel entitled to pursue other girls and add them to their collection whenever they want as well. Cory has heard this story so often from so many girls who fall for it when young and naive, but then grow up and try to escape. True love does matter, ultimately. People may pretend it doesn't, but it is a basic human need. Most people crave it, whether they admit it or not. That is nothing to be ashamed of; it's in our DNA; it's just the way we are made. Love is all there is ultimately; no amount of possessions can compensate if it is missing. As the saying goes:

> 'As you get older you find out that true happiness is not in how much you make or how many degrees you have or how big your house is or how fancy your car is. It's finding peace and joy and calmness in your life that will soon become the most important thing to you. Your family are what matters to you; love is what matters to you. Things that are of quality, not quantity'
> (Anonymous)

Cory can point to three relatively recent clear examples of relationships he had that never progressed, as that core connection and chemistry, beyond the physical, was just never there. The first involved Karolina, a beautiful Baltic blonde, tall, slim, long-legged, sexy figure and very attractive girl. She happened to work in the two main clubs Cory visited, and over a period of time, they got to know each other well. It was always one of Cory's characteristics in the clubs that if he met a girl he liked and got on well with, he would be loyal to her and ignore others. The reasons were twofold, one, it meant you could really get to know someone, as you were clearly spending more time with them, and two, it showed them you were serious and really liked them, not just another game player simply saying the same to every girl you met (a regular phenomenon apparently). They progressed from only seeing each other in the clubs to going on drinks and dinner dates around London; she became a regular visitor to his office late at night and even met his friends, who were blown away by her beauty. She was a lovely girl too. But there was one fundamental problem. Although her English was very good, you can't have that same banter and connection with foreign girls. He had tried a number of times over the years; it is not so much the language barrier, but more the cultural divide that separated them. The kind of slick interaction he had with Debbie and Layla, both street-wise, smart-ass, intelligent English girls with the gift of the gab, just wasn't there. It was a shame, as Cory and Karolina certainly had some connection, but it just wasn't strong enough to progress, and Cory could feel himself losing interest after the initial novelty period wore off. He chastised himself mentally, as here was a stunning woman, with a body and looks to die for, who he liked and got on with, and it may well have developed into something more, but the initial spark never ignited further and it faded. Cory has had various discussions about this with numerous girls in clubs; and the English girls always love to hear it, as it reinforces their feelings of superiority over the foreign girls – all very important in the ruthless competitive world that they inhabit! He's also discussed it with some male friends, including one particular chap, a Greek who has been in England for many years, speaks very good English and obviously fancies himself as something of a Lothario. He agreed entirely; said that his chat-up lines, confidence, and success with women just wasn't as good over here as at home. Unless you are a native of the language, you miss some of the vital nuances, some of the subtleties of language, intonation, or tone – all of which are simply not natural in a foreign language.

It confirmed Cory's long-held belief that whilst he could fancy and get on well with numerous foreign girls; given his need for intellectual and mental stimulation for a real relationship to work and evolve, he was unlikely to ever have this with a foreign girl. Well, not unless she had lived here for so long that not only her English was very good, but she had become immersed into the cultural nuances any nation has. Without it, there is always that slight cultural disconnect at times. It's like those delayed TV interviews by satellite overseas, where the time lag means that any quick-witted banter and dialogue can't happen, while what is said is slowly delivered and the delayed response means it's all a bit stilted. That doesn't mean it's not fun while it lasts though, and if you know someone for long enough, it may be feasible to overcome it. Two further examples were with other sexy Eastern European girls (Tatiana and Natalia), both of whom Cory met in the clubs and got on very well with. You see, for him, that's what matters. You accept that by definition, those clubs are full of attractive, sexy, scantily clad women. Most men do feel like kids in candy stores when they walk into them, with an array of beauties both to look at and choose from. But to have the spark, the connection to spend hours talking, as well as watching them dance provocatively too, is the real turn-on for him. As the drinks flow, you can quickly work out which girls are worth getting to know, which are just money machines, and which are just boring. It's the same the other way too, as the girls analyse and assess every punter, working out from their suit and clothes if they have money, from their age and demeanour if they are punters who may spend serious money, or just young flash pups with limited cash flow to match their shallow personalities. In his early days, Cory had a few occasions where he was persuaded to go with girls he hadn't yet worked out and ended up sitting bored and desperate for the time with them to end. He quickly learned from those mistakes and became fairly adept at the initial chat to work out if the girl was fun and worth spending time with. And that has nothing to do with nationality; in fact, some English girls are amongst the most boring he has ever encountered, no chat, no spark, and no real personality. It was only really outside the club, when trying to progress to something more, that the cultural divide came into play. This was the case with Natalia and Tatiana. Both great girls, sexy Eastern Europeans who spoke very good English, who he had a lot of fun with in the clubs and then outside initially. But as ever, beyond the novelty period over the first few months, the gap between them became more evident and without the ability to talk deeply for hours with him, he lost interest.

Love and Litigation

Against this background, then walked into Cory's life one of the most amazing women he has ever met: Chloe. Cory has to declare now that this will in many ways be the most difficult of his relationships to write about, as it has only recently ended. All of the others, no matter how painful at the time, have gradually faded into the mists of time (well they had, until he has stirred the hornets' nest with this book!). But his feelings for Chloe, all the reasons he fell in love with her, still burn inside him and are fully extant. He is still in love with her, deeply, passionately, and (given the way he currently feels) unendingly. As he explained to her when they last met up to talk a few months ago (for her twenty-seventh birthday), apart from Penny over thirty years ago (and that was obviously for very different reasons), she is the only woman he is still in love with after the relationship has ended. Despite his decades of experience with women and relationships, this is a new one to him and he's still trying to work out how to cope with it! Hopefully, writing the book has helped.

As he has said to Chloe innumerable times over the past five years since they first met, she is clearly his punishment for all the wrongs he has done to every other woman in his life. His dream girl in every way, but who will never quite commit to him fully enough; who is too emotionally scarred, scared, and mixed up because of her past, and therefore runs away whenever their incredible connection and amazing chemistry becomes too strong; and who can't (currently) decide what she wants from life, so they are no longer together. Heart breaking.

So let's explore now why Chloe has won his heart so strongly and he has fully fallen in love with her for really only for the fourth time in his life, in thirty-plus years of emotional involvement with women. First, there was Penny, his first love tragically taken from him. Second, there was Lisa, still the longest relationship he has ever had (is likely to ever have?) and his one true marriage. That was real love for a long time, which their boys find hard to comprehend, having only seen the divorce, its fallout, and arguments for too long. But even they say that Cory and Lisa looked happy in many photos for so many of their years together. Third, Zara, for a few years, at least.

He is very conscious of the classic Einstein quote: '*If you can't explain it simply, you don't understand it well enough*' in seeking to answer life's eternal mystery – what is love?

To Cory, the common theme in each was friendship, a closeness, a connection on every level that meant they were best friends, even soulmates. In his view, that is what love is, not lust, not infatuation, not fun, sex, partying etc. All of that is great, has its place in every relationship, and of course, problems arise when you lose those things, particularly in long-term relationships, but they are the more superficial elements, important, but not necessarily relationship-enders, as long as the problems are addressed and can somehow be rectified. But without love, without that connection, that bond that means you cannot imagine being without that one person in your life, it is all insignificant. The rest of it is transitory and generally not sufficiently strong foundations upon which to build a long and lasting successful relationship. The simple point is that nothing is ever perfect. Life isn't. Relationships aren't, and people are certainly far from perfect. Everyone has their own agenda, their own issues and baggage that they carry through their lives. Once the realities of life kick in to any relationship, once the novelty period wears off, no matter how long it lasts (as it inevitably will at some point), if there is no love, often there is nothing to keep people together. As the sayings go:

> '*Relationships are two people that might not have it all together,*
> *but together they have it all*' (Anonymous)

> '*Relationships. It's more than just the dates, holding hands and*
> *kissing. It's about accepting each other's weirdness and flaws. It's*

about being yourself and finding happiness together. It's about
seeing an imperfect person perfectly' (Anonymous), and

'We're all a little weird. And life is a little weird. And when we
find someone whose weirdness is compatible with ours, we join up
with them and fall into mutually satisfying weirdness – and call
it love – true love' (Robert Fulghum)

Cory will never know how long he and Penny may have lasted. He
knows that he and Lisa had real love and that carried them through
so much together for so many years. He will always be grateful for
that, to have experienced it no matter how sad it is that it ended and
no matter how acrimonious it has been at times since. That perhaps is
the burden of losing something that had been so strong; it can never
be replaced with anything similar. He tried with Zara, but her lack
of interest in a real family life was palpable. They should never have
married. He loved her nevertheless for everything else they had for a
few years, but resented her for insisting on marriage when it was never
real. It was just a very strong, if erratic and volatile relationship. But
they were for a number of years best friends and that brought them
back together repeatedly; as he had been best friends with Penny and
with Lisa for many years (and indeed civility has broken out between
them generally again over recent years, although of course may be
strained again, if not destroyed by this book!).

Love is complicated, or rather people in love can be. Human
emotions can be a minefield for us all to get through, particularly
given the enormous disparity between the way men and women
think, interact, and deal with their emotions. It is never simple and
means different things to different people. But Cory has worked
out what it is for him at least. He therefore knows when it is there
and when it is not. Whatever different definitions of love and of the
key characteristics we each attribute to that feeling, generally the
closeness, emotional connection, and best friend/soulmate part is in

there somewhere. The confusion arises when you think you may be in love with someone at the time, but then looking back realise you weren't. You can be close to someone and believe they are your best friend for a time, when in fact, they are just your current partner and therefore emotional support and connection for that period. No one ever said life was simple or straightforward, and human emotions certainly are not. It's clearly an issue where one person is (or at least believes they are) in love in a relationship and the other person isn't; all very tricky indeed. As Candace Bushnell states:

> 'Just because something doesn't last forever, it doesn't mean it wasn't meaningful while it did last. It doesn't mean it wasn't important'

All Cory can say is that he has been in love, truly, properly, deeply, for more than half of his thirty or so years of relationships with women. The rest may have seemed like love at stages, but it wasn't. It was just being close to someone at that time; it was transient. The acid test for him is the best friend part, not just for a few months, but for a real period of time, as he had certainly been with Lisa for over a decade and with Zara intermittently over a few years. He makes no apology for emphasising how strongly he needs that element. That's what he still craves and desires more than anything else. The rest of what he has had has been great fun and wild at times, but it's no substitute long term for true love; for the incredible connection you can only find with someone with whom you are really in tune mentally and emotionally. And that's how and why he fell in love with Chloe.

They met in a club. He had noticed her in passing a couple of times, but as they were both busy, he hadn't yet spoken to her. She had that same look as Karolina that turned him on so much. Tall, leggy, sexy, beautiful, blonde, he assumed she was another Eastern European, as she looked the part. As he chatted at the bar with others, she walked past him. He knew he had to say something. He smiled at her, apologised loudly to the girls he was chatting to, and said (so that she could hear) that she was the only woman he was interested in. Rash perhaps and risky, as the girls he was with (whom he had only just met and was making small talk with) walked away in disgust. Fortunately, Chloe returned his smile. Most women know the rules. In life, in clubs, on the streets, in public, women know that men are staring at them; it is an inalienable fact of life. How they deal with it often defines what happens next. Most women used to such attention know that if they are not interested in follow-up chat-up lines, etc. (especially in clubs and bars, but by no means limited to those environs), they should avoid eye contact completely. If they meet the man's gaze, he takes it as a sign of encouragement (he is, of course, looking for the slightest sign and often sees them when not even there). So women who are with other men, or who simply aren't interested, invariably studiously avoid his gaze and walk on by; far safer and avoids any misunderstandings (as men are prone to) about signals apparently being sent. Meeting his gaze and smiling back is his invitation to pounce!

There was something else about her, as well as her obvious physical beauty. There seemed to be real warmth in her smile and something in her eyes. Cory has always found looking into women's eyes very telling. He believes they are the gateway to a person's soul, and you can often read far more from looking into them than the person necessarily wants you to know. As they saying goes, someone's smile with their mouth isn't real unless they are smiling with their eyes too. When listening to what people are saying or even more when asking them questions, staring into their eyes can reveal a lot. All the body language experts talk of people looking away, avoiding your gaze, and the like if hiding something. But more than that, Cory has always found women's eyes so attractive and really felt as if he could see into their souls at times (although this theory had been challenged when he first met Zara, as her bright blue eyes turned out to be coloured lenses and her real hazel-green eyes were much more revealing, obviously!). He in turn had also been told over the years that he had nice eyes; they were very intense with a 'come to bed' quality. As the saying goes:

> 'Eye contact is way more intimate than words could ever be'
> (Anonymous)

and as Sophie Loren said:

> 'Beauty is how you feel on the inside and it reflects in your eyes'.

Chloe's eyes were naturally as beautiful as everything else about her, a greener tone than Cory's own hazel-green. He saw fire, fun, passion and excitement in them. They spoke; she was English. He was amazed, as she looked so Eastern European, as he told her. She said she got that a lot and sometimes even played along with it (as girls do!), putting on an affected English/Russian accent. In her high heels, she was a towering vision of beauty – think an amalgam of all the girls in the Sin City films, all the femme fatales, all the lead women, she was a collection of all the best features of all of them. Years later, his same female work colleague (from the fashion industry) who had been so full of praise for Anna's looks and body, was similarly effusive about Chloe. She said that now he had fallen in love with someone he felt so close to and who looked like a Victoria's Secret supermodel, he was stuck – it would be hard for anyone else to ever compare if it didn't work out. Vey prophetic words indeed, as that is currently how Cory feels! Here is why. In short, she was a combination of all the best bits he had loved and liked in all his exes, plus she had a number of their bad, wild traits too.

Cory and Chloe spent a long time together chatting that first night. They clearly hit it off, had similar senses of humour, and found themselves chatting so easily about anything and everything. They had so much fun that they repeated it quite a few times. But it seemed from what Cory gleaned from others, as Chloe was very guarded in chatting about her personal life, that she was in a long-term, on/off relationship with someone way up the food chain in a family that had all sorts of connections (good and bad), may have owned the club, and certainly had disparate business interests all over the place. He was told by others that she was a top gangster's girl, the archetypical beautiful, stunning girl any self-respecting man worried about his image would want by his side apparently (as this seemed to go with the territory). But Cory loved a challenge after all, and this was all part of him continuing to experience a whole new world outside the safety and security of his suburban life! It seemed that she was able to party and behave quite wildly, as people knew who she was, who she was connected to, and always made sure she was okay. She certainly had a very wild side, but was a lovely person underneath the mad party-girl exterior. Chloe told Cory that some of it was true, but she and the guy were no longer together. Others told him they were. He eventually tested it by meeting her out of the club as often as possible, where they had numerous drinks and dinner dates. More importantly than anything though, as well as their hours of chats and time together in London, they started speaking regularly on the phone. Whatever else may or may not develop between them, they had become good friends, very good friends in fact, over those first six months of knowing each other. This coincided with his (so-called) marriage to Zara getting towards its end. It had struggled on for a few years, but now finally, the divorce was proceeding. They had put it on hold, had a brief reconciliation and holidayed in Barbados as a make or break. Apart from one major argument in their hotel just before they had a tour of Sandy Lane (they were okay by the time they returned for drinks and dinner with the nouveau riche who hang out there), the holiday was generally good. But they clearly both sensed things were no longer the same; their previously seemingly indestructible bond that had always brought them back together was no longer as strong. Zara acknowledged this as they sat having a final lunch at one of their favourite restaurants, *The Lone Star*, in the sunshine before flying home; she said that she wondered if they would ever come back to the island. They never did. Although the relationship limped on a little longer, they both seemingly knew it was reaching the end.

Cory now had Chloe to confide in and she seemed keen to know all about him and Zara, partly out of usual female interest and also Cory sensed to help her work out further what kind of man he was. Cory enjoyed their chats hugely, not least as he loved talking to Chloe, loved her take on life, her views, her intuitive intelligence, her street-smart savviness, but also her sweet side. He told her after about six months that he hoped he was slowly working her out. She appeared to be something of a chameleon, constantly adapting to whichever environment she was in. When with and talking to him, she was educated and intelligent, opinionated, pretty damned smart, and yet had that little girl lost aspect to her too, hiding behind the wild party-girl exterior. He was intrigued. She remained secretive about the details of her past and recent relationships – her comment being that she was a private person and didn't want people knowing her business. She told Cory that the details of her past generally were not relevant to their friendship and to whether anything more may develop between them. This seemed to be consistent with what he was finding out about her, directly and indirectly, and was consistent with her true sensitive personality. Cory kept trying, but she just told him he asked too many questions and a lot of it was none of his business. She had that sassy confidence that added to the attraction. She did tell him about aspects of her background though to explain certain things. She had been a good girl when younger, who became a very rebellious teenager. This was in part due to her dad, who apparently was a dodgy character (so she had grown up around them, hence her affinity for such types) leaving them. She had gone to private school, but hooked up with the older boys from the local estate regularly and become the main guy's girlfriend, helping him to sell his stuff in the school. She seemed to have moved school a few times, talked of setting fire to another girl's hair with a candle when bored in chapel one day, and so many more tales. She was just a rebel. She reminded him of Alfie in many ways and of Zara too. This obviously tugged at his heartstrings.

Although she was clearly very intelligent, had evidently gained some GCSEs, by the time she was sixteen, she was in full-time party mode. Cory has told her many times over the years that she is the most intelligent woman he has ever met in that whole London party club scene. She has thanked him for the back-handed compliment! She plays the game very well but is so lovely deep down. That is, if you can break through the armour-plated barriers she puts up to ever get that close. She admitted that she could have gone to university and done so much more, but none of it appealed next to the wild party days and nights she had enjoyed in her late teenage years through her early twenties too. She had also been a very good athlete (which explained her stunning figure) with talk of her possibly even progressing to a place in the London 2012 Olympics, but that had all fallen by the wayside much to her mum's annoyance. She was, not surprisingly, hugely popular with men everywhere. In every club, she never had to buy her own drinks, as she was inundated with complimentary bottles, endlessly. She was well known across the London party circuit, in all the clubs from the chic upmarket Mayfair ones through to the leading regional clubs and in a lot of the obvious holiday party resorts too. Cory once asked her in those early days how often she was chatted up by men. The answer: constantly. She said that she was used to it. It was not just when she was dressed up, looking sexy and glamorous, but even when she dressed down, wearing a tracksuit and popping to the local shop. Men seemed to think she was more accessible and approachable then, as she certainly found some men intimidated by her when in full glamour mode. She was regularly told in clubs that she looked like a model, and some men obviously felt as if she was way out of their league. She did, and

was! She had naturally modelled at one stage, but found it too dull
and disciplined at the time compared to her wild party lifestyle. Cory
grew to like her ever more, the more he learned about her and the
more time they spent together. That's not to say he was fully hooked
quite yet. He can be cynical at times and maintained a healthy
scepticism (or the rational side of him did, at least).

Apart from still having his own issues with Zara and their near-
terminal relationship, occasionally Chloe would lapse into her
bullshit party-girl mode with him, all her barriers back up, hiding
behind her public party-girl image. A few times he walked away from
her when she was like this and told her he wasn't interested in that
superficial side of her; she should save that for everyone else, not for
him. Their friendship was solid and secure, but there was a chemistry
that was growing between them too that surprised them both. What
had started as a bit of fun in the London club world had progressed
to endless hours of talks about each other (subject to her privacy
issues) and anything and everything else too. They had by now
known each other for six months, just as a friends, but it seemed as
if it might progress to more. As well as ever more increasingly regular
chats on the phone, they spent endless hours together over those
summer months in clubs, bars and restaurants. Cory hadn't seen Zara
for months since their holiday and was feeling ever closer to Chloe.
This culminated with them spending a solid twenty hours partying,
drinking and talking together one balmy August night and day. They
had a few other long nights spilling into the next day too, and Cory
told Chloe that he felt as if they were progressing beyond friendship.
The chemistry and connection between them seemed to be growing
ever stronger. The problem was, apart from having to get back to work
post-summer, contending with the ongoing economic slowdown, he
had to deal with the much-delayed trial of his issues with his former
work colleague.

This had dragged on for a couple of years; all the usual legal
arguments had been exchanged, protracted settlement negotiations

had gone on for some time, and although it seemed they had got close at times, they hadn't achieved this. This was all against the background of the economic crash and ongoing recession, which had affected both sides' ability to pay lawyers to continue acting for them. As we all know, lawyers are often the only ones to ever really benefit from any major litigation, and this is a classic case in point. The whole case was ultimately settled a year or so ago. The full story of the issues and of Cory's working life generally is too huge to include in this book. That is a whole different tale in its own right and is the intended next volume of these tales – whose current working title is: 'Volume 2 – A Working Life: Bullshit, Egos & Parties', so workmates past and present should beware, particularly those who make Ricky Gervais' *The Office* look like a well-oiled, ultra-slick outfit in comparison! Suffice it to say for these purposes that despite business being badly affected during the recession, Cory's opponent decided to plough on and wasted a huge amount of money arguing a technical point of law in the High Court; or rather his pedantic barrister did (no doubt being paid a daily refresher on top of his initial large brief fee) fully supported by junior counsel and a huge array of solicitors from the instructing firm. What a farce! Cory knew that whatever the outcome, the arguments started years earlier pre-recession were now otiose, futile, and redundant, yet his opponent insisted on proceeding. Cory repeatedly pointed out the waste of time and money in doing so, given the effects of the recession on the business, but all to no avail.

He had previously ceased using his own expensive City lawyers when the money ran out a year or so earlier. He now decided that it would be pointless to instruct any again, as the cost would be prohibitive, and in theory at least, his previous ones had complied with all the required procedural steps, pleadings etc. when acting for him. It became clear his opponent was proceeding to trial, but not to the full claims as to the amounts of money involved (which is really all anyone cares about ultimately) but merely to this separate, preliminary hearing on a point of law that may have mattered pre-recession, but no longer did. Cory therefore had no option but to act as a litigant in person. He vaguely recalled some aspects of the trials he had been a junior instructing solicitor in fifteen years earlier, but of course had no real trial experience on his own. He could not compete with the resources of his opponent, with the clever legal arguments and arcane case law dragged up by his barristers. All he could do was play along, rely on his intimate knowledge of the facts, and hope that the truth would prevail (as naturally his opponents' case was a very different version to that of his and others from the business). But it didn't. Two days were wasted at the start of the trial dealing with the other side's convoluted legal submissions on irrelevant evidence that had no bearing on the trial (including the video clip so kindly sent to them by Zara a few months earlier, immediately after their make-or-break holiday – guess what effect that had!). They all then plodded through something like eight days of arguments back and forth, Cory doing it all on his own, from carrying all the numerous files and boxes from his office to the High Court and then running the entire case on his own, making all the submissions as well as examining witnesses and giving evidence himself. The most bizarre part was after his examination as a witness by the other side, how could he then cross-examine himself? It was a real one-man performance! He was getting up at 4 a.m. most mornings to prepare for the day ahead; it was a very intense and stressful period. Given his background, Cory knew though what was coming in advance, so had ensured he enjoyed his summer with Chloe and with his boys, the highlight with them being his holiday at the *Beaches* resort in Turks and Caicos, wonderful (though the layover in Miami en route and the intensity of US Immigration, even when just transferring flights, was an experience to behold). But as Cory said to his kids and friends at the time, he had been through worse in his life, and it was just in his nature to buckle down and do what had to be done. No point moaning, complaining, or saying, 'Oh, woe is me!' He had made realistic settlement offers that had been rejected; he had no option but to fight. We are all products of what life has thrown at us, and Cory's inner steel, determination, and desire to do the best he could came through hugely over this period. Life had thrown worse at him before and he had survived and battled back. As Jack London said:

> 'Life is not always a matter of holding good cards, but sometimes, playing a poor hand well'.

He was going to keep battling now, even though the chances of winning the legal arguments couldn't be great. He had to rely purely on the facts, but as he feared, and the other side knew, they were always likely to win. He couldn't compete with their reliance on ancient case law and endless convoluted legal arguments, strained from the cases and textbooks, as there were diametrically opposed recountings of the facts from him and his opponent. The whole thing turned out to be the huge waste of time and money Cory predicted. At the end of almost two weeks in court, the Judge summed it all up in one closing sentence: 'What if I were to find for Cory on the facts, but for the opponent on the law?' The other side were ecstatic and replied (in the usual obsequious manner) that it was the law, the legal principles that superseded the facts in answer to that question. It was however a Pyrrhic victory. There still now had to be a full trial of the quantum of the claims, which still needed to be argued fully. The reality was that most of them had now fallen away, given the effects of the recession on the business. But lawyers being lawyers will never accept what any opponent says at face value, and there followed a tortuous period of investigation into the business and Cory's finances. This was to enable the other side notionally to assess whether there were funds to pay the costs they had been awarded for winning their preliminary issue point, but actually to see whether there were hidden funds (as the opponent appeared to believe) to go after in the main trial. They talked of offshore accounts, overseas villas, yachts, etc., all very glamorous, but as Cory pointed out, if he had any such offshore tax-free bolt holes, he would probably be there enjoying them rather than acting solo facing them in court! But it still took them almost a further two years to realise this, particularly given the need to constantly go back to court for endless hearings. Cory carried on doing all these hearings himself, repeatedly facing the large, expensive legal team on the other side until finally the opponent contacted him and accepted that there was no further money to pursue. Cory ended up paying the six-figure sum he had originally offered in settlement five years earlier and a token amount on top towards the opponent's costs (a mere fraction of the full amount which he claimed were hundreds of thousands – a great result for his lawyers!). It was all just as Cory had warned his opponent at the outset – High Court litigation is always to be avoided (as even major corporations and numerous oligarchs have come to realise).

This real-life distraction meant Cory was not best placed to focus on what he hoped might be a potential new relationship with Chloe. He took her out for dinner and explained all of this to her. She understood but asked if he was going back to Zara. He said he wasn't and had no plans to. Chloe said that if there was any possibility of it happening, nothing could happen between them anyway. How perspicacious she was! All part of her intuitive understanding of people, and Cory again realised she was a very special person. But it was just not the right time for him to take things further. He also still remained slightly sceptical about Chloe, telling her that she was just too good to be true, particularly given his experiences with Zara (the last time he had felt like this). As Shakespeare put it so succinctly: 'All that glisters is not gold.'

Chloe had now elicited everything about his relationship with Zara from him over their months of talks; she knew he had loved Zara and was desperately sad that it all appeared to be coming to an end. As he focused on the trial preparation, he and Zara did indeed

get back in touch when she wrote to the opponent's lawyers trying
to retract the damaging video clip. But to no avail. They made great
play of it in the preliminary arguments before the trial, setting up
numerous laptops around the court for the judge and all participants
to watch it. Cory maintained it was completely irrelevant to the issues
before the court (it was clearly just a tactic to embarrass him). The
judge declined to view it, or take it into account and they dropped the
matter. (All part of litigation tactics, but another huge waste of time
and money). Zara was very apologetic about sending it months earlier,
following their explosive long-distance argument after returning from
holiday, when it all fell apart again (due to her broken promises).
These conversations led to a thawing in relations between them and,
as so often before, to another reconciliation after months apart. It
certainly helped Cory to have her around during the stress of the
trial, as he needed someone to talk to other than friends and current
workmates who had no real direct involvement. Zara at least knew all
the facts, the characters involved, and how Cory should best deal with
it all. She was too embarrassed to come to court though having sent
the video clip to the other side.

Cory had the previous year taken a number of clients to a charity
evening hosted by a local MP to tour and dine at the Houses of
Parliament. That had been a good night and led to a few of them
going on to various clubs after. He had agreed to take tickets again
that year, but the event now fell right in the middle of the trial. As
Cory wasn't drinking at all over this period, to keep a clear head
and all his mental faculties about him in court, he decided instead
to reduce the number of tickets and to use them personally instead.
He asked Zara to come along, and after prevaricating endlessly about
whether she would (as women do!), she finally did show up. She
looked very glamorous in a short, tight-fitting dress and high heels.
The host MP and other chaps at the event seemed to think so as well!
Unfortunately, as Cory had been in court that day and had asked
his boys to come along too, he didn't have time to commute home to

collect them as he intended when planning it all. Instead, his eldest son had to take responsibility for getting his brothers to Waterloo, where Cory met them. He brought a friend as a replacement for one of the boys who dropped out. They arrived slightly later than planned, which of course meant they were late then getting up to Westminster to meet Zara; all normal family stuff, which we all put up with and accept. Not Zara though; she was in a filthy mood, claiming that she felt like a prostitute, standing so sexily dressed on the street corner in Westminster awaiting their arrival.

Cory felt (as so often before) that she was being irrational and unreasonable. Shit happens. It was no one's fault. He clearly had to meet the boys first and their delay was unavoidable. She didn't see it like that and felt slighted that he had not been there to meet her. Cory was however stressed enough from the ongoing trial that he just accepted her rant until she calmed down, whereas usually, he would have argued his corner much more. She ultimately left earlier than Cory and the boys, but amazingly, by the time he got home with them, she was in a much better mood. Whether this was natural or due to other influences he never knew, but again reinforced that he was better off not trying to combine doing stuff with his boys and her. This extended a month or so later to attending a family christening for his nephew. They had planned for Zara to come along, but as usual, she wanted to change the plans belatedly. Cory suggested she went directly to the venue in south-west London, where they would meet. This apparently caused such offence that she ended up not going at all! They didn't see each other for months again after that, and only saw each other for two more brief periods the following year before it all ended for good. They finally accepted it was over and the divorce was finalised.

One other notable point to record from that evening was that as Cory's party arrived for dinner after the tour of Parliament, as he hadn't bought enough tickets to have a full table, they were sharing one of the long dining tables in the Commons dining room. Other guests had however got there first and sat in such a way that there weren't sufficient places together for Cory, Zara, and the three boys. Cory explained politely to the organisers the issue, who said of course they would ask the other guests, all of whom were adults, to move a few seats along. Inexplicably, they refused, saying they were fine where they were. These appeared to be rather posh, terribly well-spoken types, and Cory could only assume their arrogance at doing what they wanted outweighed any normal reaction for a parent wanting to sit with his family at such an event. Fortunately, someone else kindly agreed to move, equally offended by the posh knobs' arrogant refusal to do so – is it any wonder Cory despises such people, when every time he has encountered them in his life by chance, never by choice, he finds them so selfish and obnoxious? Unfortunately, they were still on the same table, albeit a few seats away, and compounded their offensive behaviour by ordering Cory's son's friend (who happened to be black) to open a window as he was returning to his seat from a toilet visit. The assumption appeared to be that someone of his hue dressed smartly must be a waiter. Truly shocking.

Falling in Love All Over Again

What of Chloe throughout this period? Cory realised she had been right when she asked if he still loved Zara and might get back together with her. She clearly knew how to look through what men actually said to work out the truth. Clever girl. They had a few text exchanges at the start of the trial preparation period, but nothing for a while. As Zara had come and gone yet again, Cory got back in touch with Chloe at Christmas to send her best wishes; they had a few text exchanges but nothing like over those wonderful months that previous summer. Maybe it had just been one of those short-term things. It had been great getting to know her and she had been so much fun, so good to talk to over those balmy summer months. It would be sad if so, but that was life. Real stuff got in the way and people come and go. One night, he was out in London, in a range of the usual bars and clubs, and he saw her across the bar – the first time he had seen her for at least six months, maybe even longer. He just looked at her and burst into a huge, completely involuntary grin. Eventually, he managed to work his way round to talk to her, and suddenly it was if there had been no hiatus; they were back connecting as strongly as the previous summer. She later admitted she had been nervous when she first saw him, not sure how to react and unsure how he felt, as he had walked away months ago and not really stayed in touch. But she said that as soon as she saw his smile, she could see he still cared. And he did.

As they talked and drank the night away, Cory told her about the trial, about Zara coming back and going again. Chloe commented that from all he had said about her, that he still loved her. He admitted he did, but things were coming to an end, as it was just getting worse all the time, the gaps apart ever longer, the periods back together increasingly shorter. Their ability to fix things, to repair the damage that had built up over so many years, now seemed almost to be exhausted. It was sad, but that was life. He was conscious that here he was with this beautiful young woman, who had become such a great friend and confidante, who knew so much about him, talking about the death of his marriage/relationship. When they talked like this, like last summer, he felt a very strong connection with her. The chemistry between them still seemed to be there, despite the long gap. Apart from all else, they both had that mutual lost-soul element and had enjoyed partying their nights away together. They went back to talking regularly on the phone and to meeting for drinks and dinners. The summer was approaching again and she was about to start her jet-set lifestyle, holidaying in the party hot spots, coming and going with her various groups of friends. Cory told her that he really liked her; she said she knew that and she liked him too, but she couldn't commit then. They agreed to stay in touch over the summer months and see where things stood after. Cory by then knew there was something just stronger than friendship between them. He also had worked out that despite her wild party-girl exterior, the sensitive sweet lovely girl that she was underneath was very wary of male bullshit and wasn't going to rush into anything. Cory was happy with that. Although she was beautiful and so sexy, that wasn't why he was so captivated by her. It was her personality, her mixture of strength and vulnerability, her outward confidence (almost arrogance) and inner shyness, her intelligence, her understanding of people, and the simple fact that they could talk for hours about everything and he never grew tired of her. He wasn't sure that anything would ever develop between them beyond their great friendship and connection, as there was a big age gap; they were at different stages in their lives and from such different worlds; she had a constant array of men pursuing her, rich, famous, wealthy, footballers, playboys, businessmen, bad boy types, throwing money at her, wooing and dating her. Although he clearly couldn't compete at that level, they had this amazing connection.

She went off on her various travels, he dated a few other women over the next few months, and then one day, she rang him and asked who his girlfriend was. He said he didn't have one, but that he had dated a couple of other women while she had been off on her holiday adventures. She wanted to know more. They met up in *Harvey Nichols* bar, which had become one of their regular haunts along with the *Oxo Tower* for daytime cocktails. As ever, she was very inquisitive about his personal life, wanting to know all about the other girls, why he liked them, what they looked like etc. He asked if she was jealous. She replied that she didn't know. As the cocktails flowed, she said that maybe he should think of wooing her like other men did, by buying her something. Cory laughed. He said that in his world, you dated a girl by buying her drinks and dinners, presents followed as and when you were together but not before. She countered that in her world, drinks and dinners were the minimum and most men that had ever pursued her had taken her shopping, bought her designer shoes, bags, clothes, etc. Cory reiterated that he had always bought such things for the women he had been involved with, but never for someone to try to seduce them. He explained that just wasn't his world, and anyway, he would never be able to compete financially with some of the men she encountered. She explained that wasn't the issue; it was a question of a beautiful woman wanting to be treated nicely, to be made to feel secure emotionally, physically, and (to some extent) financially. Cory said that he could offer all of that if they became an item, as he always had to his girlfriends, but not before.

She stressed, however, that she was an independent woman, worked hard, and enjoyed her lifestyle. She would never be anyone's kept woman, and men in her past had made that mistake, believing they were somehow buying her. No chance. She would never be told what to do, never controlled by anyone. Cory said he was not interested in anything like that. This line of dialogue continued between them for some months. They had clearly moved from being just friends to being on the verge of something more. Both wanted and expected it to progress in a certain way now, but had different views as to what that should be. They were both stubborn and wanted it their own way. They were at an impasse. Nevertheless, it was clear that the chemistry between them was stronger than ever, the flirtation increased, the gentle touches, looking deeply into each other's eyes, and the ongoing phone calls. One particular night, they started talking about 7 p.m. and only finished at just after 2 a.m., when (after having had to change and recharge phones at various stages) they were too tired to talk any more. As this continued, Cory eventually admitted to Chloe how amazing he thought she was. He said that though they weren't even together and he wasn't sure if they ever would be, given all the differences between them, he felt as if he was falling in love with her. It was now over two years since they had first met, and what a journey it had been! It had started just as casual flirtation, having a bit of fun out socially together and partying, to then spending countless hours talking in person and on the phone. Real life had intervened a few times, which had meant they didn't see each other for months, yet now here they were, some months further on, starting to talk seriously about whether they could overcome all the differences between them and have a relationship. He said that the En Vogue (since covered by Little Mix) *Don't Let Go* lyrics about being more than just friends were so apt!

Cory admitted that the others he had recently dated paled into insignificance alongside Chloe and the way he was starting to feel about her, as indeed most women did. Of course he was in lust with her beauty and sexuality; wasn't every man (and many women too evidently). That though was only a small part of it; lust is not love. Fun and partying is not real friendship, and the incredible connection they had was tangible. He told her that he remained concerned at the many differences between them and that he was falling in love with someone who was too good to be true. She responded that she loved their friendship, agreed they had an amazing connection, and wondered whether more might develop. She admitted she was still young and unsure what she wanted from life; she liked him but didn't know what to expect, as he wasn't her recent type. She had of course dated, and been pursued by, endless men her whole late teenage and early adult partying life. Apart from a few mistakes when young and naive, she had for years been much more cautious about who she actually got involved with properly. She knew she was one hell of a catch that men wanted, so she could afford to be fussy and choosy. She did query at times whether Cory was just another man who wanted her just for her body; who just wanted a young sexy trophy girlfriend on his arm and in his bed. Cory of course sought to reassure her, but she had clearly heard years of men's lies and bullshit to try and get her and she was wary. She occasionally let slip that she had been hurt and betrayed by men she had naively trusted in her past. She was cautious and didn't really trust anyone any more. She said that in many ways it was safer to keep her barriers up and not let anyone get too close to her. She described men as being like dogs, always sniffing around, a bit dumb, and easily controlled. They can be loyal, but do stray, always chasing the next female they see, craving affection, but mainly just sex, then always come back if you treat them properly and even keep sniffing around when you shoo them away. Cory retorted that he saw Chloe and girls of her ilk like cats: aloof and independent, self-preening, who only come back when they want or need something; otherwise love to run free or curl up alone and hate to be constrained or limited in where they can go and what they can do; who only want affection when it suits them. Of course these are broad generalisations, but hopefully they make the point. She reminded him strongly of others in his past and perhaps even of Marilyn Monroe, whose views she seemingly agreed with on many matters, including:

> 'A wise girl kisses but doesn't love, listens but doesn't believe, and leaves before she is left'.

This confirmed all Cory had worked out over the first couple of years they had known each other. She had a great social life, loads of friends, partied often, had great holidays, unremitting male attention, and that was in many ways enough. Cory said he couldn't do anything now to fix any pain in her past, and of course a lot of men would just want her as a conquest, as sadly that's the way many are. All he could say was that she knew pretty much everything about him, the good and bad, from all she had asked and he had told her over the years. As she said, he was an open book, as he had nothing to hide. She however was a very tightly closed book; with the pages even glued together to stop anyone getting in! He swore that he had never lied to her, nor would he ever. He reiterated how much he liked her, how if they ever got together he would have no interest in anyone else (as he pretty much hadn't since he had realised how he was falling for her), and that all he could do was hope that one day she would think it was worth taking the risk with him. She promised to think about it. They continued chatting regularly, getting on with their lives. Sometimes, she would say she really liked him, always had, but wasn't sure she could give him the kind of commitment he wanted. This went on for a few more months; she started opening up to him a bit more, but still very slowly and generally guardedly. He told her that this all was making him love her even more, as they had grown to know and understand each other pretty well, albeit still just as friends. He hoped they could have more one day, but he didn't want to hassle or pressurise her, so maybe he should try moving on, leave her in peace for a while and find another girlfriend. Her response blew him away. She said that he loved her, and she loved him, so why on earth would he do that? Wow! It seemed she finally trusted him enough, after knowing him for well over two years. Their friendship and connection had been growing ever stronger, enough for her now to admit what he had been telling her for months: that their friendship and amazing connection had grown into love. They agreed to meet the next evening for drinks and dinner, and so began the next phase of their relationship.

A few months earlier, Chloe had one night over drinks said they should start seeing each other, but then had immediately started making excuses, being busy working, socialising, and partying, so that they never really did. Cory told her he put it down at the time to her perhaps being a bit drunk and getting carried away in the moment. One of Cory's close friends had met her and said in true male style that he should just go for it with her, whatever may happen, as she was so fit! They got on so well, were so close, but maybe the differences between them were too great to overcome. He told her that maybe she was too much of young, wild, free-spirited party girl for him. She said that was only part of her; she had responsibilities too. He mockingly said he didn't know what those were, other than deciding which designer outfit to wear to whichever club she was partying in. She said she would tell him over the next few days. The next day, she rang him and very hesitantly told him she needed to tell him something. Her ex, the one everyone had told him about, was the father of her child! Cory was shocked. He had at that stage known her for about eighteen months off and on and would never have thought or believed she was a mother. He challenged her on it, asked a lot of questions, some of which she answered, others of which she said were none of his business in her usual way. When they next met up, she said she could tell it had put him off her. He said it hadn't, as he loved her, so would accept it. That seemed to be what she wanted to hear, although as always, she remained very sceptical of anything any man said.

Now here they were, some months on, finally about to try to convert their incredible connection and friendship into something more. So he said the same to her again now, about how the differences between them may be too great, but he agreed they should try. She told him not to be so negative about the differences and to just enjoy whatever may happen. She quoted Marilyn Monroe (again reflecting many of her own views on life):

> 'Nothing lasts forever, so live it up, drink it down, laugh it off, avoid the bullshit, take chances and never have regrets, because at one point, everything you did was exactly what you wanted'.

She said that she was still going to be busy working and seeing her friends, going on her usual holidays with them, and so on. He too had his own work and boys, so they would see each other when they could and see how things developed. As it transpired, she had various weekends away and the usual party holidays lined up, so that summer was punctuated with her absences (although she did reassuringly stay in regular contact whilst away), but their time together in between was amazing. Having spent years meeting in bars for drinks, dinners all over London, and partying the night away in clubs, they now finally added the new dimension on top of all this continuing activity, nights together too. In hotels initially, as Chloe preferred to stay in central London, and then subsequently back at Cory's house as things progressed. He told her that she was indeed very much like Marilyn Monroe, many of her quotes being so apt, especially:

> 'I'm selfish, impatient, and a little insecure. I make mistakes, I am out of control, and at times, hard to handle. But if you can't handle me at my worst, then you sure as hell don't deserve me at my best'.

On one occasion, she arrived at Cory's house just as his eldest son and friends were sitting around drinking and debating their night's entertainment. It had been a scorching hot summer's day and was one of those lovely warm summer evenings. Chloe obviously thought she was out in Mayfair or even on one of her foreign holidays, as she arrived looking as if she had just come off the pages of a glamour magazine! She was tanned, beautiful, flowing long blonde hair, wearing a white polo shirt and tiny hot pants, accentuating her very long, far-too-sexy legs, aided by her high wedges. She looked stunning. The teenage boys couldn't believe their eyes; Cory's son had to admit that this beautiful, sexy young vision standing in their lounge was his divorced middle-aged dad's new girlfriend! They walked down the road past a local pub, where the comments, cat calls, and wolf whistles rang out to the local cocktail bar. She said that when she went to the toilet in there, some of the local girls had put on mock-Russian accents, believing her to be from there, as she still had that look about her. Cory apologised and said that was small commuter towns for you. They weren't used to such beauty, particularly not so provocatively dressed. She said she wasn't. He pointed to her skimpy shorts; she said next time she'd wear an even smaller pair. He did not see how that would be possible, but knew that the wild side of her may well do it. She hated being told what to do by anyone, men especially (another hangover from her past relationships, it seems). She never did dress as provocatively or sexily ever again on any future visits. Even her normal attire of tight jeans, etc. seemed to be too much for many in the area. It helped to reinforce her view that they should spend more of their time in central London than in the sticks. She could dress as she wanted up there, as people were more accepting of stunning women who stood out from the norm.

Cory was in love, in lust, infatuated, but more than all of these emotions, regarded her as his best friend, who he could talk to about anything. He had been entirely open and honest with her about everything since they met. This meant that now they were seeing each other, she already knew so much about him, and when they had issues from time to time, she could refer back to what he had done with others in his past, in typical female style. She would be wild and unreliable, and he of course had to accept it; but if he acted like that when she wasn't in that mood, he was in trouble! She admitted sometimes she forgot who she was dealing with and said that she had learned to act in a certain way with men generally, as they all wanted the obvious from her, so she would play them back in return. She apologised and said that he should just tell her if she was ever a bitch (and not the acronym, which applied fully to her: Beautiful, Intelligent, Talented, Charming and Hot!). She was used to pushing as much as she could and needed to be told when to stop at times. However, she couldn't feel controlled or be told what to do, as she would then rebel and deliberately do what she had been told not to! But he knew that underneath all this madness on the surface, she was so sweet, so loving – if you could break through the barriers to get in that far. Cory told her all this, sometimes more honestly and brutally as a friend than delicately as a girlfriend, and she would berate him for not treating her as the gentle flower that she was. He repeatedly told her that she was indeed a delicate flower, but given how others had hurt her, that flower was wrapped in thorns and brambles, well hidden and protected, in a fairy-tale like tower, protected by a deep moat and heavily fortified, surrounded by sharp barbed-wire! She admitted that many had called her an 'Ice Maiden' over the years and accused her of having a heart made of stone or ice. She certainly was: *'a mess of gorgeous chaos and you can see it in her eyes'*.

She was beautiful and sociable and great to get to know superficially. She was intelligent and interesting. She could talk to anyone about anything, adapting her persona from posh private-school girl, to streetwise 'sarf London', tough savvy woman and anything and everything else in between. She was a social chameleon. She told Cory that she had been brought up to fight for herself and always stand up to people. If you didn't know something, always ask; if someone hurt you, you hurt them back harder; if someone dissed you, you dissed them back more; if someone hit you, you hit them back harder and so on. She had also been told, and was fully aware of the power she had over men, given her looks and personality. Her mum had brought her up to understand the value of that power and to use it always to her advantage. She was also full of banter. She was rarely outdone in any exchange, always having a slick, ready response for everything. And she hid behind this façade. She was often told that she should have been a lawyer, as she answered every question (especially anything personal) with a question back. She was, to use that famous Churchill quote, truly: *'. . . a riddle, wrapped in a mystery, inside an enigma . . .'*

But he was in love with her, not for her incredible body and beauty, but much more their chemistry and connection, their friendship, for the sweet, vulnerable lost soul behind all her barriers. He reassured her repeatedly that looks and mere physical attraction aren't enough for love; her personality was even more attractive than her outer beauty. That was why he loved her; he told her: *'Your body is what makes you sexy. Your smile is what makes you pretty. But your personality is what makes you beautiful'* (Anonymous).

He had by now spent a few years getting to know her, and finally had his prize: a new best friend. Someone who understood him, who he had amazing fun with, an incredible connection and chemistry, who he spent hours talking to every day, and who said she loved him as he did her. He had made progress, slowly but surely winning her trust and confidence so that she let him in. It had been a long tough road, but worth it. He told her that although he had obviously been drawn to her superficial London party-girl image initially, it was her sweet, lovely, little-girl-lost personality deep down that melted his heart. This was best illustrated by the fact that they would meet for the evening, and she would look stunning and glamorous as always. Many a head would turn to look at her as she walked by, particularly on the hot summer nights where she was in hot pants, high heels, and the like. She was beautiful, from head to toe. She knew it, as did everyone else. She had that confidence and touch of arrogance that can bring at times. And yet when they spent the night together and she slept curled up in a foetal position, he saw the true vulnerable person; she looked so small and needing protection – a far cry from her strident public image. He fell in love with her even more.

Chloe remained fiercely independent and incredibly stubborn, which caused issues at times, as she could also be notoriously unreliable and changeable. Cory had taken his boys on holiday to a Greek island at the end of the summer, and although they had discussed Chloe possibly joining them, they decided it was probably too soon. They talked daily while he was away, but when he got back, she started questioning him about whether he had really been away. It seemed someone had claimed to have seen Cory out in London during his holiday, and sadly, given the lies she had encountered in her life, from men generally and in previous relationships, she wanted to know if it was true. Cory was shocked, as it would never occur to him to do that, why would he? She finally believed him, but took some persuading. He commented that it was sad that her heart had obviously been broken and her trust in men so destroyed by the bullshit world she had inhabited, where people lied so readily always. They arranged to meet up to discuss it, but were both out elsewhere with other friends first. By the time they did meet, after arguing over the phone about where and when and whose fault it was, they weren't in a great mood with each other, and eventually drinks ended up being thrown over each other. The following few months became frustrating, as they were both busy at work and Cory with his boys, Chloe socially. They saw less of each other than they had over those fantastic summer months and argued more in their mutual frustration as to whose fault it was. Chloe was also travelling for work at times too. She had decided she also wanted to have some more cosmetic surgery carried out, even though she was to most people already the picture of perfection. But she is part of the modern generation of young women who are seeking complete perfection. They not only spend a huge proportion of their lives in the gym, maintaining and improving their amazing bodies, but then still always want more. Any perceived imperfection plays hugely on their minds. Their hair has to be perfect, with hair extensions and regular styling and colouring (as Chloe often said, if her hair wasn't right, she wasn't worth knowing – and she sadly meant it). This body dysmorphia appears to be so prevalent amongst so many young women these days it is scary. Nose and boob jobs amongst her groups of friends were regular occurrences and so much more too. Although they say they want to look good for themselves, it is clear from talking to them that years of having the message reinforced by society (or at least the world they inhabit) that how good you look equates to the quality of life you have, the better men you attract and so on has hit home.

That explained Chloe's near-pathological shopping fetish. She loved following celebrity women and their designer outfits, bags and shoes. Of course virtually every woman loves shopping and has far too many clothes, shoes etc. Generally, the more attractive the woman, the more extreme this is. She loved all the reality TV shows, the *Real Housewives* series, *TOWIE, M.I.C* and anything similar. In fact, her lifestyle was at times similar to the latter, and she seemed to aspire for it to be like the former. Cory kept his promise that now they were properly together, he would buy her gifts, mainly but not only for birthdays and Christmas presents. *Louboutin* and *Tom Ford* shoes, *Agent Provocateur* underwear and swimwear, *Balenciaga* and *Gucci* bags appeared to be her favourites (amongst so much more too, naturally!). He really didn't enjoy women's shopping generally, as she knew, and her raids on the appropriate departments in *Harrods*, *Harvey Nicks*, *Selfridges*, and the Mayfair boutiques were clinical and something to behold. Like a military operation, she knew exactly what she wanted, where to get it, how to flutter her eyelids at Cory to get all she wanted, and how quickly to do it while the mood was right. It was truly impressive. No endless messing around, indecision, circling around for hours - just in and out, job done. He couldn't help admiring her for it, even when paying! And that was the other incredible thing about Chloe: she actually was reasonable in her demands, never taking advantage. It is best summed up with a tale of drinks with her friends, when one of their boyfriends (a very wealthy man) offered to buy the drinks, as was expected. Girls like that rarely have to buy their own drinks. During the banter, she had (jokingly) said she only drank *Ace of Spades* Champagne, knowing the guy could afford it. He was about to do so, when she stopped him and said not to be silly; she drank vodka, diet soda and fresh lime (the classic 'Skinny Bitch' cocktail so many girls drink, as it is low calorie). He said he had thought nothing of it, as she looked like the kind of girl who would only drink the most expensive champagne, along with shopping at the top stores, wearing designer clothes etc. Although she had these latter two characteristics and no doubt had been well looked after by guys over the years, she was genuine and not a game player. She knew men would always spend money on her, but she never took advantage with him, another reason Cory loved her, as he clearly wouldn't have been with her if she was one of those girls. Occasionally, a few people had made comments along those lines to him. These ranged from other people in clubs, to his friends questioning her motives to be with him, and his boys checking she wasn't another like Zara, who, in their eyes had taken a lot and given very little in return. Cory discussed this all with Chloe and, from time to time, raised it in arguments too, particularly when frustrated that he hadn't seen her enough. But he knew that she wasn't fake. Crazy and mixed up, definitely. Infuriating at times, but so loveable underneath the bullshit exterior. He consoled himself with Bob Marley's inspired words:

> 'If she's amazing, she won't be easy. If she's easy, she won't be amazing. If she's worth it, you won't give up. If you give up, you're not worthy . . . Truth is, everybody is going to hurt you, you just gotta find the ones worth suffering for'.

She was certainly a classic example of this. He knew that she could be with many richer men than him, with men she was more used to dating, who had given her more of the lifestyle she enjoyed, but for now they were happy together. He knew that she saw him and spent time with him because she genuinely wanted to. She wasn't prone to doing much (if anything) she didn't want to. Their amazing chemistry blew them both away. Their incredible connection was stronger than all the differences between them, epitomised by their endless hours talking to each other constantly, if not in person, then always on the phone. She went off to Thailand on one of her regular girls' extended holidays, partly as recuperation from her latest surgery; Cory missed her incredibly. Once she came back, all was back on track and they carried on seeing each other and having great fun over the following months, as close as ever until her next foreign escapade came around. It was all too much like Rihanna's *Lost in Paradise*!

She had talked of going off to the United States for a few months and the impact that may have on them. She said that she wanted to do all this travelling now, while she could. Cory said that she was obviously younger and needed to do all of this, as he had at this stage of her life. He would obviously miss her, but had to accept it. The plans changed a few times, but she eventually went off on her transatlantic flight with open-ended plans as to how long she would be away. It was hard and Cory missed her hugely again. One night while he was out in London, he bumped into some mutual acquaintances of theirs and mentioned all of this and something similar about Chloe's daughter. He could tell from the reaction that something was not quite right. He pursued it, but got no further. He therefore tracked down one of Chloe's other friends (one who had not gone with the group to the United States) and proceeded to get her drunk. She seemed to have been partying already that night, so that helped. He asked about Chloe's daughter. She stumbled and ultimately admitted, when Cory finally posed the almost unthinkable question, that she did not have a daughter! Cory was shocked. He had previously asked to meet the daughter and been told he would in due course if and when Chloe was sure they were for keeps, as she didn't want her to meet a string of different men as she grew up. Apart from that, there was the complication of the bad dad to factor in. Although occasionally the daughter had been a reason for their plans to change, it had no real impact on their relationship; Cory fully accepted Chloe's reasoning as very credible and sensible. Yet now he was being told none of it was true. He said it couldn't be true; she wouldn't have lied to him like that, about something so personal, not when they were so close. Chloe's friend could see how upset Cory was and clearly worried about what he may do; she took him home to drink and talk all night long. She knew Cory loved Chloe and could offer no explanation; that would have to come from her.

But Chloe was thousands of miles away and likely to be gone for a few more months. Every time he now hears Kiesza's *Hideaway*, much as he loves the song (and finds her voice so haunting on many of her tracks), it brings back all those painful memories, as he listened to it endlessly then. He sought some kind of solace in it. That and Jonny Cash's incredibly powerful version of Nine Inch Nails' *Hurt*; having watched that heart-rending video, he realised it could apply more widely to other aspects of his own life too. She initially refused to engage in discussion with him about it (given her hatred of confrontation), but eventually they had some fraught exchanges and phone calls and agreed they would sit down and discuss it all once she got back. She actually came back early from her travels, and they spent the night at the Sanderson Hotel, initially drinking at the Long Bar (then in the Purple Bar) and talking it all through. Unfortunately, he went on directly the next day to a planned family lunch, where his alcohol intake continued apace. He thought his regular references to *Game of Thrones* characters and sayings were hilarious (having just been belatedly introduced to this awesome show and having watched all of the first few series on Sky over the preceding weeks while Chloe was away). Like many a drunk however, they are rarely as funny to others as they think and certainly nowhere as amusing as they find themselves! He even very maturely refused to take Chloe's calls when she rang to check if he was okay, instead passing her on to one of his sons and to Lisa, who had a brief chat with her.

Chloe conceded that she told him she had a kid not maliciously, but apparently when he had accused her of being just a wild party girl, as she wanted him to like her. She obviously knew from their years of chats how important his boys were to him and had decided (perhaps foolishly, she admitted) that if he thought she was a single mum, it would address some of his concerns that they were incompatible. It was also a test to see how serious he was about her; would he accept her with another man's child, or was he really just another of the constant array of men in her life who wanted her just for her body, a trophy girlfriend to show off? He understood her rationale and that had all been before they actually started seeing each other properly, but why hadn't she ever told the truth at any time since? She apologised and said she should have, but didn't know how to raise it and was scared of his reaction. She knew that she wound him up at times and didn't always like his explosive verbal reaction when she had messed him around previously, so was particularly worried with this. It was a pretty major thing for her to have to address and she didn't know how to. Looking back, he had sensed times when he had asked about her daughter that she was hesitant in her replies; she said she had been on the verge of telling him, but never quite had the nerve to do so. She hated confrontation anyway and was prone to run away from issues rather than addressing them (a regular feature of their relationship, and her life generally, it seemed). Her stubborn side also meant she found it hard to admit she was wrong ever, yet she now readily admitted she was there. She apologised repeatedly and told him she did really care about him; it didn't mean she didn't or that she had lied about anything else. In her complete honesty, she did also admit that she had occasionally used her imaginary kid as an excuse not to see him, when he was hassling her too much for more time together or she had other plans. She regarded them as white lies, but understood his anger. The question was whether he could forgive her. They agreed that he needed time to cope with this; they both needed time to reflect and decide where it left them. That was almost a year ago and is where they are currently.

Unfortunately, over the following weeks, some mutual acquaintances in the club world used the opportunity to start massively shit-stirring with all sorts of stories (as people sadly seem to do in that environment). Cory was furious. He didn't really believe them; he knew what he and Chloe had, but was very hurt by her lies, especially about something so fundamental. This had caused him naturally to doubt her. He challenged her about all these other rumours, none of which were ever substantiated and many of which were even contradictory. She reiterated that she was a private person and therefore very few people really knew the truth about her. But they argued a lot. He was hurt and angry. He asked how she could have made up something so important. She said that people lied all the time in her world; she was just so used to it and she thought nothing of it. He asked what if he'd lied about having kids. She said that she was used to such lies and would almost expect it. It was very sad to hear it all. She explained that the way she had been brought up, the circles she mixed in, you couldn't be open and honest. People would attack any sign of vulnerability, any real feelings or emotions. It was therefore just a world of blaggers and bullshitters. He said that was all desperately sad, but he wanted no part of that world; he thought she was better than that, different to all the others. She knew how Zara's lies and secrets had destroyed their relationship; how could she do the same? He lashed out verbally and said some horrible things to and about her. As the saying goes:

'Words spoken in anger leave wounds that never heal'.
(Anonymous)

All of these discussions over the next few months led Cory and Chloe to decide that they needed a break. What they had was amazing, but was tainted now by her lies about having a kid. Although he understood and ultimately accepted it, it had caused a crack; his trust in her (which had been complete previously) was shaken. His reaction, even if understandable, had hurt her in return. She said she had been hurt by people close to her too often, but wouldn't offer any further details. They talked for endless hours again about it all over the following weeks and months and about everything they had together. Cory said he wasn't sure if they had a future. Chloe was hurt. Ultimately, he has forgiven Chloe, as he still believes that everything else they had was real, but they have agreed that their break should be for an indefinite period, to get over it all and to leave it in the past. She now agrees that perhaps the differences between them are too great, they are at different stages in their lives, and maybe both want and need something different going forward. She is worried that spiritually, astrologically and emotionally, they clash too much overall, that a lot of what she does winds him up too much and causes angry reactions. And people don't change. She needs to work out what she wants from life, as we all do as we go through our twenties and beyond. She's not necessarily ready for the full-on commitment Cory wants and is used to. They have both cried, talked of wanting it to work between them, but agreeing they need this break. She suggested they stay just as friends for now, as she didn't want to lose him from her life, given their amazing connection. He replied that he can't be that male best friend he hates so much that he has encountered in so many of his other relationships, brooding in the background, hoping to get back with her, jealous of any other men she dates. He has told her that he can't ever hear about her with anyone else, as she inevitably will be, as it would hurt too much. She, as ever, has a different approach. She heard that he was seeing someone else recently, after a few months' silence between them, and rang to ask him about it. They agreed to meet up for lunch to talk and ended up sitting chatting for over seven hours together. The love, bond, connection, and chemistry is all still there. It was shaken and nearly broken, but not quite. Cory would now be ready to get back together with Chloe, having worked out his anger over those issues. She currently says that she's working out what she wants from life and that they have to:

> 'Accept what is, let go of what was, and have faith in what will be' (Sonia Ricotti).

He replies:

> 'Physical attractions are common, but a real mental connection is rare. If you find it, hold on to it' (Anonymous).

Consequently, the brief recent relationship Cory had never stood a chance; even though it was a great few months' sex and fun, it was nothing compared to what he had with Chloe. Frankly, he wouldn't want it to be (not yet, at least). He certainly wasn't looking for anything, but it was a brief distraction. He realised when he found himself in Marbella at *Nikki Beach*, *Ocean Club*, and *Plaza Beach* etc., wondering if he would bump into Chloe (and how awkward it would be if he did) and then in Ibiza, similarly at *Mambo*, *Pacha* et al, how futile it was trying to move on. You can't just stop loving someone overnight; you can't immediately switch your affections. Clearly, over time, feelings fade. This happened with Lisa and Zara over the final years of his relationships with each. But he is not yet at that point with Chloe. The way he currently feels, he doesn't want to fall in love with anyone else; he wants what they had again, what they still have, but aren't pursuing currently as they have this necessary break. But for how long?

He obviously knows that eventually, if they don't get back together, he will move on. When he's ready, he will do so but doesn't want to contemplate that at this stage. That is one of the many reasons he finally threw himself into writing this book – the usual confluence of all in his life occasionally leading to a major event. It has allowed him to channel all his energies, all his passion and drive, into various outpourings of his life's major emotional events. They now haven't had any contact again for a number of months, as she wants the space to work her life out, and he can't accept them just being very close friends. She wasn't happy with him for that, but he told her while he still loves her, he could never just be her friend. It's too painful. They discussed whether true love always finds a way; that if it is meant to be, they will get back together. But there is no timeframe on that, as she also needs to be able to cope and commit to a full relationship if she wants to try again – obviously she has trust and commitment issues from her past. Even if they never can get back together (which would be very sad, but perhaps is the reality he doesn't want to currently face), what they had was amazing and he wants more of it. Maybe it can't be with her again; the age and other differences could be too great after all. It could be that his final and ultimate act of love has to be to let her go for good, if that's what she wants and needs.

Conclusion

The simple fact is that nothing compares to true love and the depth of emotion and connection you find sometimes in life. And that really is the moral of this long, convoluted tale. It is the key message that Cory has always really known, but has certainly proved to himself repeatedly over the past decades. It is the conclusion to his very long and bumpy journey through life. It is what every man (or woman) approaching or in their mid-life crisis should take on board. That whilst sex is great, wild parties are fun and exciting (and we all crave that at times), none of that is ever a long-term solution to whatever issues our middle age brings. Frankly, this applies equally to every stage of our lives. Nothing can replace true love, and we should all pause and reflect before potentially destroying it, if you still have it. Here he firmly agrees with Ray Bradbury:

> 'Looking back over a lifetime, you see that love was the answer
> to everything.'

And that is the cliff hanger on Cory's long journey now as he approaches his fiftieth birthday; can he win Chloe back at any point? He misses her and all they had together. Or does he have to accept it was amazing while it lasted, but ran its course and move on to try and find love yet again elsewhere? If that is his new path, he sees no reason not to (when he is ready), as he is a hopeless romantic at heart, so why not?

For now, he is phlegmatic and looks forward to the next phase of his amazing adventures, whoever that may be with. This is best summed up by:

> 'Someday we'll forget the hurt, the reason we cried, and who
> caused us pain. We will finally realise that the secret of being free
> is not revenge, but letting things unfold in their own way and own
> time. After all, what matters is not the first, but the last chapter
> of our life, which shows how well we ran the race. So smile,
> laugh, forgive, believe, and love all over again'. (Anonymous)

PART IV

Growing Older: The Penultimate Chapter?

'At this stage of my life, if it doesn't make me happy, make me better, or make me money, I don't make time for it'
(Anonymous)

So as we reach the end of this tale, here Cory sits, having taken time out from the repetitive grind of life to finally write this book. He has enjoyed not having the daily commute to London for the period of months over which he has forced himself to write it. Although it has obviously been painful at times and emotionally draining, it has generally been enjoyable and certainly a cathartic experience. 'If you can't stop, pause, take a breath, and look back on your life now as you approach fifty,' he thought, 'when can you?' At the end perhaps, but it may be too late then to either have time to record it all or to fully appreciate it. This to him is like a mid-(or three-quarter) life sabbatical. He has taken stock and reflected on the madness, fun, and driven existence he has pursued for decades without time to stop properly until now. The most fitting analogy is that he has too often, over the past decades, been like the driver of a high-performance car. He has had his foot pressed to the floor, throttle fully open, recklessly burning through the gas, often running on empty with only his momentum, his zest for life and pure adrenalin keeping him going; not always in full control as he has hurtled along at top speed, worrying that he may crash, but more afraid to stop. It has been an exhilarating and often terrifying ride, but perhaps it was all worthwhile to get him to this point. Maybe it has all been part of 'The Journey' he had to go through to finally find himself. As that is what life is, after all, isn't it? He hopes that this will not be the final chapter: the denouement. He hopes to have the time, inclination, and patience to at least write the planned next two volumes he already has in mind: Volume 2 – A Working Life: Bullshit, Egos & Parties and Volume 3 – Family, Love & Relationships (as he plans to explore wider issues in both of these). Perhaps there may even be a follow-up to this book, in another ten years or so, to see how the journey has advanced and to see whether he has learned to grow older any more gracefully. He promised his boys recently that he would try to do so in his fifties, eventually and certainly by the time he reaches sixty (always good to keep your options open!). Apart from anything else, the past few months writing the book have enabled Cory to calm down and get some measured perspective on life. Long overdue perhaps!

As he reflects on it all, he is happy to have half a dozen or so close friends, who know almost everything about his life and vice versa. That's enough. He obviously knows a lot of people from his work, social, and all other aspects of his life. Unlike in your teenage years and twenties, where it is great to gather as many friends, mates, acquaintances and connections as possible; as we get older, we come to realise that a lot of people are so full of shit they really aren't worth bothering with. With age and experience comes not only knowledge, but also the realisation of what matters in life learned from all those invaluable life lessons we all go through; we also find an inner confidence to not care what people think and to cut irrelevant people and idiots out of your life. Cory has realised that many people come and go over each phase of your life, and only truly solid friendships remain. The one exception, which he still regrets, was his closest university friends who got caught up in the crossfire of the divorce. Most other people he has encountered don't interest him enough to be more than mere acquaintances, passing colleagues, or transitory friends for as long as their mutual interests and lives coexist. Many are work colleagues, who generally die away when people move on in their careers, football dads, who drift away once the kids change teams or give up football, and so on. That's just life.

That's where Cory is now and so much happier and more content. Apart from a few visits to London to party for his last birthday, to meet Chloe for hers, and to meet his mates for an old-style long and boozy Christmas lunch, he has lived in relative purdah for months, in splendid remote isolation, just at home with two of his teenage sons, writing this book day after day. He feels as if he has been in hibernation over the winter months; emotionally, he is like a slightly battered and world-weary caterpillar crawling, if not limping along, until saved by going into the safety of its chrysalis at just the right time - now about to emerge fresh and new as a beautiful butterfly! He has written the book with all his usual ebullience, immersing himself fully in the project and pouring his heart and soul into it as it has grown from an idea into a near obsession (as is his affliction with all he does in life). His view is very strongly that if something's worth doing, it's not only worth doing well, but to the best of your abilities. Otherwise, why bother? He would rather devote himself to something completely, or if he doesn't feel like that, he'd really rather not bother at all. This fundamental characteristic can be seen in every aspect of his life – his boys and family, his love life and relationships, his friendships, his working life and career, his other passions, hobbies and interests, and of course his drinking and partying! This goes a long way to not only explaining his personality and all that has happened throughout his life, but also to his impatience and frustration with those he encounters that do not feel the same. It's not just that Cory doesn't suffer fools gladly; he can't abide them at all, as he tells them brutally honestly far too often!

Over many years, Cory has been told that he is charismatic and has a strong personality. That attracts some people to him and makes others shy away, as he is too much sometimes: too blunt, direct and outspoken. Chloe (and many others) describe him as arrogant at times; he believes it is rather actually just a very strong inner confidence. He has worked his own shit out and is happy. He is far from perfect; he is fatally flawed in so many ways and has made far too many mistakes in his life. Yet it has been one hell of a ride - very bumpy, even traumatic at times. Hopefully, he has many more years to come and is in the fortunate position currently to have a relatively blank canvas as to how the picture of his life from here may develop. He knows that chronologically, he is getting older, even if mentally, he still believes he is a twenty-something cheeky charmer, albeit now with more money and life experience, which we would all benefit from having much earlier in our lives. He needs to get back into the gym more regularly, as decades of continuous alcohol intake and good living have taken their toll. As the comedian John Bishop points out, once you get into your forties, your body changes and it's far harder to control and deal with many of nature's effects than when you were younger. This is particularly crucial (and cruel!) given his penchant for very sexy younger women in their twenties and early thirties, where appearance clearly does matter and it clearly works both ways. Another of life's little tricks and ultimate ironies, no doubt!

He knows that he is getting old when (as they say) the police and teachers look so young - and his kids' teachers certainly do. It's very hard to take them seriously when they look no older than the teenagers they teach, and some are only in their early twenties. But actually, the true mark of knowing you are getting old is when women you had crushes on for years growing up start looking older. In his case, this runs from Joanna Lumley, who was his first crush as a teenager when she looked so sexy in the *New Avengers*, through so many more, who he hesitates to list for fear of causing great offence. But here goes anyway: These include Madonna, Michelle, Kim, Julia, Liz, Cameron, and Angelina – with profoundly deep and suitable apologies to each, no offence or personal slight intended. We're all just getting older sadly. That's not to say if he were ever (in his dreams!) to meet any of them, he wouldn't melt in their presence. He now looks enviously at the slightly older Hollywood hunks and musicians invariably dating his current crop of younger favourites, including Rihanna, Rosie, Amber, Tamsin, Blake, Scarlett, Megan, the Jessicas, Mila, Sienna, Kiera, Jesse, et al; he wonders if one day he can ever be in their league? We can all dream.

The sad truth of life is that most men never grow up really; mentally, in our heads, we remain the cheeky charming young chappies we either once were or in many cases would like to have been. This is probably why most men are emotionally immature for their chronological age compared to women of the same ages. Fortunately, this drives many an attractive younger woman into the arms of an older man – annoying when you're a young guy, but there's plenty more out there for you, boys; perfect, though, for us older men! As many male friends, family, and others have said (with a hint of envy) if they were single and no longer married, they too would pursue younger women. It's just one of those inestimable male fantasies (like having a threesum, especially with beautiful twin sisters, being given a BJ while watching football on TV, and so many more). Cory is pleased to be able to record that he has now fulfilled most of his desires. So what now?

He remains sanguine, as always, about life. He hopes to see his beloved Leeds United rise again; *Marching on Together*, he hopes to see them win – hard though that is to contemplate, given their massive demise and never-ending off-field shenanigans currently! At least Leeds Rhinos and Yorkshire County Cricket Club are thriving, winning, and keeping the White Rose flying high, so he has their successes to cheer from his homelands! In the meantime, he'll just have to continue enjoying his Wembley club level seats and visits to the Emirates with his Arsenal-supporting sons! For a normal guy, Cory feels he has achieved a lot. He is happy and content inside. It would be nice to have another loving relationship at some stage, but it's not essential. He still enjoys sex but knows he's had his fair share, both close emotional lovemaking with those he's been in love with as well as more than enough random shags with far too many women over the decades. Without getting too explicit, he's happy that he's tried and done everything he ever wanted to; some of it was great, some was okay, and some just downright scary, but at least he's crossed it off any bucket list he may ever have! This combined with having been married, in love, having four amazing sons who are now leaving home, having enjoyed work, made some money, lost it, spent it, made it again, had nice houses, a good life, been comfortable at home, having had extravagant times when holidaying and partying, all mean Cory has attained that inner happiness and sense of fulfilment we all strive for. Maybe it is slightly maudlin of him to feel like this now, rather prematurely, as these are deathbed kind of thoughts. Understandable though, as Cory's view of the world has been very fatalistic since the premature young deaths of Penny and Alfie. He just feels lucky to have had all he has so far. Hopefully, there is a lot more to come, but he has certainly enjoyed the ride to date. He probably does need to think about growing older slightly more gracefully at some point (but makes no firm promises as to exactly when that will be in the next decade). In short, he is ready for the next new exciting chapter of his life – hence finally writing this book. Even if no one ever reads it, it has been very therapeutic for him to set out his thoughts, which will now stand as part of his legacy.

At the time of writing, he is still in love with Chloe, but maybe has to accept it's now over and let her go. She has been one of his best friends over the past five years, fulfilling that vital component he requires to love anyone properly. But he can't be that guy, the best male friend in the background, in love with her (and not even secretly in their case)! Cory has told her that he could never meet any of her future boyfriends. Looking back, he's never had real female friends outside of work. Socially, unless they were partners of his friends (in which case, off limits, as Cory does have some moral code), they were either potential conquests or he didn't bother with them. His ex-wife said he didn't really like women, which is ironic, given that he has spent a lot of his life either involved with or pursuing them. On the basis that men patently are from Mars and women from Venus, that we really are alien creatures to each other, emotionally and in so many other ways, he agrees. In no way is this a sexist thing, though; he is like that with everyone in life. If he likes and gets on with someone, he will pour his heart and soul into that relationship, friendship, work project, or whatever. If he doesn't, he's not very good at being fake and pretending. Everyone who knows him can attest to that. Men, women, children, pets, and indeed any living being in fact. It's just the way he is made and he has to live with it. It does mean that everyone usually knows pretty clearly where they stand with him. There are no shades of grey. That inevitably immediately rules much of womankind out of his life and explains why many have said he's too direct, scary, and full on when he's interested in them. Or the complete opposite, cold, distant, uninterested, when he has no interest. He's not proud of it but has to admit that it is all true. But his male friendships are exactly the same. The difference with women though is the *When Harry Met Sally* issue, firmly confirmed so many times throughout his life; he remains vehemently of the view that men and women can't really be friends, as sex invariably gets in the way.

He is grateful to have had a handful of seriously strong relationships, to have found true love a few times and hopes he might again. If not, until he becomes too old and infirm, he has the option to carry on adding to the shag list, more flings, and short-term relationships. They are always fun for the first couple of months, but then end as there is no real substance to hold them together once the initial novelty wears off. The things that piss you off about the other person in any relationship grow to outweigh the good far more quickly without love though. He currently sees future relationships as optional, not necessary, and the way he feels presently, only Chloe coming back or meeting someone who can give him anything similar can truly win Cory's heart again. This is indeed a change, as Chloe herself has told him many times that he has just shifted his affections from one woman to the next too often over too many years. It was as if he couldn't stop in his quest for love for fear of never finding it again. But that was just stupid, and he can see how true love has always found him, but rarely (if ever) when he has been chasing it. Only time will tell if he finds it again now.

In short, Cory has done most of what he wanted to achieve by the time he reached his half century. He had no real plans or visions; he was always too busy just coping with life. But if someone had said 'By the time you reach fifty, you can be at this point, having done all you have, with four wonderful sons who are all making their way in the world', he would have taken it. His boys and family generally are what really matters. Money can be earned and lost, love comes and goes, sex is great but never enough on its own, and he has had enough parties, alcohol, and fun to last a lifetime. Maybe he doesn't need to chase it all as much anymore; if it comes, great, if not, no problem. He now just has to focus on the next stage of his life, whatever that may hold. That said, he still subscribes more towards women sharing Jerry Hall's enlightened views in her classic quote:

> 'My mother said it was simple to keep a man. You must be a maid in the living room, a cook in the kitchen, and a whore in the bedroom. I said I'd hire the other two and take care of the bedroom bit'.

To sum up, over the past thirty-plus years, Cory's main relationships, love interests, and the women he has been closest to fall into four broad categories:

1. True Love:

He has properly loved Penny, Lisa, Zara and Chloe. To the first three, he is sorry. Penny, for obvious reasons; Lisa, for the painful divorce and losing what they had for years, but very thankful for their beautiful boys; and Zara, the good bits were great while they lasted, but there was just too much shit in the end. To Chloe (and the change to writing in the first person here is deliberate), you are the only one in my fifty years I have loved and not yet reached closure with. Who knows whether we can make it work properly in the future? I hope so, but that's really up to you now.

2. A Real Connection:

Cory has been close to Abbey, Debbie and Anna. He regrets that his encounters with each seemed to be the wrong place, at the wrong time, or in the wrong circumstances and nothing ever progressed fully as he hoped it might at the time. They're the ones who got away. Sad, but thanks for the great friendships, even if it should have been so much more (Chloe could equally perhaps be added to this section in many respects too).

3. Good Relationships:

These varied and were fun while they lasted with (*inter alia*) Nina, Layla, Emma, Susie, Vanessa and Tatiana, but they all ran their course and died out; thank you, though, for all for the good times.

4. Others:

To the many others who have come and gone over the years, whether as one-night stands, brief flings, occasional booty calls, etc. that were all briefly fun at that particular time – you all helped to make Cory realise that no matter how great the sex, that alone was never enough. So, thank you all for that valuable life lesson too.

In conclusion and on a serious note, Cory knows that although he is fundamentally a nice guy, he can be ridiculously stubborn and at times controlling. He knows that when pressure built and he exploded, he has been scary, with a bad temper. He is genuinely sorry to all he has encountered who have suffered at his hands. There is much he would go back and change if he could, but he can't. All he can do is apologise for all the wrongs he has done and hope that his boys learn from his mistakes to be better men. This sums up Cory's life:

> *'In my life, I've lived, I've loved, I've lost, I've missed, I've hurt, I've trusted, I've made mistakes, but most of all, I've learned'.*
> (Anonymous)

EPILOGUE

'Life is short, live it. Love is rare, grab it. Anger is bad, dump it. Fear is awful, face it. Memories are sweet, cherish it'
(Anonymous)

Cory sat back and reflected once more on his life. This time with much of it now set out in black and white in front of him; so different to many months ago at the start of this book, when it was all just a maelstrom swirling around in his head, like a tornado at the epicentre of its destructive path, as that is how his life has seemed at times! He paused, smiled, and thought, 'Well, who knows what will happen next?' But it's sure been one hell of a journey and adventure so far. He wondered if the book would ever be published; if so, would people read it? Could it conceivably be dramatised for TV or even the big screen (as he had great ideas about actors for the main roles, the music for the soundtrack, and naturally could add in all the salacious and graphic detail he had deliberately left out of this initial tome!). Would it be feasible to send a copy to someone like Harvey Weinstein in the hope he would read and like it?

He reflected further that perhaps that was two-thirds of his life gone (God only knows!). The young deaths in his life decades ago had made him vow to live his life to the full within certain limits, at times anyway. And he had! If that was it, he had achieved a lot, lived, loved, partied and left his mark for good or bad. And that had been his aim, his rationale, and his *raison d'etre*. And yet his greatest legacy was his amazing boys. The unconditional love, time, and affection he had given them (as every parent should, otherwise why have kids at all?), which they had reciprocated, had given his life a meaning nothing else can ever really compete with. They had given him a real purpose and kept him sane and grounded, especially when the rest of it had seemed insane and out of control! Cory knew with satisfaction that whatever the scars of the divorce, they were ready for the real world, which can be cruel. He knew he had made many mistakes and hoped his boys might learn from those. He knows that they are well-adjusted decent young men of whom he is indescribably proud, and will be forever whatever they do in life now as they plot their own journeys. They know the true value of family, which is a great starting point.

He thanks his parents, his loving mum and dad from the bottom of his heart for giving such a secure, loving and stable upbringing. This has given him and Joe so much strength to cope with the bad hands fate had sometimes dealt them, and enabled them to strive through life. Finally, he reflected on the wise words of his dad decades earlier. He told Cory that maybe the bad things that happened to him in life were for a reason, so that he might one day pass on any wisdom he gained to help others. Such perspicacity again and wise prophetic words indeed, old fella – dads always know best! It's just sad that his ongoing deterioration now means that he will never read this. God bless him.

In closing, Cory knows that whenever his own end comes, his epitaph will be along the lines of this final quotation:

> 'The aim of life is not just to get through so we arrive at our grave safely intact in a well preserved body, but to enjoy the journey so much that we skid in sideways, totally worn out, shouting 'Holy shit! What a ride!' (Anonymous)